W9-DES-693

Learning To Weave
with
Debbie Redding

illustrations by Kim Jonas
photography by Joe Coca

For my students, who have taught me everything in this book, and a lot more.

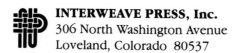

INTERWEAVE PRESS, Inc.
306 North Washington Avenue
Loveland, Colorado 80537

Library of Congress Catalog Number 84-81313

ISBN 0-934026-15-7

5M:884:JLP/VC
5M:585:JLP
8.5M:1185:JLP
8M:1086:JLP
5M:188:JLP

Acknowledgements

Very little of the credit for this book actually goes to me. Many of you will understand when I say I've been fortunate enough to be the channel for it, but in no way am I the source. To my knowledge, there is nothing original in here, only my interpretation of a lot of common knowledge, and even with that, I've had a lot of help.

First and largest credit must go to my parents, Bill and Louise Green of Greentree Ranch Wools, Loveland, Colorado, and to my good friend Eric Redding of the Weaving and Knitting Shops in Boulder, Colorado. It was the three of them who got me into weaving and started me on the path that has led to this book. If this book helps you, thank them.

No teacher can grow alone. Discussing the pros and cons of various approaches, working out ways to present information more clearly, figuring out how to best reach students as whole human beings and not strictly would-be-weavers, celebrating successes, learning from disappointments—these and much more are the things teachers share with each other. Since 1978 I have had the good fortune to have Louise Bradley as my constant teaching friend, comrade, advisor, supporter. It would be impossible to assess all I've learned from her or with her or because of her, but, most important is that I've felt her to be my own personal cheerleader. Everyone should be lucky enough to have such a friend.

Even though all of the information in this book has been used for years in the classroom, one of my concerns about putting it in a book format was, "But, will it work?!". Will it work with no instant back up, with no teacher present? Jill Schumacher was the perfect guinea pig. She always wanted to weave, knew nothing about it, and even said she had trouble learning from books. To my great relief, working from the roughest rough draft, Jill had woven off her first warp in less than a week. At the same time she gave me a wide variety of valuable feedback on the material, covering both instructions and attitudes. I'm comforted knowing that at least one person understood it and learned to weave from it. Jill's enthusiasm for the project was also a big boost.

As you will see, the illustrations in this book are essential aids to understanding the weaving process. When she started this project, Kim Jonas knew nothing about weaving but a lot about drawing, which is of course what I needed. Now she knows both. I couldn't be more pleased with the style and clarity of the illustrations. I don't think Kim is going to become a weaver, but she did tell me that in a store one day she got all excited when she recognized a twill.

While I did not have the pleasure of working with Joe Coca on the photography for the book—that was one of Jane's many jobs—I have for years admired his work, and am very grateful for his contribution to the book. The photographs are beautiful and therefore inspiring as well as educational.

Last, but certainly not least (is that too trite?), are Linda and Jane. Linda Ligon has been my editor and publisher at *Handwoven* since 1979, and a friend longer than that. She is responsible for so many opportunities that have come my way that I couldn't begin to recount them all. As my editor she has nudged me into better writing (or on occasion given me a full scale shove). As my publisher she has given me a place to grow professionally. As my friend—words can't describe, so think of the most versatile and magnificent music you know and you'll approach the feeling I have for Linda.

Jane Patrick is my editor for this book. Jane, too, has been a close friend for years, and it was exciting and wonderful when she went to work for Interweave Press. Little did any of us know that that would include her editing this book. I think she has done as much work on it as I have, adding clarity where it was needed, planning what it would actually look like. I am very grateful for her help, as can you be.

When I finished my first draft of this, some three and a half years ago, Eric, Louise, Jane, and Linda all pored over it and gave me pages of valuable feedback. I stored those in my mind (as well as my files) and went to teach at Emily Griffith Opportunity School, the adult vocational school of the Denver Public Schools. In the two years that followed I learned so much that at times I felt I must have known nothing before. That experience also improved the classes I teach, and so I send a big, big thanks to both the students and staff of E.G.O.S.

All of the people I've just mentioned have contributed substantially to this book, and I thank them more than I can say. For me one of the greatest joys of this whole project is being able to write these pages to celebrate what they've done for me. And for you.

Deborah (Redding) Chandler
Boulder, Colorado
February, 1984

Many thanks to the following students and friends who generously loaned us their weavings to illustrate these lessons:

Sharon Alderman
Jean Anstine
Selena Billington
Louise Bradley
Lisa Budwig
Awyn Combs
Ardis Dobrovolny
Betsy Holdsworth
Wanda Holmes
Helen Irwin
Janice Jones
Audrey Kick
Barbara Layne
Linda Ligon

Helen Menzel
Jane Patrick
Mary Peterson
Katie Potter
Maggie Putnam
Donna Reilly
Louie Ross
Lynda Short
Yvonne Stahl
Judy Steinkoenig
Beth Thomas
Annemarie Tucker
Margie Wortzman

Preface

Statement of teaching philosophy

When I first started teaching weaving I knew a little about weaving and even less about teaching. Since that time I've learned quite a lot about both, mostly through experience. While this may not be the most efficient means, it does have some positive aspects, perhaps the most useful of which is that none of what I do is theoretical; it all works. As I try new things, anything that doesn't work is rejected immediately; that which does work is kept, and grows.

As a new teacher my single greatest frustration was students' lack of self confidence. It was a total block to their absorbing the information. These adults, mostly women, were so full of "I can't," "I'm not clever enough," and "I don't know how," that getting them to try anything was a major accomplishment. It seemed to me that in the pursuit of teaching weaving all this psych stuff was an irritating interference.

I'm not sure when or why the shift in my perspective came, but at some point a greater truth became very clear to me, and it has been the life force of my teaching ever since. It is this: I thought I was in the classroom to teach weaving; I learned I was there to teach people. This understanding has affected my style of teaching completely, and I want to explain to you some of the ways that this is so.

I don't recall ever having students who wanted to weave ugly things, make pieces that would fall apart, create anything that they couldn't be proud of. On the other hand, at least 25% of my students have set such high standards for themselves, based not on knowledge of the subject but on a general attitude of inadequacy, that they are perpetually frustrated and self-discouraging. It isn't better standards I need to teach, it's acceptance of and gentleness with oneself, one's creations.

Each of us has our own set of priorities, our own values, our own ideas of what is important in our lives. It's not up to me to decide for anyone else what is worthwhile or valuable. (Non-judgement of others' priorities is one of my highest priorities, and like everyone else, sometimes I do well with it, sometimes I don't.) I can offer choices, set up a buffet, but I cannot serve up the dishes; those decisions are individual.

What might be in a weaving smorgasbord? Color, design, drafting, warping, original designing, craftsmanship, gifts, selling, showing, experimenting, broad knowledge, depth in one area, fun, art, companionship, privacy, relaxation, concentration, self-expression, function. Etc., etc., etc. Am I to tell you which of these is most important for you? Not a chance. Not only do I not know, as you grow and change so will your priorities rearrange themselves. If I said to you this one is most important, and you had the misfortune to believe me, you'd be stuck in a box of my making until you realized, through a degree of struggle, that while I may have been right for me, I was not for you. I don't need to give you any more oughts and shoulds, you've got enough of your own already.

So I encourage my students to understand what's happening and then make their own decisions as to how to proceed. It's a standing joke among those around my classes that the answer to most questions is, "What do you want?" While I am more than willing to help with structural problems, functional understanding, I go to great lengths to resist answering questions like: Blue or green? What size? Is this correct?.

There are lots of subjects, aspects of weaving, not covered in this book. Some are not included because they aren't necessarily appropriate to a beginning class, some because I don't know anything or enough about them yet. You'll find all of them in other books, in weaving magazines, in the minds of other weavers, in lots of places. When you are ready, when you need them, they will appear. This is only the beginning, the very beginning.

I want you to relax, to have fun. Being easy on yourself is not in opposition to good craftsmanship. Learning from and being inspired by others is not counter to originality, creativity. Enjoying something does not mean you're not taking it seriously. Mistakes are as valuable as successes, one for learning and growth, the other for reward and encouragement. There is a poster hanging in my classroom that says, "You have failed only when you failed to try." So go out and try something, and if it doesn't feel just right try something else. The journey is what it's all about, not the destination.

Contents

10 **Introduction**

13 **Part I: For the Very Beginner**

    13 **Lesson 1: Getting Familiar**
        13 What is weaving?
        16 The anatomy of the loom
        17 Equipment you will find useful
        20 Weaving vocabulary

    23 **Lesson 2: Your First Piece**
        23 The value of making samples
        25 Choosing yarn for your sample
        27 Step-by-step warping
            28 Measuring the warp
            36 Sleying the reed
            42 Threading the heddles
            49 Tying onto the back apron rod
            53 Beaming the warp
            58 Tying onto the front apron rod
            61 Tying up the treadles

    63 **Lesson 3: Weaving**
        64 Your first weaving assignment
        65 Weaving a header
        66 Winding your shuttle
        67 Selvedges
        69 Sequences of the weaving process
        72 Troubleshooting
        73 What to do about threading errors
        76 Taking your sample off the loom
        80 Finishing your fabric
        84 Learning from yourself

    91 **Lesson 4: Planning a Project**
        92 The initial drawing
        93 Warp calculations
        94 Weft calculations

101 **Part II: Now That You Know the Basics**

    101 **Lesson 5: Reading Drafts**
        101 The four parts of drafts
            102 Threading
            103 Tie-up
            104 Treadling
            106 Draw-down

    109 **Lesson 6: Plain Weave Variations**
        110 Structure variations
        112 Color variations
        116 Texture variations

    121 **Lesson 7: Basic Twills**
        123 The patterns, the drafts
        125 Miscellaneous things to know about twills
            126 Setts for twills
            126 Weaving balanced twills
            127 Using a floating selvedge

    131 **Lesson 8: Altering Drafts**
        131 Doing draw-downs to make pattern decisions
        133 More twills, a little less basic
        137 Drafting from cloth diagrams

141 Lesson 9: An Introduction to Other Kinds of Twills
    143 Offset and broken twills
    143 Waffle weave
    145 Combination twills
    146 Weaving on opposites
    147 Twill variations

149 Part III: For Those of You Who
           Know What You're Doing

149 Lesson 10: Double Weave
    150 Setting up
    150 Threading
    150 Warp considerations
    151 Sleying the reed
    151 Methods of weaving
    156 An alternate threading
    157 Yarns

159 Lesson 11: Honeycomb
    161 Size and shape of blocks
    161 Color considerations
    162 Uses for honeycomb

163 Lesson 12: Harness Controlled Lace Weaves
    164 The lace unit
    164 Blocks
    165 Threading
    166 Tabby
    166 Weaving it
    168 Yarn choices
    168 Sett
    169 Color
    169 Heddles

171 Lesson 13: Block Theory
    172 Block patterns
    174 Profile drafts

177 Lesson 14: Summer and Winter
    178 The basics of summer and winter
    180 Using two wefts
    180 Yarn and color choices
    181 Treadling summer and winter
    182 Variations
    183 Uses

185 Lesson 15: Overshot
    186 The pattern blocks and threading
    188 Tying up the treadles for tabby
    188 Yarns and related information
    190 Miscellaneous notes
    193 Wrap up

195 Part IV: Other Useful Things to Know
    195 People to People
    197 Choosing Yarns
    206 Reeds and Warp Setts
    209 About Heddles
    211 On Buying a Loom
    216 Project Considerations
    221 Finishes
    222 Further Reading
    226 Suppliers and Magazines
    227 Troubleshooting
    230 Index
    232 Formulas for Figuring Warp and Weft

Introduction

Welcome to your own home study 4-harness weaving course. Before we actually begin I want to talk about my hopes and expectations for your use of this book. First of all I want you to have fun and enjoy learning to weave. There's not much point in it otherwise. Second I want you to understand what you're doing and feel comfortable with the weaving process so that you are able to solve problems as they arise. If you understand the loom, the yarns, and the rest of the ingredients of weaving you will be able to decipher most surprises easily. My hope is that by the end of this course you will be able to plan, execute and complete a project from start to finish with full understanding of each and every step of the weaving process—and do it with confidence. What you will find here is the information you need to make these decisions, rather than the specifics for making any particular project.

So, to have fun and learn are the goals of this class.

There is one thing I want to be absolutely clear on, right from the start. I believe that taking a class and having a teacher there in person is a better way to learn than from a book. With a real live person acting as teacher, feedback on questions is immediate, and many things you didn't know you needed to ask about will be answered before they become problems. Also valuable in a classroom setting are the unique interpretations of each assignment by other people interested in the same subject you are. It's a good way to meet new people, sometimes start new friendships, and always learn more than you anticipated. So, if you can, take a class.

If you can't, however, or don't want to, it is my sincere hope that this book will help you to learn the things you need to know to become the weaver you want to be.

Without going into the details of the work that has gone into this, I do want to say a few things about this book. It is based on the classes I've been teaching steadily since 1978 and sporadically since 1972. As I've learned more about teaching and about how students learn, classes have been continually revised to encompass this new found knowledge. Even as this book goes to the publisher, the class outline has changed again. I wrote the first draft for this book over three years ago, and I was surprised at how much I'd learned and how much of it I wanted to change when I sat down now to write this final draft. And, since I expect to learn just as much in the next three years, I wonder a little what my manuscript might look like then. . . . However, I've finally realized that if I wait until I've learned everything, you'll never get it. So here it is, the best I have to offer right now, with my hope that you will grow beyond it, just as I intend to do.

Since this is intended to be used as a home study course, I'd like to talk a little about how the book is organized and recommend some methods for using it. What you will find in each lesson is an overview of the basic concepts presented in that lesson followed by an in-depth discussion of the technique or process. At the end of each lesson you'll find a few assignments to try, along with project ideas. Try them all, or only a few, or make up your own. The more you weave, the more you will know! Below are some guidelines for how you might want to proceed. Again, I prefer classes, so these suggestions are designed with this in mind.

1. Make up your own class schedule. Make it something realistic for your lifestyle. Choose a time every week or every day that is your class time. Go to class at that time and don't allow yourself to be interrupted for anything less than you would if you were attending class elsewhere. Take this as seriously as a class you'd paid for and arranged your schedule around.

2. If you have friends who also want to learn to weave, get to-gether and form your own class. Use this book as your teacher, meet and learn together. Then, one of the greatest advantages of a classroom situation will be present—seeing other interpre-tations of the same lesson. It will also help your motivation and enthusiasm stay high, both for learning and for getting your homework done.

3. Keep notes. We've left you wide margins so you can take notes as you go along. You will also come up with questions and dis-coveries that don't seem to be covered in the book; keep those in a separate notebook that you can take with you when you go to your weaving shop, guild meeting or weaving friend's house. And read over your notes occasionally. You'll be pleased to see how much you've learned (early revelations will become core knowledge that you will take for granted and think you've always known), and discoveries forgotten will be re-discovered. Reading your notes from time to time will save you some relearning.

How long it takes you to learn to weave will depend on how much time you devote to it. In my classes students complete one of these lessons each week. They spend two to three hours in class and probably four to 12 hours on their homework, more at first, less as the weeks go by. You may want to take a leisurely approach, or a more in-depth one. There are several possible as-signments at the end of each lesson, and whether you do one of them, all of them, or make up your own is, of course, up to you.

You may want to go through the whole book first fairly quickly, then repeat it with more study of each lesson, or you may want to spend a month on each lesson the first time through. How fast you go doesn't matter a bit, as long as it works for you and is a pace that let's you enjoy it, balancing satisfaction of accomplishment with not feeling pressured. Remember, enjoying it and learning are the goals.

If you already know something about weaving you may want to skim the first lessons, or skip them altogether, at least for now. These first lessons were written for people who know absolutely nothing about weaving and so are very detailed.

The other thing I want to say about reading this book is that so far I've met only one person who has read her weaving books from start to finish, and it wasn't me. I'm assuming that many of the people who pick this up will start somewhere in the middle and read only the lessons that look interesting to them. Therefore, each lesson is as independent as possible and can stand on its own. I've repeated some ideas and facts in various places as seems appropriate.

This book does not have everything you need to know in it, not even close to it. In preparing it, especially Part IV, there was a constant sense of "Oh, we should include this too!". At some point it became time to quit, and I hope you'll read lots of other weaving books for all of the interesting and useful things they've included that aren't here. There is a list of books I like to recommend on page 222, and while I suggest you don't buy them just now, because it's easier to learn from one source at a time, do consider getting some of them later. Every teacher, every author, will present ideas differently. Each will have a different idea of what is important to know.

I tell all of my beginning students that it would be ideal if they would take at least two beginning classes from two different teachers, for they would then see that they can interpret most things in many ways. The same is true with weaving books. They will appear to contradict each other; you can also say that individual perspective is another word for contradiction. There is room for us all, and in fact, a need for us all. So, let's get started so you can become the weaver you are meant to be.

Part I: *For the Very Beginner*

Lesson 1 Getting Familiar

What is weaving?
The anatomy of a loom
Equipment you will find useful
Weaving vocabulary

In writing this book, I've placed myself in the classroom, imagining you, the reader, as a student in my class. Students arrive in class with different levels of understanding about what weaving is. Some have woven a little already; others aren't so sure they know what weaving or a loom is. So as not to start ahead of you, I'll proceed as if you don't know anything at all about weaving and give you a bit of background information. If you already know these basics, you may want to skip this part.

First the *very* basics. There are many ways to make cloth. Most of you know something about knitting, that it involves two needles and a continuous strand of yarn. A knit fabric is a series of interlocked loops, just as is a crocheted fabric. To crochet, however, one uses only one hook instead of two needles.

In addition to looped fabrics there are those made by twisting yarns together, knotting them, felting unspun fibers, and others.

Woven fabrics are easily the largest and oldest category, and what we are interested in here. In woven fabrics two sets of yarns cross perpendicular to each other. One set is called the *warp*, the other set *weft* (or *woof* in some locales). You may remember as a child making potholders on a small frame, or using a needle to weave through yarn stretched on cardboard. Using cotton loops or a needle threaded with yarn, you pulled the threads over and under, over and under the threads held taut on the "loom". You were weaving then, and the only difference now is that you'll be using a more sophisticated loom.

A *loom*, whatever kind it is, is a device to hold a set of yarns taut so that it is easy to weave other yarns through them. The yarn attached to the loom is the warp. The weft is the yarn that is woven into the warp, the cross threads. On looms that are more elaborate than potholder or cardboard frames there is some kind

Knitted fabric

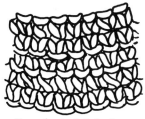

Crocheted fabric

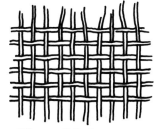

Woven fabric

of mechanism that raises or lowers some of the warp threads at any given time, making it easier to pass the weft through; the space created when some warps are raised or lowered is called the *shed*, and the tool that carries the weft through is called the *shuttle*. Different looms have different ways of making sheds, depending on what kind of fabric you want to create or how fast you want to create it. We aren't going to bother with any but the four-harness loom since that is what this class is about. While floor looms have some features that table looms do not have, what they will do is essentially the same, and this course is intended to be equally applicable to either. There is a discussion of looms in Part IV that you might want to look at if you are totally unfamiliar with your own loom.

Let's look at your loom now and get to know its parts and what they do. First, find the front of your loom, which is where the frame that moves back and forth is. That whole framework is called the *beater*, and within the beater is the *reed*, the metal piece with lots of slots (called *dents*). A beater may hang from above or it may be mounted from below, bolted to the sides of the loom. The reed is used to determine how close together the warp threads are and to keep them straight as you weave. The beater and reed together are used to beat the weft into place as you weave.

The *harnesses* are the rectangular frames hanging or resting inside the major frame of the loom behind the beater. This largest part of the loom is called the *castle*, easy to remember because it is central and kind of oversees all the rest. Hanging within each harness you'll find *heddles*, metal or string pieces with eyes in the middle through which the warp will be threaded. (If your loom is old and the heddles are very rusted, throw them out and buy new ones; they don't cost that much and heddles with corroded surfaces can cut your yarn.) On most looms the heddles are on metal heddle bars. On newer looms (those made within the last 15 years) the heddle bars are most often spring steel, a steel that will flex for removal without bending permanently. Older looms and some new ones have other kinds of metal for their heddle bars, and to remove them requires lifting the harness out of the castle and sliding the bar out rather than bending it. If you don't have a spring steel bar, don't bend it, for it will never be straight again.

If you have a floor loom, down near the floor are *treadles*, used to raise or lower the harnesses. On a table loom the lifting mechanism is a series of *levers* mounted on either the front or side of the loom, one lever for each harness.

In both the front and back of the loom, about half way up in height, you'll see two large rotating beams running from side to side which may be round, hexagonal, or made of four flat pieces of wood attached together. The one in the back will have the warp rolled around it before you start weaving, so it is called the *warp beam*. The one in front is called the *cloth beam* (or *fabric beam*) since this is where the cloth will be rolled up. The advantage of these two beams and their rotating capability, is that they allow you to weave great long lengths of cloth, something not possible on frame and cardboard looms.

Also at the front and back of the loom, higher and probably outside of the warp and cloth beam, are two flat beams, used to elevate and level the warp for the weaving process. These are called the *front* or *breast beam* and *back beam*. On most floor looms one or both of these beams can easily be removed so that you can get close to the castle for threading. On table looms you can reach through the framework to the castle. In addition, many floor looms are designed so that the whole back section will fold up or drop to the floor, getting it further out of the way. Play around with your loom to see what will and won't move.

One last part of a floor loom that makes life easier is the brake pedal. It looks like another treadle, but is off to the side, usually the right. (Some looms have cords that you pull somewhere instead of a foot controlled release; the principle is the same.) The *brake* or *tension release pedal* is used to release the mechanism holding the warp beam rigid. There are two different types of brakes, ratchet and friction, needed on both the warp and cloth beams to keep the warp taut while weaving is underway. Most looms have a ratchet and dog or pawl in front, a toothed gear and a straight or slightly curved piece that falls into the teeth of the gear to hold it still. The warp beam may have another ratchet or a friction brake. There is more information on this in the warping section, explained as you need it.

A recent development, on only two looms I know of, is a third type of brake. It utilizes worm gears for infinite adjustment both front and back. It's a nice feature, more expensive, and may eventually become more common.

This should get you more or less familiar with the basic parts of your loom. Of course you'll understand more about them and what they do as you actually begin using them, so don't be concerned if it isn't all clear now.

The loom is only one of the pieces of equipment needed to weave, and while other tools vary in their degree of necessity, I want you to at least be aware of a lot of them. Look through the illustrations on the next couple of pages, and read the descriptions of each tool. From this decide which you have and which would be useful to you. Not everything available is shown here, so browse through shops and catalogs when you have the opportunity to see what else exists, especially if you find yourself having a problem that it seems there must be a tool to help solve. The glossary, too, is here for your initial exposure. Read through it but don't feel compelled to memorize it. Use of the words will come as you get into weaving and see them in context.

The anatomy of a loom

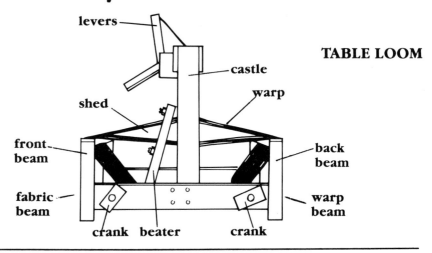

TABLE LOOM

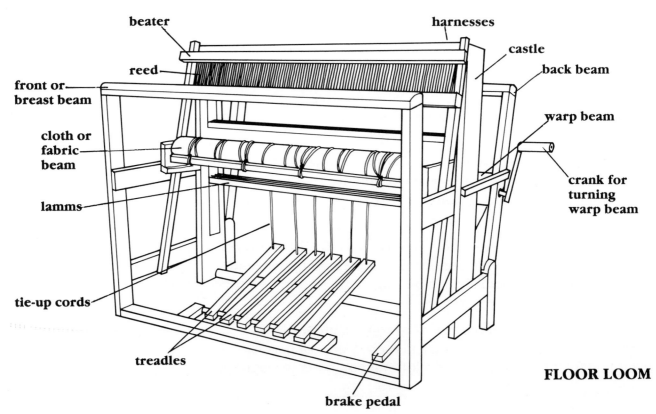

FLOOR LOOM

Equipment you will find useful

Warping pegs are the most basic of all warp measuring devices. Clamp them to a table the appropriate distance apart and start measuring.

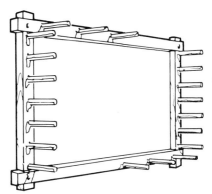

A warping board is a nice piece of equipment to own, easy to figure out, comfortable and efficient to use. This warping tool is very common and the one I refer to in this course.

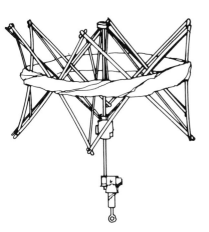

An **umbrella swift** is both invaluable and fun to look at. It holds a skein of yarn and keeps it from getting tangled. You can take yarn directly from your swift to warping board, bobbin, shuttle or whatever.

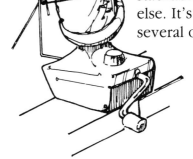

A **ball winder** is the tool to acquire right after you get a swift. In a couple of minutes a ball winder will wind a solid, stackable, center-pull ball, from which you can do anything else. It's also useful for making multiple-strand yarns, running several onto the ball winder together.

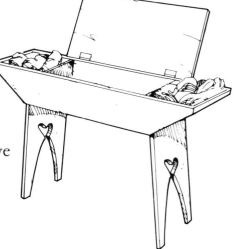

Loom benches come in a variety of styles, each with something that makes it more than just a bench. Most have some storage area for yarn, shuttles, etc. Some are adjustable in height or angle of seat.

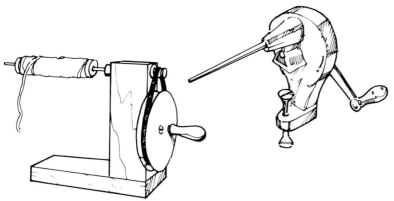

Bobbin winders come in different shapes with different drive mechanisms, and so have different prices. The purpose of a bobbin winder is to wind yarn onto bobbins for use in boat shuttles. Many people use drills, mixers or other substitutes, all of which work, but none of which are as easy or efficient as the real thing.

Electric bobbin winders go faster than manual models. They are particularly useful if you're weaving with fine threads a lot. Speed is controlled with a sewing machine style foot pedal.

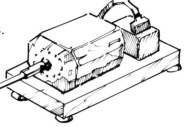

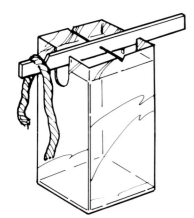

McMorran Yarn Balance is probably the greatest invention for weavers since the loom; these are still relatively new and unknown. Made of clear plastic, about 6″ tall, the arm is calibrated to measure yards per pound (or meters) of any yarn, even handspun. (A very heavy thick and thin yarn might not work, but anything else will.) It's a tremendous help to those who collect a lot of miscellaneous unlabelled yarn and keep wondering how much of it they have, or more significantly, if they have enough.

If you want to keep track of how long it takes you to get something done, buy a simple (non-digital) **alarm clock.** Set it at 12:00, plug it in while working on the project, unplug it when you leave, and then plug it back in when you start to work again, etc.

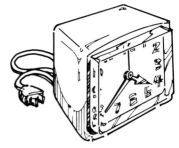

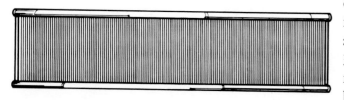

The **reed** has two functions, the spacing of the warp and the packing in of the weft. Reeds come with different spacings, called dents per inch. A 12-dent has 12 slots per inch all the way across. A 36″ reed is 36″ wide and can weave a 36″-wide warp. Reeds are made of steel and can rust if they get wet. If you live in a coastal area buy stainless steel reeds, the added expense of which is your trade-off for the joys of living near the water.

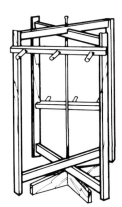

A **warping mill** is a device for measuring warp. It comes in both vertical and horizontal models; the one you'll prefer depends on which you get used to first. The difference between mills and warping boards or pegs is that instead of your arm going back and forth, they go around, saving your arm this motion. They are faster and more efficient, but take up more space and cost more. If you are measuring warps of eight yards or more most of the time, they are well worth the investment.

Pick-up stick. We won't be using this in this course particularly, but it is handy to have around. It is used for picking up individual warp threads for special patterning; it's also good for clearing a sticky shed and as a magic wand when one is called for.

A **threading hook**, also called a heddle hook, is used for threading the heddles. It can be used to sley the reed as well, though it is slightly awkward for this purpose because of its length.

A **temple** (or stretcher) is used to keep the width of a weaving constant. Many rug weavers use them always; they also get used on pieces as fine as table linens.

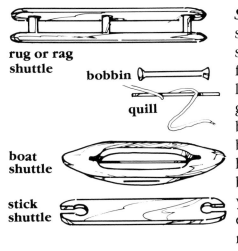

rug or rag shuttle

bobbin

quill

boat shuttle

stick shuttle

ski shuttle

Shuttles come in a variety of shapes, each designed for making some kind of weft throwing easier. Ski shuttles and rug or rag shuttles are used for holding heavy yarns. Boat shuttles are the fastest to use as the yarn is wrapped on a bobbin or quill (looks like a short straw) and then feeds off automatically as the shuttle glides through the shed. Boat shuttles are most expensive, need bobbins and a bobbin winder. A couple of shuttles and a dozen bobbins will keep you going for a long time. If you use only heavy yarn or rags don't bother with a boat shuttle because a boat shuttle can't hold as much heavy yarn as a ski or rag shuttle; you'll need to change bobbins very often. Stick shuttles are the easiest to make and the cheapest to buy. They are available in many styles and lengths.

Sley hooks, or reed hooks, are short, flat hooks used for sleying the reed, which means threading yarn through the dents (slots) in the reed.

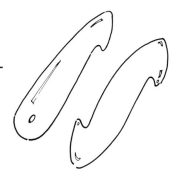

Equipment you won't need for this course (but you should know about)

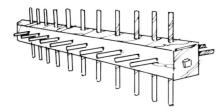

A **sectional warp beam** has pegs at 1″ or 2″ intervals. For weavers putting on very long warps all of the time, it is a time-saver. To use one as intended you also need a spool rack, spool winder, spools, a tension box and yardage counter. We won't cover sectional warping in this course but you can find out about it in other books. Ask your shopkeeper for information.

A **tension box** creates tension on warp going from spool rack to sectional warp beam.

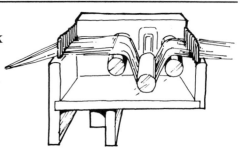

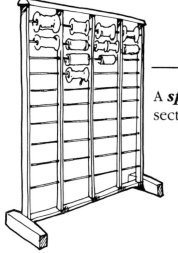

A **spool rack** holds spools for sectional warping.

A **paddle** is used to measure many warp threads at once, saving time over measuring one end at a time.

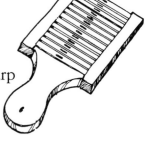

A **raddle** is used when warping back to front. It is the tool that is used when rolling onto the warp beam to separate and spread the warp to the correct width. This is another thing you won't be using for this course, but should be aware of.

Treadle Minder. Sometimes you'll weave patterns that are complicated enough that keeping track of where you are in the treadling sequence seems almost hopeless. This little board has a place for you to fill in your treadling pattern; moving a peg from hole to hole marks your place in the sequence. As far as I know these are available only from Sievers Looms, Washington Island, Wisconsin. They come in horizontal and vertical models.

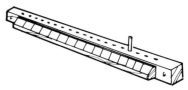

Vocabulary needed now

Balanced weave—a fabric in which the number of threads per inch is the same in the warp and in the weft. It can be loose or tight as long as the count is the same.

Beaming, to beam the warp—to roll the warp onto the back of the loom, onto the warp beam.

Cross, lease—the figure eight made at one end (or both) of the warp when measuring in order to prevent tangles later.

Dent—a slot in the reed; a 12-dent reed has 12 dents per inch.

Draft—a map of the pattern you want to weave. A full draft is made up of four parts: threading, tie-up, treadling, and draw down. Drafting is the international language of weavers. It tells you how to weave any fabric you'll ever see.

Draw-in—during weaving, the pulling in of the selvedges a little from the original warp width.

Dressing the loom—another way of saying warping the loom; or to dress is to warp.

E.P.I.—ends per inch, tells how many warp ends there are [to be] in one inch, counted sideways.

Fell—the front/forward edge of your weaving, the edge made by your most recent weft shot.

Filler—weft.

Fiber—raw material, animal, vegetable, or mineral, made into yarn. Also spelled fibre.

Fiber content—important to know so you'll know how a yarn or fabric will behave and how to care for it. Most weavers use natural fibers such as wool, cotton, linen, silk etc., each of which has its own wonderful unique characteristics.

Finishing—this word is used in two ways. One refers to finishing the fabric, which means washing, brushing, etc. The other encompasses finishing techniques—fringes, knots, hems, etc.

Lease sticks—flat sticks (or sometimes round) that come with the loom, usually as long as the loom is wide. They are used in some methods of warping for holding the cross.

Loom waste—not the fur balls that accumulate under the loom. Loom waste refers to the part of the warp that never gets woven, the ends that attach the warp to the loom at front and back.

P.P.I.—picks per inch, wefts per inch, just as e.p.i. is [warp] ends per inch.

Pick, shot—one pass of weft, often called a weft shot or just pick.

Ply, plied—when yarn is spun, it is twisted into a single strand; two singles together are called a 2-ply yarn, three singles a 3-ply yarn, etc. A plied yarn has two or more strands twisted together. A single strand yarn is often called a single ply even though it was never plied.

Problems—a word often used for opportunities to invent creative solutions, learn more. Whatever you call them, you'll have them, even when you reach that stage called "advanced". The only way to avoid them is to never try anything new, safe but boring.

Reed—the metal piece that fits into the beater of the loom which is interchangeable. Reeds may have 4,5,6,8,10,12,15, or 20 dents per inch, or others. They determine how close together your warp threads will be, what the warp sett will be. The reed and beater together push the weft into place.

Selvedge, selvage, selvege—the sides of a fabric, sealed edges that won't ravel, just like on sheets or commercial fabrics.

Set, sett—refers to e.p.i. Set is the verb, sett the noun. The warp sett was 10. The warp was set at 10 e.p.i.

Shaft—English term for the American word harness. On some types of looms a combination of shafts working together is referred to as a harness. The English term shaft takes this distinction into account. Shaft is also used in the U.S., though harness will be the term used in this book.

Shed—the space created between upper and lower warp threads when harnesses are raised and/or lowered. The shuttle and weft go through the shed.

Shot—a weft going through the shed. (See Pick.)

Sley—to put the warp through the reed.

Sley hook—a short hook designed for quick threading/sleying of the warp through the reed.

Take-up—the flexing and curving of warp over and under weft and weft over and under warp.

Threading hook—a long skinny hook designed for threading the warp through the heddles.

Warp—the yarn attached to the loom, held under tension during the weaving process.

Warp end—one warp thread, the whole thing, not just the end.

Web—woven fabric, a word more often used while the fabric is still on the loom.

Weft—the horizontal thread, the yarn running from selvedge to selvedge, perpendicular to the warp.

Yarn, thread—if I make a distinction at all it is that thread is thinner, yarn fatter; mostly I use them interchangeably.

Lesson 2
Your First Piece

The value of making samples
Choosing yarn for your sample
Step-by-step warping

Believe it or not, what to have students weave for a first piece is a matter of great philosophical debate among teachers. "Something beautiful and inspiring to get them confident and enthusiastic, and if they don't really learn anything that's okay for now," is at one end of the spectrum. At the other end is, "Now that you've woven this tapestry you must unweave it, just so you'll know that a great weaving takes a lot of learning and can't happen the first time." I fall somewhere between these two.

The value of making samples

As every student who's ever had me for a teacher will tell you, I encourage samples. Of course, I want you to be inspired and encouraged by your first weaving experience; if you're not, it's not likely that you'll go on to a second. But my own bias is that you came to class not just to weave, but to learn *how* to weave; there is a critical difference between the two. There is value and pleasure to be gained from weaving without knowing what you're doing, and I'm not opposed to that kind of experience. It's not what I have to offer, however. I want you to know what you're doing, and I think you do too or you wouldn't have bought this book. So, while I want your first piece to be wonderful, I also want it to teach you a lot. More than anything, I want it to teach you that learning to weave is easy and fun, and that you can weave nice pieces immediately.

Like most people, when I first started weaving I wanted to weave real things, things I would like to own and use and show off. I had never had any weaving instruction, consequently I had no understanding of basic things like yarn properties as they relate to weave structures, color combinations and what they do, what the loom was capable of, and lots more. So I embarked on project after project with no foundation, and was disappointed by most of what I created because they were all either ugly (experimental) or boring (safe). Two years later I took my first class and promptly started trying to weave real things again, feeling confident in my new-found knowledge. More ugly pieces, a few okay ones—again, the experimental vs. the safe.

photography in this lesson by Eric Redding

Clearly, I had to learn what was going on so I could begin to understand what was going wrong. I reasoned that weaving samples, pieces roughly 6″ × 12″ or longer, would cost me less than weaving bigger pieces and allow me to make my discoveries more quickly. I'd be saving both time and money. In the event that one ever came out well—it was bound to sooner or later—I'd have a basis for doing something larger.

So I started. And I learned.

I wove samples for a long time before I realized that I was beginning to settle down into successfully weaving "real things". The sample stage lasted a long time for me because I enjoyed it, got really excited about discovering what weaving was. There could be no disappointments because there were no expectations. I was learning how weaving worked, making up and solving puzzles, and it was loads of fun. I didn't expect that. I even remember hearing one woman tell me she liked to weave samples and my thinking she must be crazy—who'd want to waste time doing that? So, I encourage, recommend and urge that you weave samples.

Recently, I heard another teacher's wonderful reason for sampling: you have a good idea which you try out on a sample, but while you're weaving the sample something new occurs to you and you end up with something even better than you were going to have originally. There's a carrot on a stick for you!

A sample is a learning device

A sample doesn't need to be a "thing"; it is a learning device. If you have set out to learn something, and you do, then the piece has fulfilled its function. It doesn't have to have another. If it does, for instance, become a scarf or table runner, then that's a bonus. What you learn may be a positive—this I want to do again, or it may be the reverse—now I know something not to do, something that didn't work. Either way you have learned.

This is a roundabout way of getting to your first assignment. By now you won't be surprised when I say it's to be a sample. It will be nice; you'll enjoy it. Its purpose is to help you get used to your loom, to get the feel of what's going on, to play with some of the possibilities. It's to be large enough so that you get to play and enjoy for awhile, but small enough that you'll be done and still want more. So let's get on with it.

Your sample

Your sample will be 10″ wide, two yards long, two colors in the warp and two colors in the weft. You will have 12 warp threads per inch. Since I am particularly concerned with your learning to put a warp on your loom and understanding how it all works, for this assignment I'm going to give specifics as to what I want you to do. In Lesson 4 I'll discuss planning, and from then on you'll be designing on your own.

What you will need:

1. A warping board, or something to measure your warp on.
2. A 4-harness table loom or 4-harness floor loom.
3. 240 yards each of two colors of wool yarn.
4. Scissors.
5. A ruler.
6. A 12-dent reed for your loom (if you don't have one, see page 206 for what to do).
7. A sley hook.
8. Masking tape.

Choosing yarn for your sample

For this sample, I want you to use a wool yarn because it's the easiest to work with. Use it unless you have a violent allergy to it. Wool is a good yarn to start with because its elasticity is very forgiving. It will go a long way toward compensating for your inexperience at achieving consistent tension with your warp threads. I'll talk a lot about this later.

Choose a wool yarn that is plied (has two or more strands twisted together), not too stiff, not too stretchy, or not too fuzzy. A medium-weight yarn similar to a sport weight knitting yarn, about the size shown here, and which yields about 1600 yards per pound, will work well. A four-ounce skein of each color should be enough. Avoid standard knitting yarns for now: they have characteristics that require special tricks for successful weaving.

Choose a yarn about this size.

Also, your warp yarn should be strong enough to hold up during the weaving process. One method I've heard of for testing for yarn strength is to use both hands and to try to pull the yarn apart. If it breaks with a 'ping', it'll work fine; if it breaks with a 'thud', it might not be strong enough.

If you're uncertain about whether your yarn will yield 12 ends to the inch, you can wrap 1″ of a ruler with yarn. Wrap the ruler with each wrap right next to, but not on top of, the last. Push the wraps close to each other so that there is no space at all between them. Then divide the number of wraps in 1″ by two. If this number is 12, then that yarn will work for this sample. If your number is too small, then you know your yarn is too fat, and you'll need to choose a skinnier yarn.

Wrapping your yarn for 1″ around a ruler will give you an idea of how many ends per inch it should be sleyed.

I want you to use two colors so you'll see how they interact, and because that's more interesting than using only one. Two colors mean stripes; I'd like you to make them 1″ wide. Use any colors you like, though know that the more contrast there is between your colors, the more you will see what's going on. For example, black and white have a lot of contrast and it will be easy to see how they interact; navy blue and black have little contrast and you'll have a hard time seeing what's happening.

> ### *Yarn*
> *Choose two colors of plied wool yarn, not too stretchy, or not too fuzzy. A medium-weight yarn yielding about 1600 yards per pound, will work well. Use contrasting colors.*

Yarn handling

When you go shopping for yarn, you'll notice that it is packaged in a number of forms: skeins, balls, pull skeins, cones, tubes. Shape does not indicate quantity; any amount can be in any shape.

Skeins look the prettiest and are the healthiest way for the yarn to be stored, so many weaving yarns come in skeins. Of these five ways of packaging yarn, only skeins are prone to serious tangling and require special treatment before they can be used. Yarn from balls and pull skeins can be pulled from either the outside or the inside, and generally the inside is preferable because the unit will lie still instead of rolling all over, picking up dust bunnies and getting tangled up in things. Cones and tubes have cardboard in the center, and so must be pulled from the outside. A cone will stand up on its own; a tube needs to be set onto a nail or dowel or something to hold it still. If the cardboard has come out it is possible to treat the coned or tubed yarn as a pull skein, but sometimes they are wrapped with so much tension that this won't work; you'll get whole clumps of yarn instead of the single strand you want—and end up with a mess of tangles.

If you're going to own only one piece of equipment (besides a good pair of scissors) make it an umbrella swift. Most of us remember scenes of two people making a ball of yarn. One would hold the skein of yarn while the other would wind the ball. An umbrella swift, which does the job of holding the yarn, can be an invaluable tool to own. Its big advantage is of being ready and waiting any time, day or night. It's not quite as companionable, but what it lacks in conversation it makes up for in efficiency. And it's a neat looking piece of equipment, definitely related to an umbrella, but more fun.

Skein

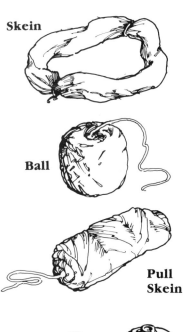

Ball

Pull Skein

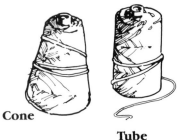

Cone

Tube

Alternate forms of swifts are squirrel cage reels and yarn reels, providing the same function, costing more, and having other advantages. Ask your local shop owner about them.

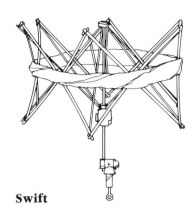

Swift

A swift holds the skein so that you can pull yarn from it as quickly as you need it. Besides making a ball of yarn, you can take yarn directly from the swift to the warping board, bobbin winder, shuttle or ball winder.

To put a skein on a swift, open up the skein to its full size. Find, but do not yet untie, the ties that are securing the skein. Make sure the yarn going through the ties is straight and not doubling back. Once all is straight put the skein around the swift and adjust the swift to the correct size, large enough to hold the skein securely but not too tightly. The ends of the skein will either be tied to each other or knotted around the skein individually; there may or may not be additional ties. Release these ends (cut or untie them) being careful to separate them from the rest of the group right away. Do not stick them through the rest of the skein. When the skein was made it had no tangles and the ends were connected last; if you put an end through the bundle you have created the first tangle and it will not feed freely again. Of course there are exceptions; some skeins do have problems that can be solved only with loving patience. Most will not have problems and will unwind easily once you've pulled the end free.

The companion tool to the swift is the ball winder. This is a clever device that will make a ball of yarn which will sit flat and pull from the center—and do it in a matter of minutes. Ball winders will easily make four-ounce balls, and many will make larger ones. The instructions for use come with them. What I will add (that it took me years to discover) is two little-known, very useful facts. First is that the plastic center the ball is winding onto weighs one ounce, so if you are trying to make a ball of specific weight, you can remove the whole top, weigh it, subtract an ounce, and keep going as necessary. The second discovery is one that I resisted for a long time because it didn't make sense to me, but it seems to work pretty well anyway. One revolution of the handle wraps on one yard of yarn. Again, it seems suspicious if only because each person will wrap yarn on at different tension, but it works with reasonable accuracy, and is useful for good approximations.

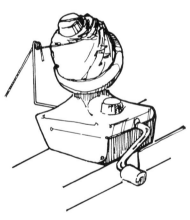

Ball winder

Warping your loom

Now that you've assembled all the supplies you'll need, it's time to start putting your warp on your loom. I've heard that you should plan on your on-loom time being about half of your total project time. There is a lot more to weaving than throwing a shuttle. Sometimes, especially in the beginning and on small projects, setting up the project takes longer than weaving it off.

Don't be discouraged by this. The more times you do it the faster you'll become and the less time it will take. There are many weavers who enjoy warping more than weaving, and, of course, many who prefer weaving.

Learning and being comfortable with the warping process puts you on the path to self-sufficiency. And since putting a warp on your loom is an essential part of weaving, and is the foundation of good cloth, I'll spend quite a lot of time on it.

In my first class, I walk my students through the warping process. They then go home with a table loom and a couple of balls of yarn to complete the warping of their looms and weaving of a sample all on their own. Here, I hope these photos and process highlights will be an adequate substitute for my class walk-through. I suggest you follow the warping process given here step by step, keeping this book next to you as you work. Each step is discussed first, followed by a brief description and a photo when appropriate. You may choose to follow the step-by-step notes for this sample, and then read over the discussion when you have a better idea of the process, having done it once. Let me stress here that you'll find learning by doing an invaluable approach to understanding warping. All these words will make a lot more sense after you've warped your loom once.

Here is a synopsis of the warping process:
1. Measure the warp.
2. Sley the reed.
3. Thread the heddles.
4. Tie onto the back apron rod.
5. Beam the warp.
6. Tie onto the front apron rod.
7. Tie up the treadles.
8. Weave.

This short list can be a quick reminder later, and give you some sense of direction now. It really is as easy as it sounds once you get used to it, but don't be dismayed when you feel clumsy and awkward, and suddenly have too many thumbs. That's normal; everyone goes through it. It will pass. Later you'll be amazed at and derive great pleasure from your speed and dexterity.

Measuring the warp

1. Measure the warp.

Though you can measure your warp on just about any stationary object, owning a warping board or warping mill will ease your work considerably. Warping boards are made with rows of pegs along each side, either a yard or half-yard apart. They are easy to use, relatively inexpensive, and nice to have around, as you can hang yarn or your coat on one when it's not being used for its first purpose.

A warping mill is easier on your arm and shoulder, faster to use, takes up more space, and costs more. Warping pegs cost only a few dollars, are less convenient to use, and they can be stored in a drawer or loom bench when not in use. If you have none of these, you can turn chairs upside down and use the legs (be sure to anchor the chairs so they don't creep together as you use them), or drive large nails into your garage wall. I knew a mother/daughter pair who, for many years, used gallon cans of food on the living room floor spaced the proper distance apart; makes my back ache to think of it, but it would work.

Because it is both common and convenient, I will discuss the use of the warping board here. First, try to find a place on the wall to hang your warping board. It should be a place that is well lit, easy to get to, and where you can install it permanently. Have someone hold it at different heights for you while you move your arms back and forth from peg to peg. You should adjust your board so that you can easily reach and move around the bottom and upper pegs. If you don't have the space to install your warping board permanently, find a place where you can prop it up to work comfortably.

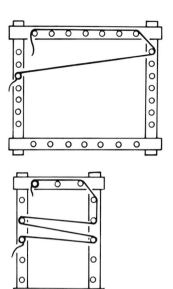

Two-yard guide string on 1-yard wide warping board (top) and ½-yard wide warping board (bottom).

Guide strings. As your sample warp is to be two yards long, you will need to find a two-yard long path on your warping board. A good way to do this is to measure a piece of yarn—a guide string—two yards long plus a few extra inches for tying it onto the pegs. Now make a path with it on your warping board until you find just the right pegs for the length of your guide string. When you've done this, tie your string to the pegs and leave it in place so that you can use it when you start measuring your warp. The guide string will be discarded after use. Using a contrasting color of yarn will make it readily distinguishable from the warp you're measuring. At top right are illustrations of two-yard warps: one on a one-yard wide warping board and one on a half-yard wide warping board.

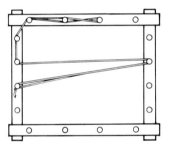

Here are some illustrations which show warps in whole-yard increments. The pegs across the top (and/or bottom) of the board help adjust for additional length. These horizontal pegs might be in ¼-, ⅓-, or ½-yard spacing. It doesn't matter what you have, just figure out what you've got and use it. You can also use the other side pegs for added inches, or go across the board on an angle instead of a straight horizontal line. At right are an assortment of paths, any of which will work.

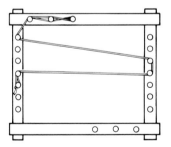

> *Find two yards on your warping board or other measuring tool. Use a guide string to help you, if necessary.*

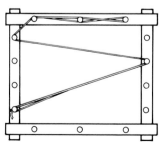

Warps in whole-yard increments. Any of these will work.

Starting to measure. Now that you have determined the path of your warp, tie on one of your colors along the vertical side where the end of your guide string is. Any knot that holds is fine. A slip knot is fast; a square knot is fine, too. Now, follow the path of your guide string until you get to the next to the last peg. Here you will need to start making the cross, which is an essential step in the measuring process. The cross (also called lease) is a figure-8 configuration. Its purpose is to prevent tangles and to keep your warp ends in order.

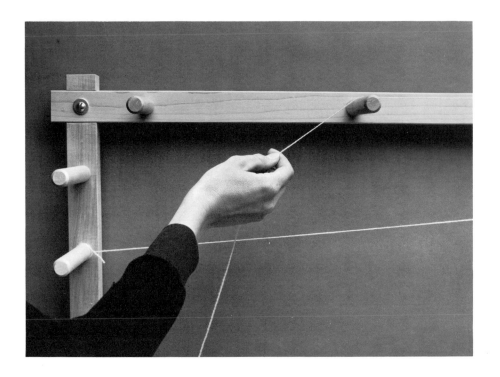

Making the cross. Go over the next to the last peg, under and around and over the top of the last peg. Then under the second to the last peg, making a figure-8. The cross helps prevent tangles and keeps the warp ends in order.

Making the cross. Again, this is one of those things which is at once apparent as you're doing it. Essentially, the cross is made around the last two pegs of your warp length. Begin by going over the next to the last peg, under and around and over the top of the last peg, then under the second to the last peg. Now go back over the top of the third peg and follow the same path of the first warp back to the beginning. From your starting point to the last peg of your cross is one warp end; when you return back to your starting point you have measured two warp ends, as shown.

Making the cross.

Go back to your cross for a minute and trace the figure-8 path of your cross with your finger. If you think "figure-8" you'll soon find that making the cross is second nature.

Measure all the threads, which is 60, of your first color. As you are measuring, try to keep just enough tension on your warp so it goes around the pegs without drooping, but is not so tight that the pegs are forced in. To make space for more ends, you may find that you need to slide the previously measured ends closer together toward the back of the peg.

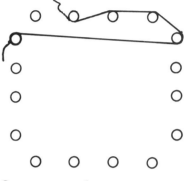
One warp end.

> *Tie on the end of one of your colors of yarn and follow your guide string. Make a cross at one end. Measure 60 ends.*

If you are alone and not interrupted it is sometimes possible to count warp ends as you go from one to 60, or whatever. For those people not so secluded, however, there are other means of keeping track of count. A counting thread is one good way. After you've measured 10 threads (that's five up and five back), tie a yarn in a contrasting color around these, leaving long tails. When you've measured another ten ends, use the tails to tie around the next group. Keep doing this, and when you have six groups you know you have 60 warp ends.

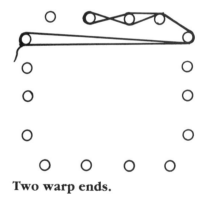
Two warp ends.

If you don't want to bother with a counting thread, but would rather just count threads periodically, there are two places you can do so. You can count all the threads anywhere along the warp path. Or look at the cross. At the point where you made your cross, half the warp is on top, the other half is below. If you count what's on top of the peg you need to count only half of the warp then multiply by two for the total number of ends measured.

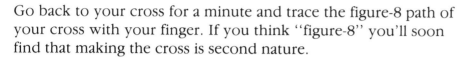
count here

Tying the cross. Once you have all 60 ends of your first color measured, you need to secure the cross so it stays intact after the warp is removed from the warping board. The cross needs to be tied in five places as shown. Four ties are used to contain the

Tying the cross. The most crucial tie is the one tying the cross. Make sure it goes *around* the cross so that the cross is held inside.

yarn on either side of the cross. These will be made on the warp above and below the pegs on either side of the cross; they help keep these sections separated for when you need to find them later. The fifth and most crucial tie is the one which protects the cross. This tie needs to go *around* the cross so that the cross is held inside the tie. Your tie yarn will go through the triangles on either side of the cross as illustrated. Your ties should be tight enough to keep the yarn contained, but loose enough to get a scissor blade in easily. Using a different color of yarn makes it easy to see what you want to cut off later and helps prevent cutting your warp accidentally.

> *After 60 ends have been measured, tie off your end at the point where you started measuring. Tie the cross.*

Two-yard warp on ½-yard wide warping board. Cross is tied; choke ties are used to contain the warp.

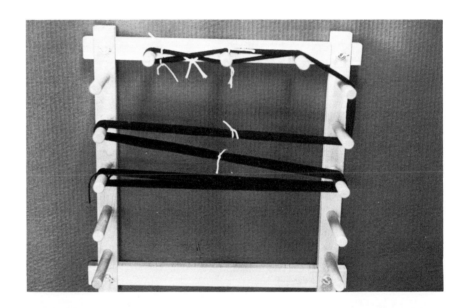

Two-yard warp on 1-yard wide warping board. Cross is tied; choke ties are used to contain the warp.

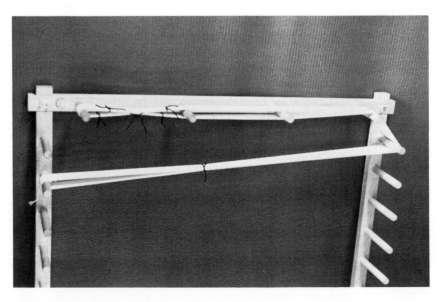

Removing the warp from the warping board. When the cross is secure, you can take the warp off the board in stages. First slide the end furthest away from the cross off its peg, holding the warp bundle firmly. Now is the easiest time to cut this end of the warp; one cut with a good pair of scissors will do the job. It is not necessary to cut this end now, however. Many people prefer to wait until the last possible moment before cutting.

Whether you've cut the end or not, tie the whole warp bundle into one large overhand knot. You will untie the knot later, so tie it tight enough to be secure but not so tight that it's hard to untie. The purpose of this knot is to contain these warp ends so that they don't get out of alignment during the warping process. Leave this knot tied until almost the very end of the warping process; it doesn't need to come out until you are just about ready to tie those ends onto the front apron rod.

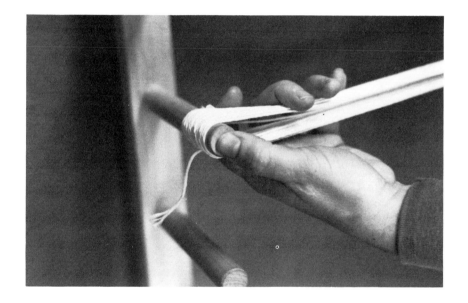

Removing the warp from the warping board. Slide the end furthest away from the cross off its peg, holding it firmly.

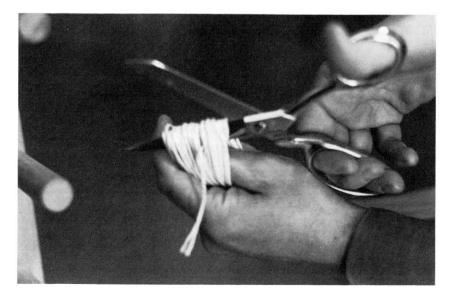

Cutting the end of the warp.

Tying an overhand knot in the end of the warp.

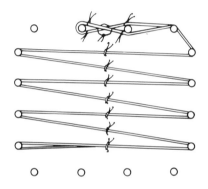

Choke ties help keep long warps from getting tangled.

Now lift the rest of the warp length off the warping board. Because you have only 60 threads and because your warp is only two yards long, you shouldn't encounter any real tangle problems. The ties in the cross and the knot at the other end will keep a short warp pretty well contained. With a long warp or very slippery yarns it is usually a good idea to put more ties, called choke ties, along the length just to keep your warp secure. In some climates and with some yarns this is even more necessary, but in any case the idea is to keep the yarn from getting disordered. Some weavers like their choke ties to be very tight to keep the yarn from slipping. If you decide to do this, then I would recommend tying a bow for easy removal of the tie. If you'd rather tie a knot, then leave the tie just loose enough to get a scissor blade in easily—it's very frustrating to cut warp while cutting ties.

> *Tie choke ties to contain your warp, as needed. Remove the warp from the warping board. Cut the end and tie an overhand knot in the end opposite the cross. Chain your warp as necessary. Repeat this entire measuring process for your second color, measuring 60 ends.*

Another common practice, done by itself or in conjunction with choke ties, is chaining the warp, which helps contain the warp and shortens your warp length so your warp is easier to handle. Chaining the warp is so common that a measured warp is often called a warp chain. Chaining is just like chaining in crochet. To begin, make a slip knot in the end where you tied the overhand knot, and begin removing the warp from the board as you chain. Your arm essentially acts as the crochet hook to make a series of loops which are easily removed later in the process. The big advantage of warp chaining is that is makes your warp less vulner-able to tangling in transport, whether you're carrying it across the room or across town.

Now your choked and/or chained warp is ready to go to the loom. Repeat the entire process with your second color; it will probably go a lot faster this time. When you have both warp chains ready, it's time to go on to the next step, sleying the reed.

Chaining the warp

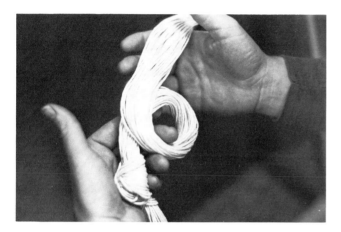

1. To start chaining, make a loop at the end of the warp.

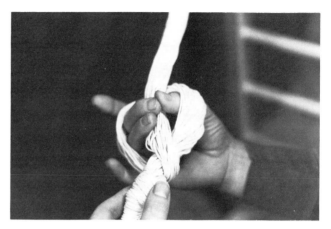

2. Pull warp from ahead of the loop (or working away from the knotted end) through your first loop.

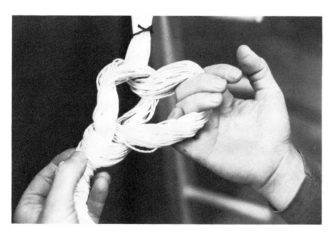

3. Pull through enough length to make another loop.

4. Continue looping loops inside of loops, as in crochet, until you reach the cross.

Sleying the reed

To sley the reed is simply to put the warp yarns through the dents (spaces/slots) in the reed. You could take any measured warp and stick the ends through a reed with your fingers and you'd have sleyed the reed. There are, happily, tools and methods that make sleying go a little faster and the steps that follow it easier. These time and effort savers are what this section is about.

1. Measure the warp.
2. Sley the reed.

Whether you're using a floor or table loom, the process is the same. First, be sure you have the right reed in the beater. With a warp sett of 12 e.p.i., a 12- or six-dent reed is the easiest, with either one or two threads per dent, respectively. If you have only one reed, then you may need to sley a sequence other than a constant one or two threads per dent to get the sett you want. For a full discussion of reeds and warp setts turn to page 206 in part IV.

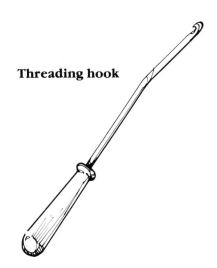

Threading hook

With the correct reed in the beater, tie it into an upright position. Some looms have a pin or other means of holding the beater in a fixed position. Most don't, and it's no big deal to have cords hanging on your loom that you use all the time for this purpose. If your loom has an overhead beater, it will automatically hang in the best position, but you may want to tie it anyway to keep it from swinging as you work. For an overhead beater, position it in the notches closest to the front of the loom so you can reach it easily.

Sley hooks come in a variety of designs and materials, long or short, from plastic to sterling silver. They all work, so find one you're comfortable with. The only significant difference is in length. A threading hook is much longer than a sley hook because it is designed to thread heddles; many weavers use one for sleying the reed and are happy doing so. I prefer the compactness of the sley hook because I can use it by simply flexing my wrist. If you have both available, try each one and see which you prefer. They are relatively inexpensive, so having both is not unreasonable.

Sley hooks

If you have neither, you have several options for immediate alternatives. First, you could use your fingers to poke the yarn through. This works fine with some yarns (smooth, stiff, smaller than the dent), but it is tricky with some others (fuzzy or fat). You can cut a sley hook out of a plastic lid, or if you have a means to dull the edges, cut a thin piece of tin or aluminum (sharp edges will cut both you and the yarn). A small crochet hook might work, or a reshaped paper clip. Cut a notch in an expired credit card. There are lots of things you can try—anything stiff enough to hold its shape should work.

Now, gather your warp, sley hook, scissors, a ruler, masking tape and whatever else you want to have within reach (coffee, Kleenex, telephone, this book, etc.) and take them to your loom.

Lay your warp chains across the front beam, approximately centered, with the cross end hanging over the top of the beater and extending 4″-6″ past it, toward the castle. Wrap the warp chain around the beam, leaving most of it (all but the 4″-6″) hanging in front of the loom. Wrap the chains several times or tie them in knots so they can't pull forward. The idea is to be able to pull threads from the cross without the chain shifting.

> *Secure your beater in an upright position. Gather all the supplies you'll need for sleying (sley hook, warp, scissors, ruler, masking tape, and whatever else you want nearby). Secure your warp chain to the front beam with 4″-6″ of the cross end extending toward the beater.*

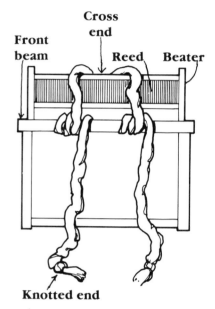

Warp chains ready for sleying.

Where to start sleying. The next step is to decide where in the reed you want to start sleying. Your weaving will be easier and your warp tension more even if your warp is centered on the loom. So, a little arithmetic is called for: your warp is going to be 10″ wide, so if your reed is 15″ wide then you'll have 5″ left over. To center your warp, leave 2½″ of reed empty on each side. Take your ruler, measure 2½″ in from the end of the reed, and that's where to start sleying. If the reed is 36″ wide, you'll have 13″ empty on each side.

If, after you've sleyed the reed, you discover that you measured wrong and the warp is not centered, don't move the threads yet.

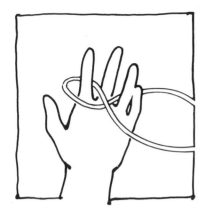

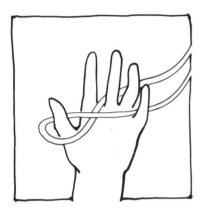

Two ways of holding the cross; use the method which feels more comfortable to you.

Many looms have beaters longer than the reed, or have open-ended beaters, allowing you to slide the reed back and forth. If yours does, then simply slide the reed over. It's the warp that needs to be centered, not the reed.

Holding the cross. Beater secure, warp chains secure, all tools within reach, starting place found, you are now ready to pick up your cross in preparation of sleying. Take one of the warp bundles in your left hand and drop the cross over it in such a way that the figure-8 is held open. (If you are left-handed, put the cross over your right hand and from here on use left when I say right and right when I say left.) Try both of the positions shown and use the one that feels more comfortable.

Close your fist down around the cross to protect it; you still have the use of your thumb and index finger. Tuck the yarn down to the base of your fingers and palm of your hand and try closing your last three fingers and flexing your first two. It should not be uncomfortable. Weird, maybe, but not uncomfortable.

Whether you start from the right or left is up to you and depends on how you hold your left (cross holding) hand and wrist. The idea is not to drag your hand across the warps you've already sleyed, risking pulling them out. My own comfortable position is to hold the cross as in the first illustration and sley from right to left. I think this works for the majority of right-handers, but not all, so see what feels best for you.

With the cross in position in your hand, carefully cut the ties off the cross and cut the end of the warp. With your right hand lift the top thread off the pile and quickly close your hand again to keep the rest of the warp threads of the cross in place. To determine the order in which you want to take the threads, look at the

Cross on hand, ready for sleying.

Cutting the ties off.

Cutting the end of the warp.

cross from the side and observe their Lincoln log-like stacking. You need to take the top thread off the stack each time, which means they'll alternate as to whether the end is coming from the left or right of your index finger (or thumb if you used the second illustration). To choose, look at the stack right where the threads are crossing each other, at the center of the X.

Lift the first thread off, fold it to make a loop at the end and hold both ends between your left thumb and index finger. With your right hand insert the sley hook through the chosen dent in the reed, pointing it from the back toward you. Catch the loop of yarn with the hook and pull it through the reed so the yarn is pointing toward the back of the loom. Then take the next warp from the cross, sley it through the next dent, and continue on. As you pull the threads through the dent, pull them as far as they will come, making each taut from where it is wrapped around the beam. Doing this will cause the warp to lie flatter, and you'll be able to see where you are much better than if your ends are loose and jumbled.

Since you're going to have a striped warp, first sley all the threads of one color where you want them, i.e., sley 12 ends, skip 12 dents, sley 12 ends, skip 12 dents, and so on. Then take your other color and fill in the spaces. When that's done, you're through sleying.

Find where to start sleying. Hold the cross in your left hand, cut off the ties and cut the end. Sley all 60 ends of one color, sleying 12 ends, skipping 12 dents, sleying 12 ends, skipping 12 dents, etc. Repeat for the second color. Check and correct any sleying errors.

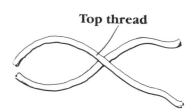

Top thread

When selecting the threads from your cross, always take the top thread. To find the top one, look at the stack right where the threads cross each other.

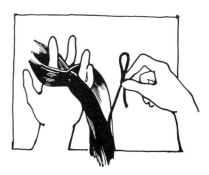

Removing threads from the cross. Lift thread off with right hand; close left hand to protect cross; hold single thread with left thumb and index finger to hold for sley hook.

Sleying the reed

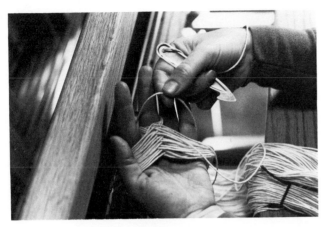

Lift the top thread off the stack. Notice that the sley hook is kept in the hand.

Fold the end to make a loop. Insert the sley hook through the chosen dent in the reed, from the back towards you, and catch the loop with the hook. Draw it through the reed.

Sley all ends of one color. Sley 12 ends, skip 12 dents, sley 12 ends, skip 12 dents, etc.

Sley all ends of the second color in empty dents.

Sleying errors. There is one more thing to discuss: mistakes. It is very likely that you'll skip a dent or put two threads in one dent. This is not traumatic. Especially this first time, it is a good idea to check each stripe as you complete it. This way, if you have to move a thread, it is easily done—and you can hardly go wrong with the second color, as the spaces are already counted out.

If you have an empty dent simply take the next warp off the cross and put it in the empty space; if you've finished sleying when you discover the error, just take the warp from whichever side is closer to the error and put it in the space. It will not be in perfect order, but that's no big deal. As you beam the warp (roll it onto the back beam), you'll be doing a lot of combing of it with your fingers. A few out-of-line threads won't create problems. In the same way, if you have two threads in one dent, simply take the extra one out and sley it where you need one.

The purpose of the cross is to make warping easier. If you are so rigidly attached to its perfection that you end up moving dozens or hundreds of threads just to keep them as they originally were, the cross has done you no favor. It's made you more work instead of less. Using the cross will keep your warps more organized than tangled, and for that we are grateful. A few threads out of line won't create a tangle, and even a few dozen out of a few hundred won't cause enough of a mess to get excited about. Part of why you're weaving is to handle yarn anyway, and combing out (gently fondling) some minor irregularities just gives you more opportunity to enjoy that pleasure.

As you may have realized, once the ties are cut off the cross, the only thing keeping it intact is your hand. In the strictest sense, that means you cannot leave your loom until you've finished sleying the bundle in your hand, and that always leads to the question, "What if the phone rings?"

There are any number of answers to this, but your concern is that the cross doesn't disappear. If you are working with a fairly sticky/hairy yarn, you can gently lay the cross down on the beam and it will hold its shape. I keep a roll of masking tape near my loom and put a piece about 4″ long across the X of the cross if I expect to be gone awhile; then I know it will stay on the beam where I left it. The trick is getting the tape off the yarn without scrambling it; use cheap tape, only slightly sticky, and it's pretty easy.

Other answers to this question come from the other direction: planning ahead. If you have small children or some other activity that may require frequent or instant jumping and running, keep your warp groups to a number that won't take long to sley. I

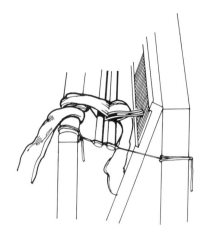

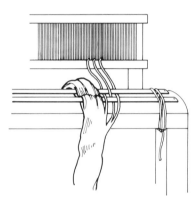

Sleying the reed from lease sticks.

don't get interrupted so I let my groups go up to 18″; wider than this creates hassles while threading. How many threads that is depends on my warp sett. At six e.p.i. that's only 108 warp ends, while at 24 e.p.i. it would be 432 threads. If you expect to need to get up, keep your count down, to say 50-75 threads per group. I knew one young mother who always kept her groups to 10 threads. If you feel the need to stop that often then I suggest you use lease sticks. It's slower, but you can get up whenever you want.

Using lease sticks. Lease sticks are long flat sticks that come with the loom, usually two or three of them. Instead of putting your hand in the cross, you slide the sticks through it in the same places the pegs were when you measured it, or that your index and ring fingers would have been had you used the first illustration. Put all of the warp on the sticks at once, then tie the ends of the sticks together and tie the pair onto the loom, either between the front beam and beater or directly to the front beam.

Once the warp is safely on the sticks, with enough warp length extended forward to reach a few inches beyond the castle, take off the cross ties and spread your warp out, loosening it up so you can pick off individual threads. Sley the reed as you would with the cross in your hand, this time lifting the threads off the sticks and sleying from right to left or vice versa, putting them in the reed in the same order as they are on the sticks.

Once the reed is sleyed, by whichever method, the cross has done its job and is gone. The threads are all lined up in the same order as they went onto the warping board, and there should be virtually no snarls. Of course, it is possible to warp a loom not using the cross, and if you drop one and lose it, just continue sleying, doing your best to maintain some orderliness. Loss of the cross simply means you'll have more combing to do when beaming, rarely a really terrible task, and not bad at all on short or narrow warps.

If you plan to leave your loom for awhile, tie bunches of the warp into slip knots or bows behind the reed to keep it from falling out. Kids, cats, curious adults, falling objects, any number of things can cause the reed to move or·the warp to be jostled, and tying the warp ever so slightly can prevent lots of frustration and "if only I had's . . .".

1. **Measure the warp.**
2. **Sley the reed.**
3. ***Thread the heddles.***

Threading the heddles

As you can now begin to see, the warp is making some forward progress. The ends are pointing in the direction they want to go, and if you remember that, it may be easier to remember the sequence of events.

Threading the heddles takes longer to describe than it does to do. And like all of this, each time you do it, it will get a little faster and less awkward. There are some things about this whole process that are small time savers, especially as long as your warping is still at a very conscious level. Soon many parts of the warping process become so automatic that they will not require concentration at all, and by then it's useful to have good habits developed. My recommendation is that you use this guide for the first couple of times, possibly taking notes in the margin on your second time through. Then, after about eight or 10 warps, read through it all again and see if you pick up some of those time savers that didn't register in the beginning when it was all new.

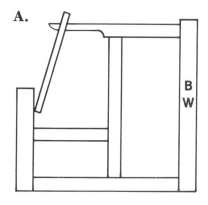

So, to threading. Loosen or untie the warp chain from the front beam and pull the warp forward until it reaches 6″ past the castle (or the last harness you'll be threading). Then be sure the chains are tight again because now it's even more important to be able to pull against them.

Once that is done release your beater and tip it back so it's leaning on the castle. Now go to the back of the loom and arrange the loom and your body in such a way that you are sitting as close to the castle as possible. You'll be reaching through the castle to get to your threads and sitting closer contributes substantially to ease and stamina.

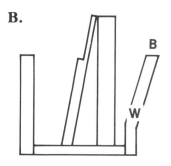

Reaching the heddles for threading. If you have a table loom you'll be reaching over or around or through the back. Floor looms come in a variety of basic designs, and the means of getting close to the castle vary. Some allow you to remove beams, others fold, others are large enough that you can sit inside. The drawings here are pretty generic, showing four structures that are most common. B stands for back beam, W for warp beam; sometimes one is removed, sometimes the other, sometimes both, sometimes neither. Look at these illustrations and your loom, try things and decide what is most comfortable to you.

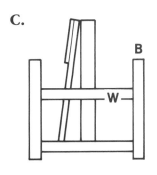

A: Sit inside, don't remove anything.

B: The whole back end will fold up close to the castle, or may drop to the floor. Removal of the back beam (B) may be of additional help; try lifting it off. The warp beam (W) is probably fixed and not in the way.

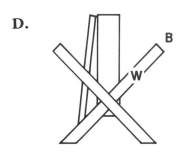

C: While parts of the back may fold, the majority won't. It's very likely that the warp beam (W) lifts out easily; the back beam (B) either folds up or lifts off.

D: How to work with an X-frame loom depends partly on how large or small it is, how stable it is when folded up, and how long your arms are. On larger looms, the back beam (B) and/or the

Basic loom designs.

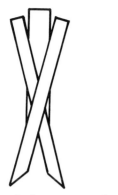

Some X-style looms may be folded up for threading.

warp beam (W) may lift out. With the warp beam (W) out and the back beam (B) in, you may be able to sit inside between the back beam and the castle to thread. Some looms are designed to leave the back beam and the warp beam in place and instead lift out the harnesses and reed, putting them all in a rack on a table, to be replaced after threading is done. Another alternative is to fold the loom up, which puts the beams right next to the castle and makes reaching through easy. Some X looms are stable enough to do this easily, others will do better if up against a wall. If you have long arms and a small loom, you can reach over the back beam and thread from the back; this will work, but I think your back will get very tired.

Whatever type of loom you have, sit low enough so that your back is straight. A footstool, milk box, wastebasket on edge, sewing machine cover—try sitting on an assortment of things until you find something practical and comfortable. You'll be most comfortable and efficient if your eye level is somewhere between the heddle eyes and top heddle bar. With a table loom you might find standing at a counter the best position. It's easier than sitting on the floor, which also works for short periods of time.

> *Prepare your loom for threading. Adjust warp and back beams for comfort; place table looms at a comfortable height.*

Positioning the heddles. Any loom wider than 20″ will have some kind of hook(s) connecting the heddle bar to the harness frame for support. When you are about to start threading, unhook all the hooks on both the upper and lower heddle bars so you can slide the heddles around as you need them. Rehook them just before you start to weave. It's a good idea at this time to check to see that you have enough heddles on each harness before you begin to thread. If there will be 15 warps threaded on each harness, for example, then each harness will need to have 15 heddles. This is not a big concern for this narrow project with relatively few threads, but something to consider when you're threading wider pieces or one with many threads. (See Part IV for more on heddles.)

Now, slide all your heddles to your left. (Remember, lefties, do the opposite.) If you know that you have many more heddles than you'll need, slide some of the extras back over to the right side of the harnesses if you want to. In theory, this gives the harnesses a better balance because the weight is more evenly distributed, though in my experience, I've never found it to make much difference. It does look nice, and occasionally it's useful to have some over there for fixing mistakes.

There will be times when you are using the full width of the loom and still will have many extra heddles. Instead of removing these extra heddles, just space them out among your warp threads. Thread a dozen or so warps, then pull over and leave some empty heddles, then thread some more warps, then leave some more empty heddles, and so on. This way, your heddles are out of the way and require no extra time to remove and re-place later. If you ever have to take heddles off, slide them onto a string or wire to keep them lined up, then when you return them to a harness just slide them off the string onto the heddle bar. (It's a known fact that loose heddles contribute to insanity.)

> *On wider looms, loosen heddle hooks. Check to see that you have enough heddles on each harness.*

Threading. Back to our sample warp. From the heddles on the left, pull out one heddle from each harness (assuming you have a four-harness loom. If you have more harnesses, take a heddle from each of the first four.) These four heddles represent one complete repeat of the threading pattern I want you to use for this sample. You will continue threading harness one, then two, then three, then four, repeat, until all your warps are threaded. The harness closest to the beater is harness one; the harness closest to you is harness four. To begin threading, put the yarn that is furthest right in the reed through the heddle on harness one. Put the yarn from the second dent in the reed on harness two. Keep going in this manner, pulling out new groups of four as you need them, until you've threaded an inch. With your warp sett at 12 e.p.i., this will be 12 threads.

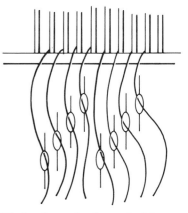

Eight threads threaded in a straight draw.

Important to know about heddles is that they have a directional twist to the eye. If you twist a heddle either toward you or away from you, the eye appears to be more open one way than the other. The purpose of this twist is to allow a warp threaded through the eye to travel in a straight line from front to back. If your warp were required to bend, it would wear and possibly break. Try threading a heddle from both sides of the eye and you'll immediately see that when the warp moves in a straight line through the heddle, the heddle is easier to thread. The heddles will want to naturally twist so you can thread them easily and correctly.

> *Thread from the right and thread 1,2,3,4; 1,2,3,4; etc., until all warps are threaded. Thread 1"-2" at a time, tying each group in an overhand knot as you go.*

Tying overhand knots. When you have an inch worth of warps threaded tie them all in an overhand knot with the ends reasonably even. Any unevenness or other extra length not necessary is your first contribution to loom waste, yarn and money thrown away. Tie the knot tightly and as close to the end as you can get it. Once you are even a little adept at what you're doing you'll see that it's easier to separate 12 heddles from the group at once than to pull out four heddles three times. What these small, separated groups do is make it easy to see which heddle you want to thread next. Without these you must keep looking at the confusion of heddles with threads to see what you've already done. This sounds like a picky thing, but when you're doing it, you'll see the difference.

Threading the heddles

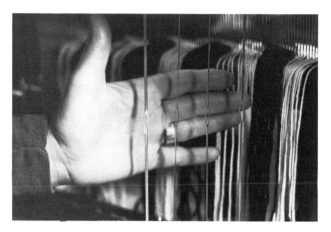

Having slid all heddles to the left (or right, depending on the direction you're working), separate out four heddles, one from each harness.

Hold the heddle steady with one hand; thread with the other one. Thread a fold, not an end.

Catch the warp with the same hand that threaded it. It'll feel awkward at first, but will be much faster later.

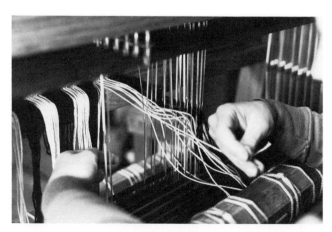

After you've threaded the heddle slide it over by pulling the warp sideways.

After you've threaded 1″ of warp ends (12 ends), check for correctness and then tie them in an overhand knot.

Threading finished.

Developing a threading method. Now about threading itself. You'll develop a method that is comfortable and fast enough for you, so I won't go into inch by inch detail. I will throw out a few things for your consideration, though. Some people enjoy using a threading hook, also called a heddle hook; others prefer using their fingers. I'm a finger person myself, figuring by the time I get the hook through the eye, which requires some sense of aim, I can be long done using my fingers. If you have a threading hook, give it a try; you might like it.

When using your fingers, the most important thing is to feed the heddle a folded yarn, not the cut end. A folded piece gives more stiffness, so the yarn helps itself through the heddle and there isn't any fuzzy end to catch on the edge of the heddle eye.

The second thing I've found useful is to pull the threads taut against the front beam as I'm threading. With the beam as an anchor I can develop a pattern for my hand and arm motion that makes the process become automatic, instead of always being a series of conscious decisions. Look at the illustrations and read the description of what I do, and from this, develop your own methods and style. As with all of this, whatever works best for you is the right way to do it.

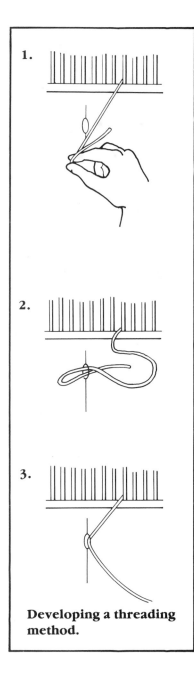

1.

2.

3.

Developing a threading method.

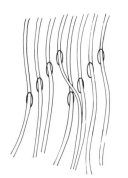

Threads crossed within the heddles.

1. I pull the warp taut, then about 3″ past the heddle I fold the yarn over my index finger.

2. Holding the heddle still with my left hand, my right hand goes back to the heddle and I slide the loop of the warp off my index finger and push it through the heddle eye. With the same right fingers, I pull the thread through the heddle, and as I pull it toward me, I also pull it to the right, sliding it over to make room for the next threading operation.

3. I keep pulling until the thread is taut again. That keeps all the warps neatly lined up, and then making the ends even is a very minor operation.

No matter what you are threading, what your warp sett is, always tie your back knots in groups of 1″-2″ reed width. (At 12 e.p.i. this is 12-24 warps; at eight e.p.i. it would be eight to 16.) If you tie more than this together, the warps on the edges of the group will act as if they are shorter than those in the center, and the effect will be an increase in loom waste and a concurrent decrease in how much of your warp can be woven.

I told you to tie a knot after you'd threaded 12 heddles. You can wait until after you've threaded everything to tie your knots, but there are several reasons to do it as you go. First, it's a small task to even the ends of 12 threads or so, especially compared to lining up hundreds. If you do it one bundle at a time you won't get sick of doing it. Second, and perhaps more important, as you tie each small bundle you can check your threading for errors, correcting them early and easily. And finally, tying off groups as you go decreases the likelihood of loose threads falling back into the heddles and coming out in the wrong place, resulting in crossed threads.

Threading errors. Crossed threads are the most common mistake in warping and can occur in either of two places. (They are easy to fix, and I'll tell you how in a minute.) To avoid them, first be sure that you take threads from consecutive dents in the reed, first thread to first heddle, second to second, etc. If you have more than one thread per dent in the reed, be sure to thread all threads from the first dent before going on to the second. If you cross threads between the reed and heddles, one thread won't always be able to go up when its harness does because it will be held down if the thread crossing over it is in a harness not being raised. (That may not be clear until you do it, but then it will be very clear. Clear or not, try to avoid it.)

The second place to find crossed threads is among the heddles. If, as you threaded, the end of a warp went around another heddle and came out in a different space, the twisted threads will not allow each other clear sheds, the same as with the other type of crossed warps. The difference is that these are harder to see and so can create problems more difficult to track down.

With either type you'll have mistakes in your weaving, and the strain of being pulled up and down at the same time may well break the thread. Crossed threads are a nuisance, but are common and easy to fix, so don't get too upset by them. You'll discover crossed warps when you start to weave and something isn't quite right. Look sideways through the shed.

Once you've found which threads they are, untie them from the front apron rod, pull them out of the reed (and heddles if necessary), uncross them, and put them back in where they belong, uncrossed. Tie them back onto the apron rod and proceed. If you've already woven some, don't unweave it, just pull the warps out of the weaving and tie them back on over the top of it; after you take your weaving off the loom, you can weave them into their proper place with a yarn needle if necessary. Crossed threads are usually easy to fix, but also easy to avoid by watching carefully as you thread. (Having good light is more important during sleying and threading than at any other time in weaving.)

When you've finished threading all of the heddles and tying your warp into small groups, put your loom back into its weaving position. If you folded the back up, extend it out again and put the beams back on. Time-wise, most of the work is done. What's left is very important but relatively speedy.

Tying onto the back apron rod

At this point the ends of your warp are hanging behind the heddles in small knotted groups. The next step is to securely attach these bundles to the apron rod. Any way you can do it is fine as long as it holds. Beyond security, the only concern is waste. As this yarn back here will never be woven, you will want to keep it to a minimum. I'll show you three ways to attach warp to the back apron rod; other weavers can show you more.

Most important, with any system, is to remember to *pull your apron rod out from the warp beam toward you and then up over the back beam toward the castle.* When you look at the loom from the side the warp should go horizontally from the front/breast beam to the back beam.

Every weaver I've ever known has forgotten this at least once, and even years of experience does not make one immune. If you forget to go over the back beam and your warp is going from the warp beam straight up to the heddles, you will get a poor shed at best, possibly no shed at all. Fortunately, it's an easy error to fix, requiring at most a screw driver or wrench. You *don't* need to

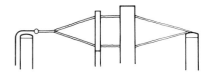

Clean shed; no crossed warps.

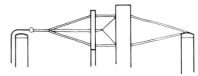

Shed with warps crossed between reed and heddles.

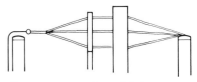

Warps crossed amidst heddles are harder to find.

Look sideways with the shed open to check for errors.

1. **Measure the warp.**
2. **Sley the reed.**
3. **Thread the heddles.**
4. *Tie onto the back apron rod.*

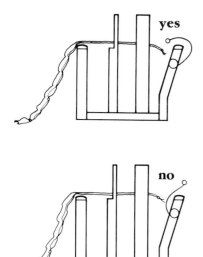

Pull your apron rod up over the back beam as shown at top.

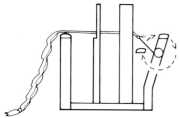

If you forget to go over the back beam and have already tied on, you can correct this by simply lifting off the back beam and sliding it under the warp and apron rod. Lift the yarns up with the beam and return it to its original position.

untie and retie unless you have a very unusual loom. Instead, simply lift off the back beam (which may be screwed or bolted on), slide it under the warp, and replace the beam with the warp lying on top of it.

I also want to talk about the various kinds of apron rods. Every loom manufacturer uses different rods and a different means for attaching them. My theory about the term apron rod is that long ago, when weaving vocabulary was being developed, looms had cloth aprons attached to both the fabric and warp beams. These aprons were simply large pieces of sturdy cloth with hems at the ends, and slid through the hems were long sticks or rods—thus, apron rods. These days, some looms still have cloth aprons, some have apron cords, some have webbed straps, any of which work fine as an apron rod holder.

The rods themselves may be of wood or metal, square or round. I myself prefer round apron rods, because it's so much easier to tie the warp around them. Or, I use a method for attaching my warp in which I don't actually tie the warp onto the rod, easy in back, but (for me at least) less desirable in front.

Types of apron attachments. One last thing before we go on to tying on. If you have cloth aprons use two apron rods instead of one. Slide the first through the apron hem, then lash a second one to it (through small cuts in the apron) with a strong cord, 3"-5" away. The reason for this is that it allows you to tie onto the rod anyplace, rather than needing to work around the fabric. This saves wear and tear on the apron itself, not to mention wear and tear on you.

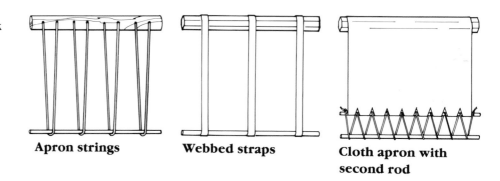

Apron strings   **Webbed straps**   **Cloth apron with second rod**

Methods of tying on. Try all of these methods for tying on, only one per project, and decide which you prefer. I've provided photos for the first method only; I suggest you start with this one. In my opinion, the first method is the simplest, the second the fastest once you're use to it. The third method is good for emergencies, which I'll explain later in the book. Method I wastes the most yarn; methods II and III are good if you need to conserve yarn.

Tying the warp on to the apron rod using the overhand knot method.

1. Loop over the apron rod.

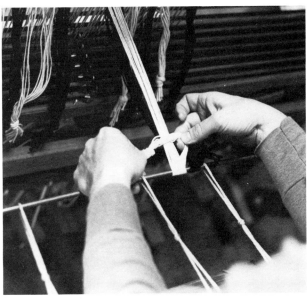

2. Bring first knot over top of the warp group.

3. Bring knot around and through.

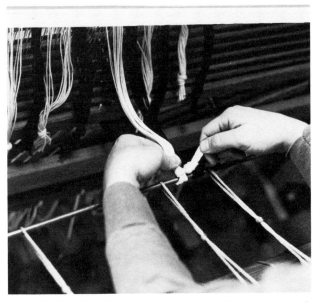

4. Pull the first knot snug against the apron rod.

I. Overhand knots method. The overhand knot you tied after you threaded a group of heddles serves as the first knot in this method. The second step is to tie another overhand knot around the apron rod. Pull this new knot tight, with the first knot right up against the new knot to keep it from slipping. (This is important! It may not slip now, but it will later, as you approach the end of your weaving.)

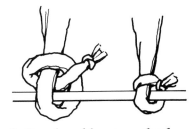

I. Overhand knot method.

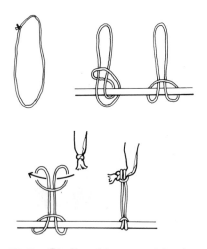

II. Lark's head knot method.

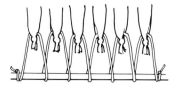

III. Lash cord method.

To prevent bent or broken apron rods on narrow warps, slide the outer lash cords off.

II. Lark's head knot method. By attaching cords to your apron rod you can decrease your loom waste and have a quick way of tying on. First, make a bunch of loops all the same size with a strong, non-stretchy yarn. Now, attach these to the apron rod as shown. To attach your warp, make a lark's head at the other end of the loop and put the knotted end of your warp through it. Pull tight, being sure the knot in the warp is close to the lark's head knot.

III. Lash cord method. This method uses a long cord which lashes the warp bundles onto the back beam. Start at one side and thread your cord through a warp bundle, bring it around the apron rod and through the next bundle and so on until all warp groups are lashed onto the rod. Tie your lashing cord to the apron rod and adjust your cord until all groups are even. The more even they are, the less waste you'll have. Of these three methods, this one is the only one which can be used to tie onto the front apron rod, too.

Regardless of the method you use, it's easiest if you start at the center and work your way out, or tie both edges first; either way you'll be supporting the apron rod, making your work easier.

As you tie your warp to the back apron rod, come in a straight line back from the reed. If your warp is 20″ wide in the reed, then it should be 20″ wide on the apron rod. Don't crowd the warp on the apron rod as it increases abrasion on the yarn and may adversely affect your tension while weaving.

> *Tie onto the back beam rod using one of the methods described here. Make sure your apron rod goes up over the back beam before beginning to tie on.*

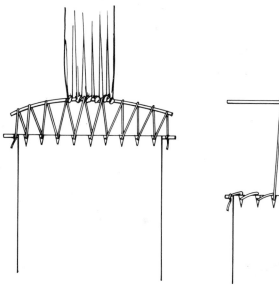

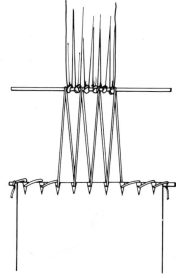

If you are putting a narrow warp on a wide loom the strain of the narrow warp will try to bend or break an apron rod. The solution to this is very simple, and while it sounds odd, it does work. Slide the supporting apron cord off the apron rod for all the width not being used, i.e., only have the apron cord pulling the rod toward the beam in the same area as the warp is pulling it toward the castle. Until the warping process is done, and for that matter, until the weaving is almost done, the strain won't show up, so don't be overly concerned now. Just try to remember when you see your apron rod bend that there's a note here about it.

Beaming the warp

Beaming your warp properly is without question the most important part of the warping process, no matter which method you use. How well you do it will be one of the biggest factors in how much you can enjoy weaving the warp off. Here your goal is even tension. I've referred to this earlier and probably will again later because it's so important. Let me discuss a little of the function of tension in weaving.

1. **Measure the warp.**
2. **Sley the reed.**
3. **Thread the heddles.**
4. **Tie onto the back apron rod.**
5. *Beam the warp.*

As you know, the loom's biggest job is to hold a set of yarns under tension so that it is easy to weave other yarns into it. Different kinds of looms have different mechanisms, but all looms are warp holders, tension providers—that's the definition of a loom. If the warp is tighter, the weft packs in easily, beats down fairly closely. That's why it is important to be able to get a great deal of tension on a tapestry or rug loom. If the overall tension is looser, the weft will not pack in as much. The lack of resistance results in a softer fabric. If you are braiding something, either hair or ropes, you know you can get a tighter braid if the end is well anchored. The difference between how you handle a warp or braid that is tighter or looser is tremendous, and at any given time one or the other may be what you need. Rugs require tight tension, shawls looser.

Now, imagine a warp that is tighter in some places and looser in others. The tighter areas will pack closely, the looser ones will not. Your weft cannot possibly stay straight. The tighter warps will very possibly break, because as you tighten the overall warp enough to have sufficient weaving tension the tighter threads will get so tight that they'll snap.

The too loose ones, on the other hand, will create a different set of problems. If they are slack enough, when the harness rises, they may not bother to go up since they have enough length to allow them to stay put. If this happens, your pattern will have skips. Furthermore, your shuttle will be obstructed when a loose thread hangs half way in the shed, neither up nor down. When your shuttle hits the thread, it may well break it.

These are just the simplest of tension problems. See the trouble-shooting guide in Part IV for more. Then put your best effort into a good beaming job so you'll experience as few of these frustrations as possible.

Enough explanation; let's get started. It is time to untie or unwrap your warp chains from the front beam. Unchain part of the length, and let the loosened warp relax and fluff up, opening it up to the width needed to go through the reed. If there are any tangles visible (shouldn't be) or the warp is crossed over oddly anywhere, gently shake the chain and comb it out with your fingers so that what is in front of the reed is fairly orderly and parallel. Now pull the beater forward until it is resting on the front beam. Go to the side of the loom and *without touching the warp or beater* crank the back beam and begin rolling the warp toward the beam. It will be awhile before your warp actually reaches the beam, as first you'll be rolling on the apron strings or apron.

Getting ready to beam

Unwind the warp chains from the front of the loom.

Open up the warp to its full width. Shake and comb it out so that all the warp in front of the reed looks fairly orderly. Pull the beater forward.

54

Determining warp beam direction. On some looms the warp goes around the outside of the beam and then in toward the loom, while on others the warp goes to the inside first, then around toward the outside.

Both work just fine, neither is preferable to the other. It is important for you to determine which direction your beam goes because if you beam the whole warp in the wrong direction your brake won't hold and you'll have to redo it all. To determine the direction your beam goes do either or both of two things. Hold the apron rod; start winding it on using the beam's handle, and then try to pull it away again. If it unrolls try again in the other direction. The second method is for looms with ratchets in back instead of friction brakes. Be sure that the dog or pawl is engaged, is lying on the ratchet and not flipped off of it. Turning the beam one way you'll hear a clicking sound as the pawl falls across each ratchet tooth. You shouldn't be able to turn it the other direction at all, for this is your brake mechanism. When beaming your warp, listen for the clicking, knowing that hearing it means you're going the right way. On floor looms it's better to disengage the brake while beaming (by stepping on the brake pedal); do so after you've determined the proper direction to go.

Now for beaming your warp. From this point on you will be doing three things. You will be cranking the warp beam around, combing/shaking out tangles, and being sure there is some kind of separator between the layers of warp as they roll onto the beam.

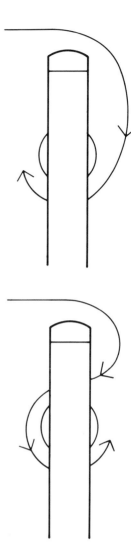

Your warp beam may turn either direction to wrap the warp on.

> *Prepare for beaming by untying or unwrapping your warp chains from the front beam. Shake out the warp so that it lies parallel. Pull the beater forward so it rests on the front beam. Determine which direction your warp beam should turn.*

Warp separators. The separator, be it heavy brown paper, corrugated cardboard, or warp sticks, needs to be inserted as you roll on to keep the layers of yarn away from each other. If they are not separated, some threads will sink down into the roll and others will not, causing the threads to travel different circumferences. Those that sink in will end up shorter when you start weaving and so will become increasingly tighter as you weave. Don't rely on newspaper, plastic bags, or cloth; they are too soft and won't do the job, and newsprint rubs off on yarn. Grocery bags opened up are pretty good and easily available. Be absolutely certain that your separator is wider than your warp so the edge threads won't fall off.

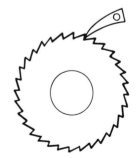

Be sure the dog or pawl is engaged. If it is, you'll hear a clicking sound as you beam.

Tension during beaming. The big question, of course, is how to get even tension. It's very simple, actually. Don't apply any. Having people hang onto the warp means you are relying on different hands to do identical work; that's not likely to happen. Trying to put some kind of weight on the warp that you know would be consistent is time consuming and troublesome, as well as unnecessary. The yarn passing through the reed and heddles encounters enough friction, all identical, to travel evenly.

So as you roll the warp onto the beam, don't touch it at all. Use the beater as a visual gauge. Start cranking with the beater tipped forward. Continue to crank until either the beater comes back to the castle by itself or you've turned the beam three full turns (past the insertion of the separator).

When the beater tips back to the castle it is time to shake and comb out the warp again, finding and eliminating any errant snags. Every three revolutions or so you need to tighten the whole roll. The tension is even, but it's too loose for weaving. If you don't tighten the roll now it will tighten as you're weaving, a subtle change that will cause uneven beating. To tighten it, grab large handfuls of warp on the left and right sides (with only 10″ you may be able to grab the whole thing). Brace yourself against the loom and pull hard until you feel the roll tighten. Then, go back and forth across the entire warp, and in a series of large handfuls, keep pulling until the entire width is tightened. Pulling warp is like pulling hair—if you pull just one, it will break, but a whole handful is much stronger; it can withstand much greater pressure.

> *Begin rolling on. Don't touch the warp during beaming so that the tension across the warp is even. Shake and comb out the warp in front of the reed whenever the beater tips back to the castle. Insert separating paper. Tighten your roll about every three revolutions. Stop beaming when there's just enough warp in front of the reed for tying onto the front apron rod.*

When the roll has been tightened, once again comb out the warp with your fingers, gently so you won't create knots; pull the beater forward and crank the back beam with no hands on the warp or beater. Etc., etc., etc.

Continue until there is only enough warp left in front of the reed to tie onto the front apron rod. I've found that a good measure is for the ends of the warp to just reach the front beam. The knot you tied in the very beginning is your protection against cranking the warp through the reed while you're not watching. Leave it in until you're ready to tie onto the front apron rod, for a curious visitor could easily pull the beater forward and "unsley" all of your warp. (If your warp does come out of the reed, simply resley it, this time from back to front, taking the threads in the same order that they are threaded in the heddles.)

Beaming the warp

When beaming, cranking the back beam, *do not touch the warp!* Keep cranking until beater hits castle.

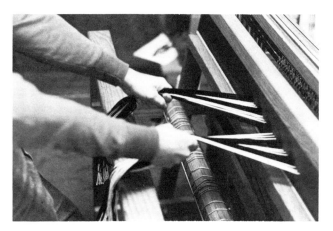

When the beater hits the castle, stop beaming and come around to the front of the loom and shake out the warp in front of the reed. Comb it out with your fingers if necessary. Tighten the roll every three revolutions by pulling hard on the warp as shown here. Move beater back against breast beam and continue beaming.

Adding separating paper.

Leave the knots in front of the reed tied until you are ready to tie onto the front apron rod. This will protect your warp ends from accidentally 'unsleying' themselves.

1. Measure the warp.
2. Sley the reed.
3. Thread the heddles.
4. Tie onto the back apron rod.
5. Beam the warp.
6. *Tie onto the front apron rod.*

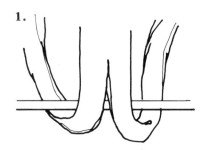

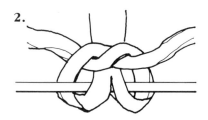

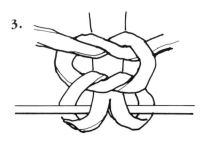

Tying onto the front apron rod.
1. Pull the warp over the apron rod, then split it in half.
2. Tie the first half of a square knot.
3. Finish tying the square knot after the tension is adjusted.

Tying on

When you tied the warp to the back apron rod, your primary concern was wasting as little yarn as possible, so your knots were designed to be as close to the end of the warp as possible. When tying onto the front apron rod, you still don't want to waste any yarn unnecessarily, but your primary concern is even tension.

There are several ways to attach warp to the front apron rod; I'll discuss two of them and show photos of one. You'll need to try them out and pick your favorite.

Methods of tying on. The first of the two ways I'll show you is probably the most common but not the only one by any means. Pull 1″ width of warp over the rod, split it and pull up two groups to be tied together over the warp in the same way you start to tie a shoelace. You will eventually complete it as a square knot, or if you prefer, a bow. For now, tie just half of the knot.

If the yarn is at all sticky, a variation you might like is a surgeon's knot. Do the first half of the knot (center illustration) with two twists through instead of just one, often eliminating the need for the second half of the square knot.

In either case, start at the center of your warp and tie 1″ of warp (12 threads at 12 e.p.i.) around the rod with *the first half of the knot only*. Then tie one or two groups to the left, then to the right, and continue tying half knots from side to side until all your warp is tied on. If you didn't cut the far end of the warp when you took it off the warping board, now is when you'll need to cut some of the ends so that you can separate the groups for tying. The advantage of waiting until now is that you can cut at the point that will allow each side to have equal length. You may not even need to cut any. At any rate, your needs and options should be fairly obvious as you look at what you have before you.

Starting at the center is not critical, and you can start anywhere you want. I like starting at the center because of how it supports my apron rod; if I start on one end, the rod is pulled askew and there's a balancing problem. Once I've tied onto the center, this tie supports the rod, and I can then tie the outer edges with no problem. If it's a wide warp I may do that for added stability.

Tying onto the front apron rod

Starting at center, take about 1″ of warp and bring it around the apron rod, spliting it into two groups.

Tie half of the square knot.

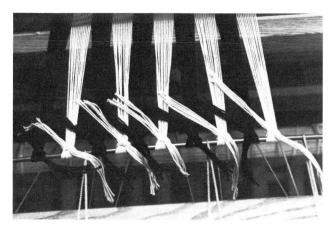

Tie the first half of the square knot all across the width of the warp.

Pat across the warp to check for unevenness.

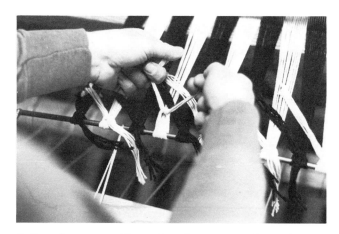

Adjust knots until tension is even. It doesn't need to be tight, just even.

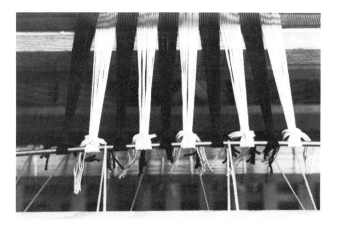

After tension is adjusted, tie the second half of the square knot.

Evening the warp tension. So, now you have all the warp tied on with half a knot only. Feel the center, the first groups you tied. They are much looser than the rest of the warp, and you can even feel a steady progression of increased tension as you pat the warp from center to edges. This progression is normal and is why you tied only half a knot. Go to the center and your first knot, take hold of the warp ends, pull them and their knot forward, away from you so the warp slides around the apron rod, then pull the ends sideways to tighten the knot. Now, go to the next one and do the same thing, repeating back and forth all the way across. It may take a couple of rounds of adjusting to get all of your sections of warp to have equal tension, but no matter how many times you need to go back and forth, do it. As the tension on your warp becomes more consistent, pat the warp with your hand to feel how even it is. Remember, it doesn't matter how tight or loose it is, you can adjust that with your ratchet any time. Experience will teach you how precise you need to be. Don't spend an hour trying to be absolutely perfect, but do spend enough time that the tension is reasonably even. When you are satisfied that it is, tie the second half of the square knot to keep it that way. (For those of you who've forgotten what you learned in scouts or on boats, to tie a square knot tie right over left and then under, left over right and then under.)

Another way to even up the tension as you tie the front knots is suggested by Cay Garret in her book *Warping All By Yourself*. Because the progression of loose to tight is remarkably consistent, start by tying the center knots, then tighten the ratchet a click, tie a few more knots right and left of center, tighten the ratchet another click, etc. How many knots to how many clicks will vary with your particular tying skills, the type of yarn you're using, and the size of your ratchet's teeth. It's a good system and one you may prefer to retying and adjusting by hand.

A second way to attach the warp in front is to tie overhand knots in 1″ segments all the way across, keeping the lengths as even as possible, then lace those groups to the apron rod with a strong cord, as discussed in tying onto the back beam.

This works, and if you're trying to squeeze every inch possible out of your warp it will save you a few (or more). You must spend time adjusting the cord to make sure that the tension on all groups is the same. Their length will not be the same, but their tension must be. I find it easier to even my tension on individual groups tied directly to the rod, but no doubt that's because that's the way I learned. With most aspects of weaving, the way you learn first is the way you'll be most comfortable with, so try both of these while they're still new and decide for yourself which you like better.

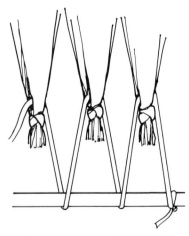

Lashing onto the front apron rod.

Remember, with either method keep your warp groups small, usually about an inch and never more than an inch and a half. If you tie wider bundles, you will have tension problems and it will take more inches of weaving from the start to get your warp spread out evenly, something you have to do before your "real" fabric begins.

> *Tie onto the front apron rod using one of the methods described. After all warp is tied on, adjust the tension until it is even. Tie the other half of the square knot if the first method is used.*

When you're tying your knots in front, your warp ends will not all be exactly the same length no matter how careful you are. Among other things, variations in the yarn will affect each warp's stretch. You will discover quickly that your knots will need to be tied accommodating the shortest ends you have. The ones that are shorter at this end are that way partly because they were longer at the other end; wrapping your warp chain around the front beam when you sley and thread should keep this to a minimum. Generally, you shouldn't have a big difference in lengths, so it's not of much concern. What you do want to remember, though, is the more tail you have hanging out of your knot, the more yarn you are wasting, unless it will be fringe. So don't tie long flowing knots unless you can't think of anything else to do with your money. Your time is valuable too, so use enough length so that the tying process is easy; lost time is even worse than lost yarn, for yarn can be replaced.

If, after you've woven a couple of inches, it is clear that one section is looser or tighter than the others, simply untie it and readjust it to a more appropriate tension. The first inch of weaving might look a little funny, but this is insignificant when contrasted to the problems that will occur if you don't make the adjustment now.

Tying up the treadles

Multiple tie-up floor looms need to have the treadles tied up before weaving can begin. On table looms and direct tie-up floor looms each lever or treadle is permanently attached to one harness, i.e., one treadle or lever always operates one harness. As you might expect, there are a variety of multiple tie-up systems: wires through holes, cords through slots or holes, or chains or cords that attach with hooks. If you have a multiple tie-up system, check your loom instructions to see how yours works.

1. **Measure the warp.**
2. **Sley the reed.**
3. **Thread the heddles.**
4. **Tie onto the back apron rod.**
5. **Beam the warp.**
6. **Tie onto the front apron rod.**
7. *Tie up the treadles.*

The multiple tie-up system allows you to lift more than one harness with one treadle and aids in helping establish a rhythmical and orderly treadling sequence. Usually, four harness looms have six treadles, eight harness looms have 10.

Since I want you to really understand what's happening, for this lesson I'd like for you to tie your treadles up as for a direct tie-up loom (tie harness one to one treadle, harness two to another one, harness three to a third treadle, and harness four to a fourth) and use both of your feet to raise the different combinations of harnesses.*

With this done, you're ready to weave!

---

*If you have a counterbalance or countermarche loom: In theory, with a counterbalance loom, harnesses will move up or down only in pairs. In fact, however, some will work with one harness against three. Try doing a direct tie-up and see if you can get a clean shed; that means that one harness will lower when you step on the treadle, the other three will raise, and you'll easily be able to see where to put the shuttle between the two layers of threads. If you don't get a clean shed, choose two treadles, any two (see drawings on page 188), and to one of them tie harnesses one and three, to the other one tie harnesses two and four (this will weave tabby, or plain weave). To the other four treadles, tie the following pairs: one and two, two and three, three and four, and one and four. You'll weave twill with these. If you have a countermarche loom, use this same tie-up. While you can tie up one treadle to one harness as you would for a direct tie-up, you cannot depress two treadles at once.

Notes and comments

Lesson 3
Weaving

Your first weaving assignment
Weaving a header
Winding your shuttle
Selvedges
Sequences of the weaving process
Troubleshooting
What to do about threading errors
Taking your sample off the loom
Finishing your fabric
Learning from yourself

Sample weaving with 1″ black and white warp stripes. At left is plain weave; at right is twill. Warp sett is 12 e.p.i.

Your first weaving assignment

And now, to weaving! First, with this sample, I want you to get used to your loom and how it operates. So that you get a feel for the process, there are a few things I'd like you to try: weave plain weave (also called tabby), which is done by raising harnesses one and three together for the first weft shot and two and four together for the second weft shot, repeating this sequence over and over. You'll notice that in plain weave the weft travels over one warp, under the next, over the next, under the next, etc. (This is the most basic of weaves.)

Using the same yarn for weft as you did for warp, I want you to try three different beatings, i.e., packing the weft in at three different densities. For one, try to get a balanced weave, one in which your p.p.i. (picks per inch, weft shots per inch) equals your e.p.i. (warp ends per inch). Use a ruler to measure an inch and count how many picks you packed in. Weave 3″ of balanced weave, another 3″ where you beat very hard (more p.p.i. than e.p.i.), and 3″ with very loose beating (fewer p.p.i. than e.p.i.). Use only one color for each 3″ section. Alternate colors between blocks if you want.

After this 9″ of plain weave I want you to repeat the three methods of beating while weaving a 2/2 twill. A 2/2 twill is a weave structure which occurs when you have two harnesses up and two down (that's what the 2/2 stands for) for every weft shot in a sequence such that a diagonal line is created. To weave a 2/2 twill, raise harnesses 1&2 together for the first shot, 2&3 for the second, 3&4 for the next, and finally 4&1. Continue on with these four combinations. You'll notice now that your weft travels over two warps and then under two, then over two, under two, etc., and that with each weft pick the weft moves over one place, creating a diagonal.

A twill behaves differently from a plain weave, so your beating will yield somewhat different results; remember to count your weft shots to find a balanced weave.

Once you've woven these 18″, play around. Try more of what you liked, change colors of yarns, lift different combinations of harnesses (which means change your treadling sequence), do anything you can think of. Weave as far as you can, then untie everything and take it off the loom so you can measure your loom waste and take-up.

In summary here's your assignment, but before you begin, I suggest you read through the rest of this section on weaving. Then come back and weave this sample.

Sample I

10″ × 2 yds, 2 colors of wool.
Weave plain weave for 9″.
    3″ beating for balanced weave.
    3″ beating for weft predominant (harder beat).
    3″ beating for warp predominant (softer beat).
Weave 2/2 twill for 9″.
    3″ balanced.
    3″ harder.
    3″ softer.
Play around.

Now let's have a vocabulary lesson. I don't ever want to hear any of you say, ''I weaved a scarf.'' It hurts even to write it. I weave, I wove, I have woven, I will weave. I am a weaver. There's a huge philosophical debate about when that is appropriate to say, or by whom, much like the phrase, ''I am an artist.'' Much as I'd like to get into this, I'll resist. The point is, you are a weaver or you weave; you don't do weaving.

How to weave is really the easiest part of the whole process. Open the shed, throw the shuttle, beat, repeat. There are a few details beyond this, some finesse to develop, but the mechanics are this easy. Just in case this isn't all clear, let's do some review.

The shed is the space created between the upper and lower warp threads when you raise or lower some of your harnesses. You can throw a shuttle, pass it, or stick it through the shed; which word you use will probably be determined by your mood and the type of shuttle you are using. You can throw a boat shuttle; a stick shuttle won't flow as smoothly across, so it's probably passed or handed through the shed. Beating is using the beater to push the weft shot into place. If it's a tight weave, then thinking of it as beating is good. If you are weaving a loose fabric such as a shawl, ''beating'' has too much force; thinking in terms of gently pushing is more appropriate.

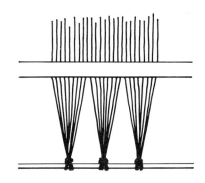

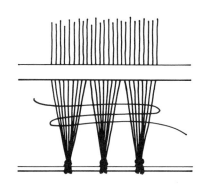

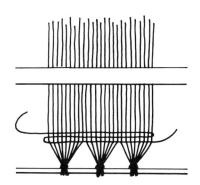

Weaving a header. Here three weft shots are woven before beating them in. This closes the V's so that all the warps lie parallel.

Weaving a header

Before you start weaving, you can see that your warp is not parallel in front of the reed, that from the knots on the apron rod to the reed the warp forms a series of V's. Your first job is to get the warp ends in the V's to lie parallel. There are several ways to do this, all using the same principle.

As you weave, the warp will straighten out, but since the weaving doesn't look good until this has occurred, you want to reach this point as soon as possible. Many weavers start with what's called a header, a weft that is not the same yarn you'll use for your project but a special one, usually fatter. It can be yarn, old stockings, rags, toilet paper, or even flat sticks, for it is not considered part of the weaving, and is pulled out when the piece comes off the loom. Whether you are using a special weft as your header or starting with your planned weft, the fastest way to reach parallel is to put three weft shots into alternating tabby sheds* without beating in between. Then, beat all three together. Repeat the sequence and the threads of almost any warp will become parallel, even with a very skinny weft. If it's not working even after three repeats of the sequence, check the width of your knotted groups; if you've used much more than an inch of warp (reed width), it will take much longer to spread it out.

An added benefit of beating the first three shots together instead of individually is that it does a very nice job of fine tuning your tension. Looser warps will pucker or loop in front of the weft and are held there by the three shots. The result is that the warp still to be woven is now very even. The effectiveness of this varies with the yarn being used, stickier/hairier better, slipperier less so.

Winding your shuttle

Before you begin weaving, you'll need to put some weft yarn on a shuttle. Any shuttle, whether commercial or homemade, will work, though some shuttles are more efficient or work better for different types of weaving. Boat shuttles are faster and more expensive; stick shuttles are slower and less expensive. You can use either one for this project.

If you'll be using a boat shuttle, you'll need to wind the bobbin which fits inside it. If you don't have a bobbin, you can use cut down straws or paper rolled up—anything on which you can wind yarn. A bobbin winder, either hand or electric, is an invaluable time saver.

There are many different ways to wind bobbins. One popular technique is to build up yarn on the outside edges of the bobbin, then build up the center, as shown here.

A stick shuttle needs to be wound by hand. About any way you do it will work, though the figure-eight method shown here allows you to put more yarn on at one time and still maintain a fairly low profile on your shuttle for going through the shed more easily.

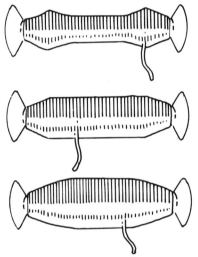

Winding a bobbin. Fill the bobbin at both ends first and then build up the center.

Winding a stick shuttle using the figure-8 method. Both sides of the shuttle may be filled.

Alternating tabby sheds is a new phrase. Plain weave is woven by raising harnesses 1 & 3 together and then 2 & 4 together. Tabby and plain weave are the same thing, just different words (couch/sofa, car/automobile). The treadling (harness combinations) given is two pairs alternating; thus alternating tabby sheds are 1&3 vs. 2&4. This is true on the threading you've just done, 1,2,3,4. On a different threading you might need to do a different treadling to get tabby. We'll talk about this as we go, when differences come up. At this point, I just don't want you to think that tabby is *always* treadled 1&3 vs. 2&4.

Selvedges

When the weaving of the piece actually begins, the first questions that arise have to do with selvedge (side) control and how much weft to leave in the shed. The goal is to have selvedges that are parallel and reasonably straight. This takes practice, and just what you need to do varies with every piece, so don't let wobbly edges discourage you. While different yarns and different patterns each have their own peculiarities, there are some common factors useful to know.

When the shed is open and the weft is put through you have available the old rule that the shortest distance between two points (the right and left selvedges) is a straight line. For a 10″ wide warp this means that a 10″ piece of weft would be long enough to reach from side to side. When the shed is closed, however, the straight line no longer exists. The weft must actually curve and go under the warps that were raised and over those that were in the lower position. As you can see by the illustration, a longer piece of weft is now needed.

This has everything to do with how straight your selvedges are and how much draw-in you'll get on the sides. The extra weft needed to travel the extra distance must come from somewhere, and the only available place is the edges. The take-up will pull equally from the two sides, or try to. On one side there will be plenty of yarn to draw from as it is simply pulling more from the shuttle (if the shed is still open). On the other side, the side on which the weft is already woven, it will pull just as much, and in the process will draw the edge warp(s) in with it. That is where draw-in comes from.

Minimizing draw-in

To keep draw-in to a minimum, and to keep it consistent, you'll need to leave more weft in the shed than would seem necessary. When you weave, instead of having your weft travel straight across the warp, make an angle or curve or some other non-horizontal trail.

There is one other factor to be aware of. If you leave excess weft on the edge, as opposed to within the width, the packing in of the weft shot will create a loop or bubble on that side, resulting in a loose or sloppy looking selvedge. This refers to the side that the shuttle is coming from, not the side it's going to. To prevent those bubbles and loops, pull the weft close to the selvedge thread and leave the excess arc further in. Practice everything you can think of, remembering you are now developing habits that will stay with you.

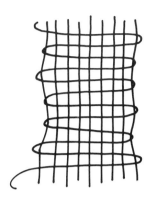

Uneven selvedges.

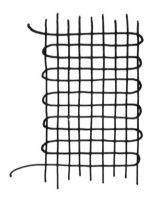

Nice, even selvedges.

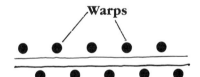

Open shed with weft going through.

Closed shed, weft going over and under.

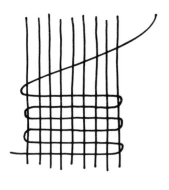

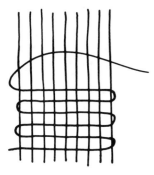

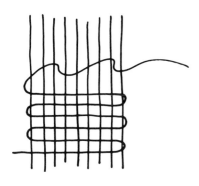

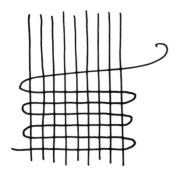

To minimize draw-in allow extra weft in the shed. Angling or curving as shown here are ways to add length to the weft in the shed.

Some miscellaneous information about draw-in and selvedges is in order here. Most important for you to know is that every weaver has one better selvedge and one not as good; there are habits you can nurture in yourself to get them as consistent as possible, but know it won't be automatic. Watch yourself and see what you're doing differently with your right and left hands, and work from there.

One way to have very even straight selvedges is to pull your weft tight and go for a maximum amount of draw-in. I've seen this done and sometimes it works. The hazards, however, are that if you are using a firm yarn the strain on the pulled edges will likely break them. On the other hand, if you are using a soft yarn it may stretch. If one selvedge pulls in more than the other, the stretching will result in one side of your weaving being longer than the other side (a trapezoid), one of the few problems in weaving that is virtually unrepairable.

A temple or stretcher is a tool that is designed to keep selvedges straight. Some weavers use them all of the time, for every kind of project; others never do. Basically, they are adjustable tension bars with teeth on both ends that sink into your weaving (without hurting it) and hold it to a fixed width. It is placed in the web (cloth) in what was just woven, and then you weave a few inches. As soon as you've woven a few inches you lift it off and move it forward, always keeping it within a couple of inches of the fell (front edge, last weft shot).

While the tendency when you first start to weave is to pull at the selvedges, resisting the urge will lead to developing a smooth weaving rhythm, especially if you are using a boat shuttle. An even weaving rhythm does a lot for selvedges, as well as making your weaving progress more rapidly. Practice, though, is probably the main factor in achieving good, even selvedges.

Special selvedge considerations

Twills have a special selvedge oddity that plain weave doesn't have. With plain weave you are alternately raising every other thread every other time, so your edge threads go up, down, up, down forever. With a twill this is not the case. Because of the treadling order, a harness will stay up for two shots, then down for two. Depending on the direction your shuttle is going, and which side it is on when you change which shed, the edge threads may or may not be caught by the weft. If they are not, then you'll have a warp float on the side, sometimes for a short distance, sometimes for the whole piece where the weft never catches that warp. I'll give you a variety of ways to deal with this and you can choose the one(s) that seems most reasonable to you.

The easiest thing to remember is that the problem stems from when the shuttle passes by the selvedge relative to when the selvedge thread is going up or down, so that much of the time you can solve this problem by simply changing the direction of the shuttle. To do this either cut the weft and start again from the other side, or skip one shed in the treadling sequence; e.g., instead of 1&2, 2&3, 3&4, 4&1, treadle 1&2, 3&4, 4&1. Skipping a shed will cause a skip in your pattern, so you may not want to do this. Try it just to see what it looks like, then if you don't like it, unweave it (reverse your treadling and pull the weft out).

Sometimes changing the direction of the shuttle only changes which side has an uncaught warp, no real solution at all. If you are weaving this twill for a short distance, you can manipulate the shuttle around the edge warp thread, simply going over or under it by hand instead of entering the shed as you normally do. This can be a strain on the warp and is tedious if kept up for very long, but it works well for short distances.

If you know that this will be a recurring problem in a piece, you can use a floating selvedge. I'll tell you about this when we discuss twills.

Finally, there is a formula for minimizing the occurrence of this unwoven edge thread. This is guaranteed to work only if your threading begins on harness one and ends on harness four (or vice versa). When weaving a 2/2 twill, if you first treadle 1&2, start your shuttle from the 3-4 side, i.e., if the furthest right thread is on harness one, start the shuttle from the left, or if the left selvedge thread is on harness one, start the shuttle on the right.

Whether or not you need to use any of the above solutions depends on whether or not an uncaught warp is a problem. This depends on what the project is. If you are making a sample, then practicing these methods can be good; but it doesn't really matter to the sample whether the edge thread is caught or not. Likewise, if you are making something that will eventually have the selvedges cut off or sewn up, then again this doesn't matter. If one thread *never* catches, then eliminate it and your piece will be one thread narrower. If the selvedges will be forever visible, as in a table runner, vest front, or wall hanging, then yes, you need to choose a way to make your selvedges look nice.

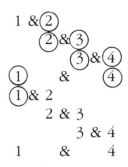

Twill weaving order. Here a harness stays up for two shots, then down for two.

Sequences of the weaving process

Next comes the actual sequence of events, the order of changing the shed, throwing the shuttle, and beating the weft in. The only question of any real significance is whether to beat with the shed still open, after closing it, or after changing to the next shed. In weaving tabby, for instance, after you've thrown the shuttle

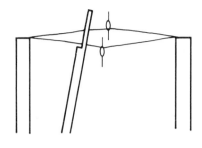

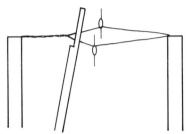

As the fell of your fabric gets closer and closer to the reed, you will find your shed getting smaller and smaller. When you can't get your shuttle through it easily, it is time to advance the warp.

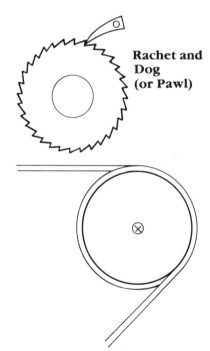

Rachet and Dog (or Pawl)

On or off, a ratchet brake can hold only at intervals, in a tooth of the rachet. On a friction brake a cable or wire clamps down and holds tight. It can be loosened a little for slight tension release. It can hold tight at any point around the drum.

through the 1&3 shed, do you beat with the 1&3 still raised, after you've lowered 1&3 and have no harnesses raised, or after you've raised 2&4? There are positive reasons for all, and weavers with every preference. It probably makes the most sense to vary your decision with what you are weaving, by project or yarn distinction. Some yarns are more fragile than others and that makes a difference in how they need to be handled.

The argument for beating with the same shed still open, and changing the shed with the beater still forward, is that it creates less friction on the yarn, much safer for a delicate or hairy yarn. Also worth considering is that with the shed still open any more weft needed to accommodate take-up is available, i.e., can easily pull from the shuttle end of the weft shot.

The case for beating after the shed has been closed or changed is used most often for rug weaving, though it applies to other weaving as well. With the shed changed, the weft is locked into place, so once it's beaten in it will not slide back out or shift.

Either sequence can give you a consistent beat, an even density. You are responsible for that, and if you are consistent, the fabric will be.

When weaving on a floor loom with a boat shuttle you'll develop a rhythm that is so smooth and flowing that the beat sequence is almost imperceptible, both things happening almost simultaneously.

Advancing the warp

As your weaving progresses you'll notice your shed getting smaller and smaller. This is due to the decrease in the allowable weaving space between your reed and the fell of your fabric and because of the increased tension that is put on the threads which restricts the shed which can be made. How far you can weave depends on your loom; in most cases this will be somewhere between 2″ and 6″. When the shed has gotten small enough that it is difficult to get the shuttle through, or even an inch or so before that, it's time to advance your warp. (Weavers needing great consistency advance their warp quite frequently, for as the fell advances the angle of the beater changes, causing a different beat if the weaver doesn't compensate for the changes.)

If you have ratchets front and back, release the front ratchet first to relax the warp tension, then release the back ratchet to be able to advance the warp. On a table loom this is done by hand. On a floor loom there is a brake pedal, usually to the right of your treadles, and stepping on it will release the back ratchet.

If you have a loom with a friction brake, lightly tap the brake pedal with your foot until the brake releases a little bit. You don't ever want to release a tight tension all at once (with either type of brake) because the sudden release will cause your warp beam to spin and unwind a lot of warp, necessitating the rewinding of it. If you have a brand new loom, the friction brake may require some adjusting and breaking in to compensate for new stiffness. Try releasing it over and over, being careful to never bend the cable that wraps around the drum. If this cable gets bent it will never hold tight again, nor release reliably.

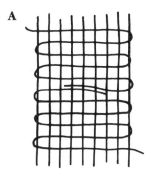

Once you've disengaged the back brake, whichever type it is, keep it released and crank your warp toward the fabric beam, again listening for the clicking of the dog on the front ratchet this time. There should be a handle or crank of some kind attached to the fabric beam for rotating it forward. When your fabric is almost far enough forward to get a good shed, reengage the back brake (take your foot off the brake pedal or manually flip the dog back on the ratchet). Then crank the fabric beam forward enough to make your warp tension tight enough to resume your weaving. On table looms all this is done by releasing the ratchet and advancing the warp by hand.

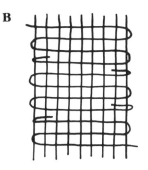

Advancing the warp too far is very common in the beginning, the result being that either your beater will hit the front beam before it hits the fell, or the angle of the beater will be such that it won't beat the weft in well. When you have advanced your warp too far, simply reverse the process, rolling the warp toward the back again.

Ending and starting weft

The last thing I'm going to cover under the subject of how to weave is what to do when you end one weft and start another. There are so many variables that for starters I'll say that the only constant is *don't* knot them together. Knots cause bumps that are there forever, and they are both unattractive and unnecessary.

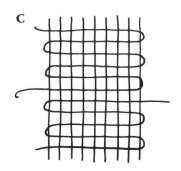

I think that illustrations are more appropriate and easier for showing you the various options than words, so here are some.

A. Overlap anywhere, 1"-2".

B. Tuck ends in on opposite selvedges; changes direction shuttle is going, which may or may not matter.

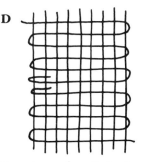

C. Leave ends hanging out while weaving, cut back to selvedge or sew them in after piece is washed and shrinkage is final.

D. Tuck ends in on the same side; may cause excessive build-up on one side, especially if you're using a fat weft yarn.

Ways to end and start weft.

Any of these overlap methods will work. There are times when one or another will be preferable, and determining factors include thickness and color of yarn, how loosely or tightly the fabric is being woven, whether or not the selvedges will show in the finished piece or be sewn into hems, how often you are changing wefts, and no doubt many others.

As you weave more and more, you'll discover and develop numerous tricks of your own. The basic process—opening the shed, throwing the shuttle, beating—is that simple. What makes your weaving yours is the little extras you'll add. Every weaving book will have a few special tricks that the author has found to be useful, and letters from readers in weaving magazines offer many more. There is no aspect of weaving that can be done only one way, so never feel restricted or required to do something that doesn't feel right to you. If you don't like it, try something else, and if you can't think of an alternative (which is to be expected in the beginning), ask other weavers what they do. Eventually you'll develop a style that is uniquely your own and helps you to enjoy weaving as much as you thought you would when you first dreamt of it.

Troubleshooting

In part IV there is a whole section on troubleshooting which is a quick, at-a-glance reference for different kinds of problems, with possible corrective measures to take for solving each one. You'll find this a handy resource as you do more weaving. For now, I'd like to discuss just a few things which could go wrong (at any time) and what you can do about them. Know that almost all problems have solutions.

I discussed what to do about crossed warps in the warping lesson. After you've woven an inch or so is a good time to check for them. Open the shed and look through it from the side. It should be clean, no warps hanging in the middle or crossing it. If there are, find these threads and see what the problem is. Are there crossed warps between the reed and heddles? Are there crossed warps amongst the heddles? Does a warp end or section of ends not have enough tension in one place? For crossed warps, simply untie the group of warps which contains the crossed ends, pull them out of the weaving, through the reed and untwist them between the reed and heddles or amongst the heddles. Rethread as necessary, then resley and retie. For loose warps, simply tighten and retie. If many threads are twisted in the heddles or crossed between the reed and heddles, you might not even get a shed. (Check the troubleshooting section for other possible causes of not getting a shed.)

Another thing you might notice when you look at your first few inches of weaving is whether you've made a threading error. Some signs of these will be if two warp ends right next to each other are weaving together, that is, always acting as the same thread by going over and under the same wefts at the same time. This means that you've threaded these two warps on the same harness. Sometimes you may want this, but if it looks like a mistake because it's the only time it's happening, then it is a threading error and needs to be corrected.

If a warp isn't weaving at all, it might not be threaded in a heddle. If this is the case, you probably noticed it when you looked through your shed sideways and saw this end hanging in the middle.

Other errors are noticeable because a thread is out of sequence and is not making the pattern it should make. If there is a straight diagonal line, as there is in a straight twill, you'll notice a jog in this line. If this occurs vertically it is a threading error; if this occurs occasionally along a horizontal line, this is a treadling error.

What to do about threading errors

If you have determined that you have one, first trace the thread or threads in question to the heddles. Possibly, you threaded one group of heddles incorrectly, and fixing the error means only rethreading this group. To correct, untie the group of warp threads in error, pull them out of the weaving, through the reed and the heddles, and rethread and resley them in the correct order.

Another thing which you might see when you look at your heddles is that you threaded two adjacent threads on the same harness and don't have a heddle to thread one of these warps onto the correct harness. Don't panic. This can be easily solved. You can simply take one of your unused heddles and cut the sides of the top and bottom slots where the heddle attaches to the heddle bars and remove it from the heddle bar. Then slide it onto the bars in the place where you need it. Save this heddle and reuse it again when you need it; when the metal fatigues after many uses, just replace it with another repair heddle.

One thing which will happen at some point in your weaving career is a warp thread will break. This is not a terrible problem and can be easily repaired. There are numerous reasons a warp will break. Maybe there's a thin spot in the thread which gives way, or a knot in a warp which breaks as it goes through a heddle eye when you are advancing the warp. Uneven tension can often cause warps to break. Abrasion in the reed, where the yarn is too fat for the reed and too much draw-in will cause warp threads to

Woven by Yvonne Stahl

Color play and treadling variations can produce exciting results, as seen in this weft-faced pillow. Here, cotton carpet warp is set 8 ends per inch, and is completely covered by the weft. The threading is a point twill, rosepath (threaded 1,2,3,4,3,2,1,4 repeat), woven on opposites (see page 146 for more on this). By using different color and treadling sequences, all kinds of patterns are possible. In this example, the use of rich purple, pink and red, with zingy specks of yellow, produce an electric effect. You might explore neutral, pastel or close-in-hue color schemes for equally interesting results. Though complicated in appearance, this pillow is really quite easy to weave. Let your inspiration guide you!

Woven by Audrey Kick

This overshot runner was done in a beginning weaving class. It is a good example of how a class sample can serve a functional purpose. The simple plain weave border is a nice contrast to the heavily-patterned body of the runner; both the royal blue background and the red pattern weft play equally important roles in the overall design. Generally, you can plan on your pattern weft yarn being twice as large as your background weft in order for it to show up effectively; a steady, even beat is important to achieve a balanced pattern.

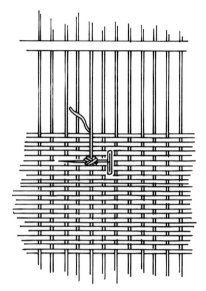

Tying a broken warp end. Place a T-pin in your fabric in line from where your replacement warp comes from the reed. Anchor your replacement warp by making a figure-8 around a T-pin.

break. As you weave and come across problems, check the troubleshooting section, it'll be a helpful guide to diagnosing and curing any weaving problems which occur.

For now, I'll mention what to do should a warp thread break. Simply measure another warp which is long enough to reach the broken thread coming from the back. Pull out the broken warp and leave the end hanging at the front so you can sew it in after you remove your warp from the loom. Then sley your new end through the reed, thread it through the heddle and then find the broken end at the back of the loom. Tie your new warp to this broken one with a sturdy, small knot. Tie it so you have about 2" of each thread left for a good overlap when repairing after the fabric is removed from the loom. Now, go around to the front of your loom and take up any slack on this replacement warp. Place a T-pin in your fabric about an inch or so from the fell of your fabric, in a straight line from where your replacement warp comes from the reed. Adjust the tension on this replacement warp so it matches that of the rest of your warp, and then anchor it by making several figure-eights around the pin. This pin stays in place until the weaving holds the new warp in place. The ends are sewn in before your fabric is washed. Also at this time, you'll want to take out the knot you tied in repairing your broken warp. It will be woven into the cloth, so you'll need to coax it loose and sew these ends in as well. This is explained further in the next section.

You'll find that as you get more accustomed to weaving and how your woven fabrics look, your eye will be alert for these kinds of errors, most of which are easily remedied. Again, check the troubleshooting section should you come across problems.

Taking your sample off the loom

You can tell you're almost done when you see the back apron rod approaching the castle. Just as the fell getting closer to the heddles made your shed smaller, so the back knots getting closer will close your shed. How far to weave depends entirely on you and the project. If you are weaving the last half of the last placemat, then you'll want to weave until it's done. If you are weaving a long scarf and you're short on time, you may quit as soon as the shed begins to be less than ideal. If you are meticulous and thrifty you will probably weave until the shuttle won't go through anymore; you can buy or make some very thin shuttles for those last few inches, or use a 5"-6" yarn needle. If the piece is a sample and you've already learned what you set out to discover, you may quit long before the end of the warp. Each piece and each day call for a different answer to the question, "How far should I weave?"

As the warp comes off the loom the tension will of course relax, and among other things your last few weft shots will begin to slide out. There are numerous ways to deal with this, and which one to use will depend on what you're doing. I'll give you three; there are many more.

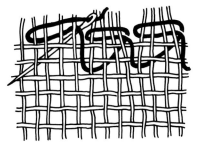

Hemstitching.

If you've been weaving a piece that will be essentially done when it comes off the loom, say a table runner, then hemstitching is pretty and secure, and is easiest if done while the warp is still under tension on the loom. Generally speaking, if you do it at one end you'll probably want to do it at the other end as well. To do this requires some planning ahead. After you've woven your first 3″ or 4″ at the very beginning of your project, is the time to hemstitch the front end. When the piece is all done you can hemstitch the other end. For more on finishes and finishing see Finishes, page 221, in Part IV.

If you want to use the warp ends to create a fancy fringe, or just to tie overhand knots, you'll want the weft to stay in place until you are ready to work with them. One good way to assure this is to use another weft, maybe fat, and weave a header such as you did at the front. Then what's ravelling is the header; your project weft is staying in place. Tying overhand knots is probably the most popular way to make a fringe. How many warp threads you include in each group will depend on your yarn and sett, and what you want your fringe to look like.

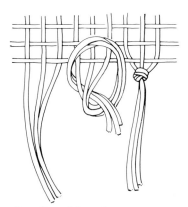

Overhand knots.

Finally, if you are weaving yardage, simply a large piece of fabric, a few weft shots loosening up won't be of much consequence. If the yarn is at all fuzzy or textured the weft will probably stay locked in pretty well anyway. In this kind of project you don't need to bother with any special end treatment, just take it off the loom and zigzag across with the ends with a sewing machine if necessary.

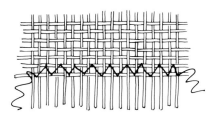

Machine zigzag.

The actual process of removing a piece from the loom is remarkably simple and magnificently gratifying. All during the weaving process you've never seen more than 6″-8″ of the piece at a time unless you unrolled it to look (which you can do, by the way). Now you will finally get to see all of what you've done, and the longer the piece is the more exciting it can be.

To get your piece off the loom, reach behind the heddles and cut the warp as far back as you can. If you've used lark's head knots or a lash cord, be sure to cut the warp, not the loops or cord. If you need to measure take-up or loom waste, then you can untie all the knots and pull the warp out intact. Because this is so time

Woven by Yvonne Stahl

Plaids are always fun to weave and lend themselves well to all kinds of things: shawls, tablecloths, towels, vests, caps, scarves. Think of weaving plaids in plain weave or twill, knowing that either weave structure will produce a different result. The plain weave scarf and matching twill hat are examples of where the combining of weave structures on one warp produce varied, coordinated results. There's room for lots of experimentation here.

Placemats are an all-time-favorite project of weavers. This set is woven of durable cotton and will take lots of everyday wear and tear. One inch stripes of white and brown alternate in the warp; this sequence is repeated exactly in the weft for a checkered mat. Warp sett is 12 ends per inch; 12 weft shots per inch are woven in for a balanced and square pattern. Experiment with color: try mats of blue and green, red and white, gray and pink, brown and beige. Explore! Create!

Woven by Bethany Thomas

consuming, if the warp is fairly even in length you can untie and measure a sampling of knots instead of all of them and cut the rest.

Once you've cut the warp from the back beam, pull it forward, out of the heddles and reed, release the front ratchet, and unroll the whole piece from the fabric beam. In front you may be better off to untie the knots, for usually the weaving starts so close to the front apron rod that cutting leaves no fringe to work with and results in a far greater danger of ravelling weft.

If your front apron rod is actually tied to the loom and won't come free, then you'll need to untie the knots to get the piece off the loom. If your rod is lashed on and so will slide away from the apron cords, then you don't need to untie the knots now. Grab one end of the rod firmly with your stronger hand, use your other hand as a knot-stopper, and slide the rod out of all that is tied to it.

That's it; you're off the loom. And after a few minutes (or days) of enjoying the pleasure of viewing your weaving, it's time to proceed with the next step, finishing the fabric.

Finishing your fabric

There are whole books written on this subject, and I'm not even going to begin to give you a full discussion of it. The point I want to get across is that 99% of the time a piece is not finished until it has been washed (including wool). While technically speaking fixing errors is not part of fabric finishing, it's far easier and more successful to do it before the piece is washed so I'll mention it now as well.

Repairing errors

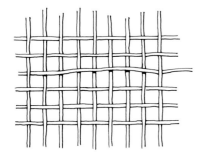

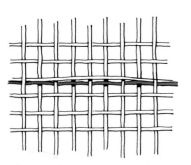

To repair errors, stitch in a new piece of yarn where the thread was suppose to be. Stitch along the original thread on both sides of the error. Cut the old one off where it was floating in error.

It is important for you to know that almost any mistake you make can be fixed; a weaving error is not a crisis. It is also true that should you notice an error while weaving, it's easier to fix it now, than later. Stop weaving and unweave your errant pick, or if you've woven quite a bit before noticing the error, fixing it now under tension on the loom will be easier than later.

One of the things that is nice to own is a yarn needle at least 5″ long. When you find a thread that skips over some it wasn't supposed to, warp or weft, take your needle and a new piece of the same yarn and stitch into the fabric where the thread was supposed to be. Stitch along the original thread on both sides of the error for a little way. After you remove your piece from the loom, simply cut the old one off where it was floating in error; the overlapped area will keep everything secure.

Often you will want to use the original thread to make its own repair instead of a new one. In this case, cut it at one end where the error begins, and stitch it into the correct place. If the error is near one end of the fabric and can be repaired by reweaving a warp, instead of cutting anything, pull the warp out of the weft and reweave it back to the end.

When a piece of fabric comes off the loom, it will relax and be softer to the touch, more flexible. With the tension released, the yarns can begin to bend and curve around each other, and with some patterns the fabric can even take on an entirely different look. Relatively speaking, however, you are still seeing lots of threads together as opposed to a homogeneous cloth. Once the piece is washed all of the yarns find their true relationship to each other and so are no longer as likely to shift. That settling will make most repairs/reweaving practically invisible.

Washing to finish your fabric

While washing a fabric may also be for cleaning purposes, that's aside from the finishing process necessary.

I don't want to go into great detail about washing. Different fibers require different handling, as different project characteristics will also be factors in washing methods chosen. At this point I will mention gross generalizations and say use care and common sense, and perhaps some further research. Most often abuse or shock are the things that ruin fabrics. Use warm water, soap or gentle detergent, and squeeze, don't wring. A spin cycle's okay, but agitation is dangerous. Lay your fabric out to dry instead of hanging it, as water weight has a tendency to pull fabric out of shape. If you have a very large piece of fabric, wash it in the bathtub. Dry cleaning is not the same—remember it's shifting, fulling, you're after, not cleaning.

A lot of what you need to know about finishing comes with an understanding of yarns, how they're made, how certain fibers behave, etc. Read the section on yarns when you want to know more, and especially watch yourself, learn from your own experience. Given the exact same assignment and materials, no two people will produce identical results. Therefore, each of us needs to learn what is unique to each yarn and to our own use of it.

And that brings us to the last section in this lesson, learning from yourself.

Towel woven by Yvonne Stahl; napkin woven by Helen Irwin.

As you gain more experience and confidence in your weaving abilities, before long there's a good chance you'll want to try weaving some fine threads. At left is a simple, plain weave fingertip towel with pale green overshot borders. The warp is a white cotton set 24 ends per inch; the weft is a natural beige linen packed in for a balanced weave at 24 picks, or shots, per inch. Shiny perle cotton, used for the borders, is a nice contrast to the mat finish of the background yarns.

The napkin at right is woven of fine linen. It has lace borders on all four sides which give liveliness to the plain weave background. Hemstitched hems add to the heirloom quality of this piece. These two fabrics are especially appealing for their simplicity. If you're not yet ready for fine threads, try these ideas out in heavier yarns for placemats or table runners. Don't let fine threads scare you, though; you'll be pleased at the joy of weaving fine fabric and surprised that the weaving progresses more rapidly than you supposed it would.

Woven by Katie Potter

Simple plain weave and a cotton novelty yarn work well together to make the shawl and matching purse cover shown here. The warp is a bleached white, 5/2 perle cotton; the weft is a natural cotton boucle. When woven, the two yarns produce a fabric with a pleasing texture and a lot of drape.

In planning, keep in mind what you want your finished product to look and feel like, and then choose your yarn, sett and beat accordingly. The choices made for this ensemble give it a special appeal, both visual and tactile, for cool summer evening wear. Think of some of the yarn and texture choices you might make for a fall or winter version.

Learning from yourself—record keeping—self evaluation

You don't have to keep records if you don't want to, any more than you have to weave samples or do anything else. Most of us keep records of what we've done on a fairly sporadic basis I'd guess, doing very well for awhile and then forgetting for awhile (at least that's how I do it). I know two weavers who have detailed records of every warp they've ever put on; I know lots more who have none. There are some very valuable reasons for keeping records of what you've done, and these reasons are why we continually try to keep it up.

First of all, you have to do some figuring in advance anyway, so why not do it in a notebook reserved for just this purpose? It's probably even easier than scrap paper because you know where it is, you'll develop a system that works efficiently for you, and you'll be able to refer to it easily. Being able to refer to it is, of course, why you'd want to have it available.

While you're working on a project you'll need to check your notes to find out how many warp ends you need, how long, what colors, where they go, what the threading order is, how you want to weave it. Your planning calculations are the first part of your record sheet but probably the least important in the long run.

Other information to include in the beginning is the cost of a project, which is usually two different amounts. If you have many stripes and you've used yarn that came premeasured (four ounce skeins, two ounce tubes, whatever), rather than in the exact quantity you need, you will no doubt have some left over. It may have cost you $40 to purchase all the yarn, but you may have $12 worth of yarn left with which to weave another project. Your out-of-pocket expense is therefore $40, but the project really only cost $28. Your next project may use some of this left over yarn and so may have an out of pocket expense of $3, with the project's real cost being $10. You need to keep track of both numbers because it is not at all unusual for someone to see something you've woven and ask for one for themselves. Sometimes you'll say yes as a gift, other times you'll say yes if they buy the yarn, and sometimes you'll want to charge them for the yarn and labor. In any case, it is much faster and cleaner to make such arrangements if you can quickly look up what was involved in the way of money and time.

Time. Now is not when to begin watching it. When you are just learning, everything you do will take longer than it will later, and it could give you a very distorted idea of how long it takes to weave something if you kept close track now. Sooner than you think, however, you'll be accomplishing feats of weaving in half the time you do now. If you expect to ever sell anything or to weave for a deadline (birthday presents, etc.), you'll have a much better sense of what's feasible if you know how long something took to make, from conception on through to delivery. The most clever idea I've seen for keeping track of time, is to buy a cheap alarm clock (not digital) and set it at 12:00 at the beginning of each new project. Every time you start to work on the project plug the clock in; when you quit, unplug it. It will count your time cumulatively and if you finish at 9:30 you'll know it took nine and a half hours to do that project. The only catch is coming up with some trick to remind you to plug and unplug the clock.

At this point, you may well think that each thing you weave has so much invested in it—time, planning, worry, love, decisions, frustrations, joy, and money—that you'll never forget it, and so keeping records isn't really necessary. At least that's what I thought for a long time. It's not so; you will forget some of them. I've been to friends' homes in other parts of the country and seen things that looked surprisingly familiar, only to realize I had woven them years ago. One of the biggest reasons for keeping thorough, dated records, is that a friend of a friend will see a pillow you wove and say, "Oh, I'd like one just like it only in blue!" Can you imagine remembering the threading for a pillow that you wove several years ago and haven't seen since?

What all goes into a record sheet? Everything you might ever want to know. I've included a sample record sheet on page 88. There is more information that could easily be included as circumstances call for it: your name, special equipment needed, loom used, finishing techniques, to name a few. If you like this one, feel free to photocopy it for your own use.

If you are keeping these notes only for yourself, then any paper is fine. If you are sharing the sheets or attaching samples to them, stiffer paper such as card stock is probably better. Putting sheets into a looseleaf notebook makes them easy to remove for copying and sharing.

Discoveries

For me, the most important part of the whole record sheet is the section for other discoveries. This is where I record surprises, disasters—all the true learning experiences: Sett too close for yarn; friction-caused breaking. Colors bled. Colors worked just right for couch. Selvedges terrible; floating selvedge needed. Beautiful yarn lost its character; finished piece not as pretty as I'd hoped. Softness and bumps perfect for slightly textured baby blanket. Pattern didn't show with this color choice. Forgot to compensate for stretchy yarn; piece ended up too short. Beat is just right; I'm getting better. Etc., etc., etc. There is no end to the discoveries you'll make, and it's a rare project that doesn't teach

Woven by Louise Bradley

You can have a lot of fun playing with twills: you can combine twill threadings, vary treadlings and explore color. Another variation worth experimentation is scale. Here, three brown wool yarns are used as one for warp (you could also use one very heavy yarn) and they are crossed with a doubled weft for a straight-forward, bold design. The squatty-looking rows separating the rows of large diamonds result from using the weft singly in these areas. The warp sett for this piece is 10 ends per inch; think of what would happen to the scale of your design if this threading were sett 15 ends per inch, 20 ends per inch, or at 40 ends per inch (you'll need to change your yarn size, too).

Woven by Maggie Putnam

Mixing yarns and colors in the warp can produce subtle and rich fabrics, as in the shawl shown here. A single weft, similar in color, serves to further blend the warp colors and textures together. Because some yarns are stretchier than others, wide stripes can potentially cause tension problems in weaving because some yarns will stretch, or give, more under tension. If you're not sure about whether certain yarns or stripe widths will work together, do a sample first. A scarf, because it is small, is a good project for your first mixed warp. Though this technique is appealing in itself, it is also a good way to use bits and pieces of leftover yarns.

Record of a Project

Name of project: _____

Date woven: _____

Approximate time project took: _____

Yarns used: warp _____

weft _____

Pattern: _____

Source: _____

Length of warp: _____   Dimensions on loom: _____

Width of warp: _____   Dimensions off loom: _____

Sett: _____   Dimensions after washing: _____

P.P.I.: _____   Cost of project: _____

Total yarn used: _____   Out of pocket expense: _____

Goal of project:

Was goal met?:

Other discoveries:

you something new. Mostly I've discovered that if I don't record what I've learned and then read over it once in awhile, I have to learn the lesson all over again.

If this is your first experience with weaving, you probably don't know what everything on this record sheet refers to or what all the surprises listed above mean. Don't worry about it, you will in time. For now, just fill in what you do know; leave the rest for later.

Self evaluation

Self evaluation is a real mystery, especially if you live in weaver-isolation. On the one hand, the real truth is if *you* like it it's good; if you don't, it's not. Assuming (always a dangerous thing to do) that you are weaving for your own pleasure and satisfaction, the only thing that matters is that you are enjoying what you're doing or what you're getting, or better, both.

While this is true, most weavers also want to know how their work rates alongside what other people are doing, what the standard is. If we never see what other weavers are doing, it's difficult to know what we could be striving for, either in quality or new ideas. I can't give you any absolute answers because there aren't any, but I can offer some guiding questions.

Is your piece structurally stable, or is it likely to fall apart easily?

Is the yarn appropriate to the project? Wool bikinis and linen rugs leave something to be desired.

Does your piece look finished, or are there pieces of yarn hanging out? Look for evenness of beat, reasonably straight selvedges, good finishing of fabric and finishing techniques, no mistakes in the pattern.

Is your fabric aesthetically pleasing—good color, design—to you?

Does the piece fill the need for which it was intended?

Is it better than your earlier work, either improving on old skills or experimenting with new?

Are you proud enough of your piece to show it to your best friend, a total stranger, your parents, or your third grade teacher?

Actually, no one needs to feel totally isolated from weavers anymore because of the number of weaving magazines available. Weaving magazines show weaver's work, some by professionals and some by beginners, many in between. As of this writing there are four or more magazines being published just for weavers, several others for the fiber arts in general. A subscription to any one of them will connect you to thousands of other weavers. Each magazine has a different emphasis, and by reading them you can get a very good idea of what's being done and how people feel about what they are seeing. Read the letters to the editor, find one you like, and ask that person to be your weaving pen pal. Or write you own letter to the editor and offer yourself as one.

Meanwhile, if you're just starting out and you are alone, don't spend much energy wondering how your work ranks alongside others. Now is the time to learn, to let yourself explore all that's new and exciting and easily available. Look at each piece you finish and decide what *one* thing about it you want to improve on in your next piece, then work on that. Most of you will be way too hard on yourselves anyway. You are not going to be the world's greatest weaver this month, you are going to be the weaver you are. Enjoy it. Enjoy it. Enjoy it.

Notes, discoveries and ideas

Lesson 4
Planning A Project

The initial drawing
Warp calculations
Weft calculations

Now that you've woven a sample, you should have a pretty good feel for how your loom works and what weaving is all about. While knowing how to warp your loom and throw a shuttle are essential, they are not all you need to know to become a self-sufficient weaver. To be able to truly weave on your own, you need to be able to make all the decisions for planning a project before you ever begin to measure your warp.

One of the most astonishing things I have ever witnessed was a student whose first step was to go to the warping board and begin measuring her warp. After awhile she asked me if she had measured enough.

"What are you making?" I asked.

"A shawl."

"Well, how many warp ends do you need and how many do you have?"

"I don't know."

"Where are your warp calculations?"

"I didn't do any."

"How did you know how long to measure your warp?"

"I thought this looked long enough."

It was one of the few times in my life I was speechless. Only later did I learn that any number of people, for a variety of reasons, guess at their yarn needs, bluff their way through their projects, hoping they'll get something usable. Aside from the fact that that's unwise and unnecessary, planning can be as much fun as any other part of the process, and it's a shame to leave it out.

For your first piece I told you just what I wanted you to do, but that will be the last time. Even though I told you what to do, I wanted you to understand what it was I was asking you to do, because if you don't understand, then you won't be able to do it on your own. Your ability to do what you want is my goal, and I hope it is one of yours, too.

Front loom waste

Mat 1

Fringe between mats

Mat 2

Mat 3

Mat 4

Back loom waste

Draw a picture of what you want to weave.

The initial drawing

Planning a project is really very easy. I have learned to draw on paper whatever it is I have in mind, and that way I rarely forget anything. For an example, let's start with something easy, like a set of four placemats. All four can be woven on one warp, made long enough to accommodate them.

This is what the warp and mats would look like after being woven if it were all stretched out on the floor. The loom waste in the front and back is the warp that never gets woven. In front you need some yarn to tie onto the front apron rod. In the back all of the warp behind the reed, through the harnesses, and tied to the back apron rod never gets woven because there is no way to get to it. We'll talk about how much yarn gets "wasted" when we discuss warp calculations.

I want to have fringe on these mats, so I need to be sure to leave unwoven warp between mats for it. If I were going to hem the mats I could weave continually and simply cut and sew the ends.

So, the first step in planning is to make an initial drawing of what you want to weave. Then, it's simply a matter of filling in the details. To make your plan, you'll need to ask and answer these questions:

How many mats?

What dimensions?

Fringed or hemmed?

How much length is needed for fringe or hems? If your mats will have fringe, even if the final fringe is to be only 1″ long you'll need at least 3″ to work with; it can be trimmed later. If you're planning hems, you'll need to decide how much to allow to turn under.

What fiber do you want to use? Cotton, silk, rayon, wool, nylon, acrylic, linen, a blend?

Shrinkage? Wash a piece of yarn a yard long and see how much it shrinks.

Thick or thin? Generally, you can think that thin yarn makes thin mats, thick yarn, thick mats.

Design. There are many design questions you'll have to ask yourself, but right now I'd like to keep to the basics of planning. I'll talk about design gradually, throughout the lessons.

Warp calculations

Let's get on with specific warp calculations. The formula is very easy; there is nothing magical about it at all. First, we need some answers to the questions above.

We already decided we'd make four mats. (Somehow saying "we decided" is like the teacher saying, "Now *we* are going to take a test," when you know full well the teacher is *not* taking a test. However, if you were in my classroom "we decided" would be accurate since I always have the students make the decisions; so, I'm going to go ahead and use it since I want you to feel that you are in a classroom.) Four mats. Placemats come in many sizes, from 9″ × 11″ to 17″ × 22″. I like large mats myself, and I usually aim for around 14″ × 17″, finished.

Fringe or hems? Let's go for fringe, hemstitched with a needle and yarn to match the warp. Hemstitching is an edge treatment and gets done on the loom while the warp is still under tension. It looks nice and means you don't need a lot of extra length to work with afterwards.

Cotton is good for placemats. It will barely shrink at all if it has been mercerized, and may shrink a lot if it has not. (Mercerized cotton is shiny; non-mercerized has a duller finish.) Since this is an exercise in warp calculations, not a real project, let's just decide that the cotton is pre-shrunk and allow only another 5% for shrinkage.

As with choosing a fiber, choosing yarn is very arbitrary when we're making up an example. Let's have a thinner warp and a thicker weft.

Figuring your warp needs

Now to the formula. First we'll figure out the warp, then the weft. Let's start by drawing the picture again and adding some dimensions.

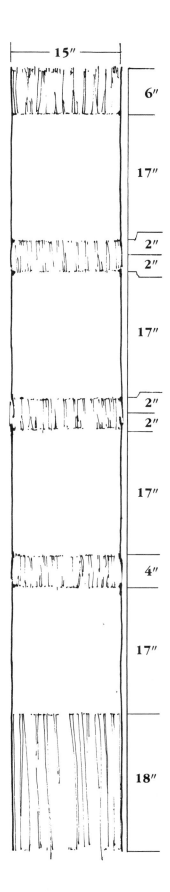

Warp Calculations

finished project length	4 mats × 17″ = 68″
fringe (ends can come from loom waste)	
	3 sections × 4″ = 12″
shrinkage (5% of mat length)	.05 × 80″ = 4″
take-up (10% of what's to be woven)	
	.10 × 68″ = 6.8″ or 7″
loom waste (front and back)	24″
total warp length	115″
	115″ ÷ 36 = 3 yds, 7″

As yarns are woven they curve and flex as they go over and under each other. This flexing and curving acts to shorten the distance a yarn is able to travel, and is called take-up.

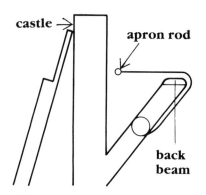

castle →

apron rod

back beam

Extend the apron cords or lash a second rod onto the first if additional length is needed.

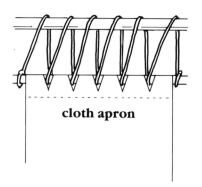

cloth apron

If you have a cloth apron, lash a second apron rod onto the first.

Take-up is something we haven't discussed yet but it is very important to account for. In any woven fabric the threads are going over and under each other, flexing and curving as they go in and out. That curving of the yarn shortens its length, and while it doesn't matter a lot on a placemat it matters a great deal on anything that needs to be a particular size, be it clothing or curtains. (Before I believed in take-up I had made two sets of curtains too short for their windows. I finally moved to a house with shorter windows and could use them.) Most of the time 10% is a reasonable take-up estimate. For very fat yarns you'll need to figure more; for very thin yarns you can get away with less. Remember that if the weft is fatter, it's the warp that will take up more, for it is the yarn going over and under the fat weft. If the warp is fatter, the opposite will take place. Also, remember that only the woven part experiences take-up, the mat length in this instance. That's why in the calculations above the shrinkage is based on a different number than the take-up. The fringe will shrink, so shrinkage is figured on 68″ (mats) + 12″ (fringe), but take-up occurs only in what's *woven*, the 68″ of mat length.

Loom waste varies with the loom and the weaver. An experienced, stingy weaver on a small loom may well have only 12″ of waste, whereas a beginner on a large loom may have 30″ or more. To determine what yours will be pull your back apron rod (the rod attached to your warp beam) over the back beam and to the castle, getting it as close as you can. If it won't reach up to almost touch the last harness, then do something so it will; either lengthen the cords holding it or, if you have a cloth apron, lash a second apron rod onto the first. Practically any wood or metal rod will work as an apron rod as long as it's reasonably sturdy. I prefer to use round ones because the warp knots roll and shift around them more easily. Hardware stores carry dowels and aluminum rods, among other things, that will work fine if you decide to change.

Now tip the beater back against the castle. Measure the distance from the front of the beater to the back apron rod. That will be the largest part of your loom waste but not all of it. Tying the warp around the apron rods takes at least another 2″ front and back, and often people use 6″ though that's not necessary. Finally, it is rare that you will keep weaving until the apron rod reaches all the way to the castle, for reasons you'll understand the first time you approach the end of a piece. The closer you get to the castle the smaller your shed will be, until finally you can't weave any further. That's how you know you're done, or one way anyway.

Those are the places your loom waste goes. The easiest way to determine your own amount is to measure it when you take your piece off the loom. You can measure your take-up at the same time.

From the calculations above we know how long the warp needs to be. Next is to determine how many warp ends are needed. While it can be avoided, most weavers experience some *draw-in* as they weave. What that means is that the *selvedges*, or edges of the weaving, are pulled in a little from the original warp width. Most of the time this doesn't hurt anything, for consistency is more important than actual width. As you weave a variety of projects with a variety of yarns you'll find each drawing in in its own unique manner. Over time you'll be able to predict how certain yarn and pattern combinations are likely to behave.

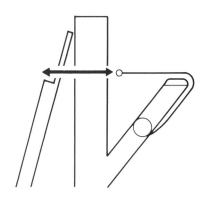

The distance from in front of the beater to behind the castle is the major part of your loom waste.

finished width	15″	*(Shrinkage of 5% = less than an*
draw-in	1″	*inch, so in this case we can leave*
total width on loom	16″	*it out.)*

So we know that we want to put a 16″ wide warp on the loom. The warp yarn I'm thinking of will be good set at 12 e.p.i. (ends per inch), that is 12 warp ends per inch in the reed.

12 e.p.i. × 16″ wide = 192 warp ends total

If you have a huge cone of yarn then you now have enough information to go measure your warp. You know you need 192 pieces, each 115″ long. However, if you are going to go purchase the yarn, you need to find out how many yards you'll need. 115″ × 192 ends = 22,080″ ÷ 36 = 613.3 yards of warp needed.

Formula For Figuring Your Warp Needs

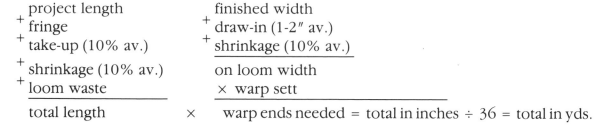

The formula above is for you to use to figure your warp needs. The formula is really very easy. It's also printed on the last page of this book for quick reference.

Determining weft needs

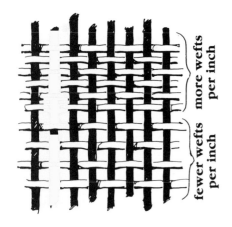

more wefts per inch

fewer wefts per inch

Now for weft. The formula for determining weft needs is as simple and straightforward as the one for warp. The difference is that unless you've woven a sample you can only make an educated guess at how many weft shots you'll pack in per inch. Warp ends per inch are determined by you and the reed and stay constant. Weft shots per inch or *picks per inch* (p.p.i.) are determined by the tension of the warp and how hard you beat, and can vary with every inch. For that reason weft calculations are rarely as precise as warp, but they can certainly be close enough to be valuable.

Formula For Figuring Weft

	length of one weft shot in inches	
×	shots per inch	
=	inches needed to weave one inch of fabric	
×	inches to be woven	
=	inches of weft needed to weave all of project	
	÷ 36	
=	yards of weft needed	

Open shed with weft going through.

Closed shed with weft going over and under warps.

Before you start filling in numbers, remember take-up. It works in the weft essentially the same way it does in the warp. As the weft goes over and under the warp threads it is no longer in a straight line, therefore it needs to be longer than just the width of the warp.

Ten percent take-up in both warp and weft is a reasonable amount to allow for a balanced fabric, one with about the same ends per inch as picks per inch. (If a fabric has many more warp ends per inch than wefts per inch, there will be more take-up warpwise. A fabric which has many more wefts per inch than warps will have more take-up in the weft.) Therefore, if the warp is 16″ wide in the reed then one weft shot will be approximately 16″ + 1.6″ (10%) = 17.6″, or almost 18″ long. Theoretically, it could be rounded either up or down, but realistically it's always better to have a little more yarn than you need than a little less.

So, let's fill in the blanks in the formula.

	length of one weft shot	18
×	p.p.i.	10 (for instance)
=	total weft per inch	180″
×	inches to be woven	68″
=	total inches needed	12240″
÷	36	÷ 36
=	total yards needed	340

When you get to the inches-to-be-woven line, remember not to add in the inches that will be fringe and not woven. You won't need weft for these areas. For our example, the mats themselves account for 80″ of warp length but only 68″ of this amount is woven. The rest is fringe.

If you haven't woven a sample to find out how many weft shots per inch you'll have, you can try a couple of different things to get a number to use. If you've decided that your piece is going to be a balanced fabric (equal e.p.i. and p.p.i.) and your weft and warp are the same yarn, you can say that the p.p.i. will equal the e.p.i. Then when you're weaving, be careful to beat so that it is. Or, you can try wrapping your weft yarn around a ruler at the density you think you'll pack it in, then count how many wraps there are in 1″. If you are weaving a balanced weave (e.p.i. = p.p.i.) your weft needs will be approximately the same as your warp needs. You won't need quite as much weft because you aren't weaving up the loom waste. This is your cushion. This ratio varies with the proportion of the project, i.e., the longer the total warp (and therefore the lower percentage of waste) the closer the warp and weft quantities will be. If your whole warp is only 1 yd long, then half or more will be waste, so you won't need nearly as much weft. If your warp is 10 yds long, then the waste is only about 5%, making your weft and warp needs much closer to equal. This only works with a balanced weave. If your weave is unbalanced (more weft per inch than warp, or vice versa), use the formula to determine how much weft you'll need.

That's really all there is to it. The math is not difficult, and once you've woven a few pieces and know what all those parts of the formulas are for, you'll even remember them all most of the time.

Planning a shawl

Let's go through another project planning exercise, this time without so many words.

Shawl: 24″ × 72″, in wool, loosely woven, smooth warp in two colors, fuzzy or bumpy weft in one color.

			WARP		
project	72″	+	finished width	24″	
+ take-up	7″	+	draw-in	1″	
+ shrinkage	7″	+	shrinkage	2″	
+ fringe	3″*		on loom width	27″	
+ loom waste	24″		× warp sett	× 8 e.p.i.	
total	113″ long	×	warp ends needed	216 = 24,408″ ÷ 36 = 678 yds	

*The rest is coming from loom waste.

WEFT

length of one weft shot (27″ + 10%)	30″
× p.p.i. (estimate)	× 8
inches of weft needed per inch woven	240
× inches to be woven	× 72
total inches needed	17280″ ÷ 36 = 480 yds

Total needs are 678 yards of warp, 480 yards of weft. Because there are two colors in the warp the total needs to be broken down into two numbers, one for each color. Say you have two blue stripes on a white background. The two stripes of blue are different widths, one 2″ wide, one 1″ wide; that gives a total of 3″ of blue, or

8	e.p.i.	216 total warps needed
× 3″		− 24 blue
24 blue warps		192 white warps needed

You'll need to figure the total yardage for each color using the warp formula above.

There are many routes to determining how much of each color you'll need. If there are four colors and you need equal amounts of each, simply divide the total by four. Sometimes you won't figure the total first, instead you'll figure each color on its own. Whichever way seems easiest at the time is the one to use.

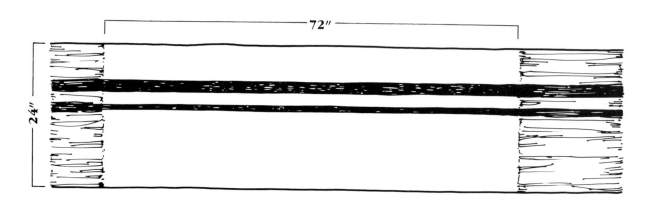

A shawl, 24″ × 72″, in wool, two colors in warp and one color in the weft.

Another planning exercise

Here's one for you to figure out. Six dishtowels, red and white checks, cottolin (a great cotton/linen blend yarn), 18″ × 24″, short fringe, stitched across the ends with a zigzag stitch. Checks are done by striping both warp and weft, in equal size stripes for gingham, other proportions for other looks. Equal sized stripes would mean you needed half red yarn and half white.

Check designs

Six dishtowels

WARP

	project length		finished width
+	fringe	+	draw-in
+	take-up (10%)	+	shrinkage
+	shrinkage (10%)		on loom width
+	loom waste		× warp sett (15 e.p.i. for this)
	total length	×	warp ends needed	÷ 36 =

Add the column on the left, add and multiply the column on the right, multiply the two totals, and divide by 36 to get a more reasonable number to work with. That's all you need to do to determine your warp needs.

WEFT

length of one shot (warp width + 10%)
× p.p.i. (15 p.p.i. for this)
_____
inches of weft needed per inch of weaving
× inches to be woven
_____
inches of weft needed
÷ 36
_____
yards of weft needed

Warp and weft are the same yarn this time, so the two totals can be added together for total yarn needed. Then decide how much is red, how much white, unless you did that stripe by stripe already.

By now you should be getting the idea, seeing that the process for finding out how much you need is really quite basic. Getting comfortable with calculating yarn needs is a matter of practice more than anything else. The first time it takes just short of forever, but later it takes only a few minutes. If you want it to become easy, do this simple exercise: every day figure out one project. It doesn't need to be real; that's not the point. Repetition will make it automatic, and in time you'll be able to figure yarn needs for the most complex project in 15 minutes, or for an easy one in two or three. You'll find a calculator speeds up the process even more.

Because warp and weft calculating is dependent on many subjective factors, there are no exact right answers to the above exercise. To find out if your totals are somewhere in the ballpark, however, look on page 232.

Notes

Part II: *Now That You Know the Basics*

Lesson 5
Reading Drafts

The four parts of drafts:
   Threading
   Tie-up
   Treadling
   Draw-down

Drafts are the weaver's blue prints. They tell the weaver in what order to thread the heddles and when to raise which harnesses. Just as musical scores tell musicians what notes to play, drafts are the weaver's notation for creating weaving patterns.

True weaving literacy comes with the understanding of drafts and drafting. As with reading, it's not at all difficult once you understand the basic principles. And, as comfort with reading eventually allows you to write, so comfort with reading drafts will allow you to make up your own designs. Just as some people write as little as possible and others write constantly for the sheer joy of it, so some weavers use their drafting skills only to adapt existing patterns while others invent their own patterns for everything they weave. It doesn't matter what your preference is, what I want to give you is enough information about drafting so that you will be comfortable with the basics of reading and designing. When you want to learn more I suggest you read Carol Kurtz's *Designing for Weaving*, an excellent book that contains a very thorough section on drafting. So let's start at the beginning.

The four parts of drafts

There are four parts to a draft: threading, tie-up, treadling, and draw-down. The threading tells you in what order to thread the heddles. The tie-up tells you which combinations of harnesses to raise together. (On some looms the harnesses are lowered, not raised, and I'll address this later. But, because most weavers in the United States use rising shed looms, for the sake of simplicity I will always refer to raising harnesses. For most of the discussion it doesn't matter which type of loom you have, but when it does, I'll say so.) The treadling tells you the order in which to raise the harnesses. The draw-down is a graphic picture of what the pattern will look like.

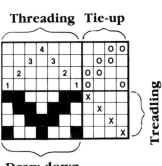

Threading   Tie-up

Treadling

Draw-down

Threading

Many different symbols are used when drafts are written, but the differences are not worthy of confusion. *Where* the symbol is located is the important factor, not what it is.

4	X	1	a	■
3	X	1	a	■
2	X	1	a	■
1	X	1	a	■

Each of the above says the same thing. The bottom row represents the first harness, the second row up the second harness, the third the third, and the fourth the fourth. Remembering that the location of the symbol is what matters, each of the above notations says to thread 1, 2, 3, 4. That means that the farthest left thread will be threaded through a heddle on harness one. The second thread will go through a heddle on harness two, and likewise with three and four. This particular pattern is the most basic of all and is called a straight draw because warp ends are threaded on one harness after the other in a straight line from harness one to harness four.

The threadings below are not straight draws and yield different patterns. The threading on the left, a point twill, says that after you've threaded the first four threads onto each harness respectively, thread five goes onto harness three, thread six onto harness two, and the seventh thread onto harness one.

4				■	■		1	1	1
3	3				■	1	1	1	
2		2		■		1	1	1	
1			1	■	■	1	1		1

For the second pattern the threading reads 1, 2, 1, 4, 3, 4. The third threading says 1, 2, 1, 2, 3, 2, 3, 4, 3, 4, 1, 4. Threading variations are unlimited, and each change results in a different pattern. What makes it all manageable is that there are families of weave structures or patterns related by common characteristics that make it possible to predict how a particular threading (in combination with specific treadlings) will look and behave. Later on in this course we'll cover some of the families; there are many more.

Each of the threadings above shows one repeat of the pattern. For reasons I don't know, "a repeat" is what one time through a threading (or treadling) pattern is called, even though you don't repeat it until you thread that sequence a second time. Most drafts will show you only one repeat of a threading sequence for the sake of space economy, and because there is no need to re-write the same thing again and again. It is up to you to start over,

102

to repeat the repeat. You may thread it as many times as need be to achieve the width you want.

There are different styles for writing drafts; some read from right to left, others read left to right. Either way is correct. What is important is that when you are reading a threading, be sure you always work in the same direction. Most books and magazines will tell you which direction to read for how they've laid out their drafts. Most threadings may be read from either direction so it doesn't matter.

> *The threading tells you on what harness and in what order to thread the heddles.*

Tie-up

The tie-up tells you in what combinations the harnesses need to work. Each horizontal row of the tie-up represents the same harness as found in the threading. Thus, the bottom row is harness one, the next one up harness two, etc. The circles or markings in the boxes indicate harnesses to be raised during weaving. The marks in each individual column tell which ones to raise together. In this tie-up it says that at one time you'll raise harnesses one and two together, at another time two and three, another three and four, and at another four and one. The combinations could be anything, depending on the pattern to be woven. There are fourteen possible combinations with four harnesses (eliminating raising all or none at once since that's of no value), shown here. A tie-up will include only those combinations necessary to its particular pattern, so you'll probably never see all fourteen combinations at once. Four or six are most common, and sometimes two are enough (for tabby, for instance).

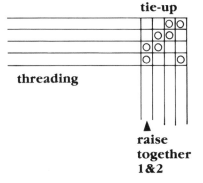

The reason that this part of the draft is called the tie-up has to do with floor looms. Many floor looms have treadles designed so that different combinations of harnesses can be tied to each treadle. Four harness looms usually have six treadles. Therefore, it is necessary to be able to tie different combinations of harnesses to the treadles so that you can get what you want. A tie-up for a given draft may not require all six treadles, it may only need two or four. That is of no consequence, simply use however many you need. (The only exception to this that I know of is for some countermarche looms, which require the weight of the treadles for the counter-action, and so all treadles must be tied up even if not being used.)

There are fourteen possible combinations with four harnesses. A tie-up will include only those combinations necessary for a particular pattern.

When translating the information in the tie-up to your loom think of each column as a treadle and tie the harnesses indicated to that treadle. On the first tie-up shown, that would mean you'd tie harnesses one and two to your farthest left treadle, harnesses two

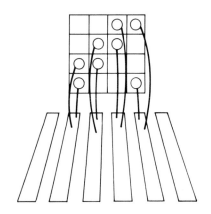

When translating information from the tie-up to your floor loom, think of each column as a treadle and tie the harness indicated to that treadle.

and three to the second treadle, etc. Whenever you need to raise that combination of harnesses simply step on that treadle. Other looms, including table looms, have what is called a direct tie-up. This means that there are four harnesses and four treadles (levers on table looms) and they are tied directly to each other. Treadle one is tied to harness one, treadle two to harness two, three to three, and four to four, and none can be changed. With either floor or table looms you'll need to raise each combination of harnesses individually, frequently using two or three fingers or both feet simultaneously. Since most drafts use essentially this tie-up and treadling format you need to know how to read it no matter which type of loom you use.

Now that you understand the tie-up, in theory anyway, I must tell you that the treadles on jack-style looms are not actually tied to the harnesses. They are tied to the lamms, which are connected to the harnesses. The lamms are horizontal pieces that act as intermediaries between the treadles and the harnesses. When the treadles are pushed down, the lamms push up or pull up the harnesses. They are part of the jacking system of the loom and provide the lifting action.

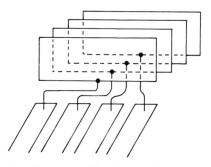

On looms with direct tie-up systems, each treadle is tied directly, and permanently, to one harness.

> The tie-up tells you which combinations of harnesses to raise (or lower) together.

Treadling

The treadling tells you in what order to raise the harnesses. It is most often read from top to bottom. If you have a loom with multiple tie-up treadles where several harnesses may be tied to one treadle, and have tied them up according to the tie-up, then all you need to do is follow the pattern reading down. In this example you would step first on the left treadle, second on the second treadle, third on the third, fourth on the right treadle, fifth back on the third treadle, sixth on the second from the left, and seventh on the left treadle again.

If you are working with a direct tie-up or a table loom you'll need to translate the information to exactly which harnesses are being lifted. (And even if you have multiple tie-up capabilities you certainly need to know what it is you're really doing.) The picture below shows you how to translate the information.

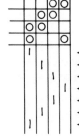

◄says that for the 1st weft shot you should raise harnesses 1&2.
◄says that for the 2nd weft shot you should raise harnesses 2&3.
◄says that for the 3rd weft shot you should raise harnesses 3&4.
◄says that for the 4th weft shot you should raise harnesses 1&4.
◄says that for the 5th weft shot you should raise harnesses 3&4.
◄says that for the 6th weft shot you should raise harnesses 2&3.
◄says that for the 7th weft shot you should raise harnesses 1&2.

To read the treadling, look directly above the treadling mark (whatever symbol is used) to the tie-up at the top of the column; whatever harnesses are indicated are the ones you want to raise. The column the mark is in tells you which harnesses to raise. Where this mark is in vertical sequence tells you when to raise those harnesses. Like the threading, different symbols will be used in different books. If two or more symbols are used in the same draft, it indicates a change in weft threads, by color, thickness, texture or something else. Another treadling notation which you need to watch for is when numbers appear in the columns. Instead of different wefts, numbers note how many weft shots should be woven in a given shed before moving onto the next number (usually this involves other factors which I'll explain later in the lessons on summer and winter and overshot).

Look now at the differences between these treadlings: the one on the bottom of the opposite page tells you to use one weft; the top one at right tells you to alternate between weft A and weft B; the bottom treadling at right tells you how many weft shots to throw in each shed.

When working on a table loom or a direct tie-up floor loom it might be easier for you to rewrite the treadling in numerical form. That way you won't need to keep looking up and down the columns to see what's next. If you write the numbers in a staggered sequence, so the angles of the pattern show, in time you'll learn to recognize the pattern of the weave even before you do the draw-down or actual weaving.

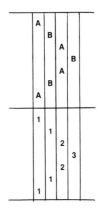

When different symbols appear in the treadling, it means that different wefts should be used. When numbers appear in the treadling, this indicates that more weft shots should be put into the same shed.

```
12        12
23        23
34          34
14        1   4
```

The treadling tells you in which order to raise the harnesses.

One last very important thing to be aware of about tie-up and treadling is that some are written for rising shed looms, others for sinking shed looms. The difference in the looms is that on a rising shed loom the harnesses go up to make the shed, on a sinking shed loom they go down. On a rising shed loom, for example, if harnesses one and two are raised, three and four are left down. To get the same thing on a sinking shed loom you would need to tie up harnesses three and four; they will be lowered, and harnesses 1&2 will be raised.

At one time it was reasonably safe to say that o's in the tie-up meant rising shed, x's meant sinking shed. While this is still true most of the time, it is not always the case. You'll find many other symbols used as well. Older books are usually written with a sinking shed in mind. Newer books, those written since the surge of jack looms in America, are written expecting rising shed looms. Some books plan for both.

If you weave on a rising shed loom and use a sinking shed tie-up you'll be treadling the exact opposite of what's intended. The result is that you'll still get the same fabric only you'll be weaving it upside down. Instead of the pattern facing you it will be facing down and you'll be looking at the back side. (Often you won't be able to tell the difference.) When you take it off the loom turn the fabric over. If you want to weave a sinking shed tie-up right side up, simply tie-up the empty boxes instead of the filled in ones.

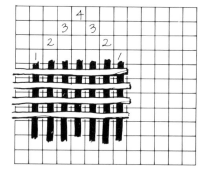

Rising vs. sinking shed looms: most often O's equal rising shed and X's equal sinking shed. Both of these say, from left to right:
1&2 up/3&4 down
2&3 up/1&4 down
3&4 up/1&2 down
4&1 up/2&3 down

The draw-down

With the information you have so far you can read a draft and weave the fabric. Equally important is being able to do a draw-down. The draw-down will show you what the fabric will look like (in most cases), and where to begin and end the threading and treadling to have a centered or balanced pattern. In some books, while the full pattern threading is given, what is written may start in the middle of the design instead of on the edge. If you've done a draw-down you can easily determine where to begin and end to get what you want. More on that later, in the lesson on altering drafts.

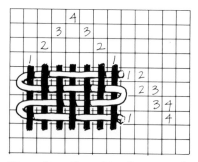

Think of each column of the draw-down as a warp thread, as if you were facing your loom; think of each row as a weft crossing the warp.

Filling in a draft's draw-down is something like doing a puzzle only easier. First think of each column on the graph paper as a warp thread, as if you were facing your warp on your loom. Think of each row as a weft thread crossing the warp. If you were to take yarn and lay it in the spaces between the lines on the illustration at left, each warp thread would be threaded on the harness indicated at the top in the threading. Now take the yarn away and know that the column of boxes on the page represents the yarn. The same is true for the weft; each horizontal row represents a weft thread. In the upper illustration the yarns are laid on the paper, not woven together at all. If you were to do a drawing of woven fabric that showed the actual interlacements of the threads as called for in the draft, it would look something like the lower drawing. As you can see, when the treadling calls for harnesses one and two to be raised, the warp threads go over the weft threads. The same weft shot goes over the warps on harnesses three and four because they were not raised. The second weft shot goes over the warp threads on harnesses one and four because they were left down when harnesses two and three were

Drawing showing the actual interlacement of threads as called for in the draft. When the treadling calls for harnesses one and two to be raised, the warp threads go over the weft.

raised. For the third shot harnesses three and four were raised, so those warp threads are on top of the weft, or on the surface of the weave. The fourth row shows that harnesses one and four were raised, for those are the warps passing over the weft. Another way to think of this is, when threads are raised, they have been lifted up out of the way and will be on top; the threads that remain unlifted may then be crossed by weft and are on the bottom.

This is a pretty explicit illustration showing the pattern a draft will give, but drawing it like this for each draw-down would be ridiculous—you could weave it faster. So, a shorthand version of the same idea is used. The boxes representing the warp going over the weft are filled in; those where the weft is on top are left blank.

To do your own draw-down from a draft is very simple. If the treadling says to raise harnesses one and two, go across that row filling in all the boxes under the 1's and 2's in the threading. When it says to raise harnesses two and three, fill in the boxes under the 2's and 3's. Etc.

Trace along the weft shots that are drawn in until you see how it all works. Then take a pencil and fill in the rest of the draw-down below yourself. You should have no problems, but just so you can check yourself the completed draw-down is on page 232.

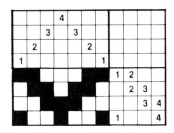

To do a draw-down from a draft, if the treadling says to raise harnesses one and two, fill in the boxes across that row under the 1's and 2's in the threading.

The draw-down is a graphic picture of what the pattern will look like.

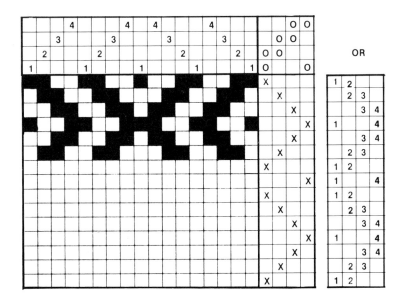

Your assignment

That's what you need to know for now about reading drafts and doing draw-downs. From here it's a matter of practice and getting comfortable with the system. I've given you some exercises to do that will give you practice at doing draw-downs and start your library of drafts. I recommend you use a pencil since being able to erase comes in handy. Filling the squares in all the way makes a beautiful draft which is easy to see. Other alternatives for filling in the squares which take less time are to use x's or dots or o's or vertical lines (to look like warp). You can put anything you want in the squares as long as the ones you fill in are the warps on the surface of the weave. It will be evident almost immediately that the denser or bigger the mark the more clearly the pattern will show; use whatever is a balance of fast enough and dark enough to please you. And have fun.

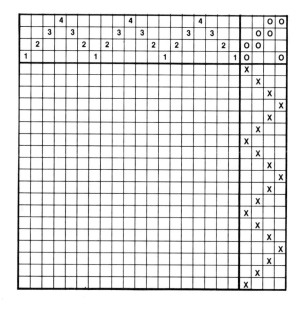

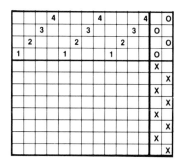

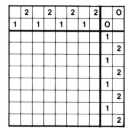

Lesson 6
Plain Weave Variations

Structure variations
Color variations
Texture variations

Fabrics by Bethany Thomas, Jane Patrick, Yvonne Stahl, Linda Ligon

Plain weave and its variations, though simple in structure, can be tremendously complex. One way to achieve fabrics with dramatically different qualities is by altering how much warp or weft shows. Here, working clockwise from the far left, we see a balanced plain weave fabric where equal amounts of warp and weft show. This fabric will drape well and is suitable for a shawl or non-tailored garment. The next two fabrics have the warps set very close together; the first is referred to as a warp-emphasis fabric because a little of the weft shows; the second is called a warp-faced fabric since no weft shows at all. The first of these two would be ideal for table runners or placemats; the second fabric would make a sturdy belt. The fourth fabric, bottom right, is a weft-faced rug sample where the weft completely covers the warp. For a weft-faced fabric the warp needs to be set wide enough so that the weft will cover it easily. While warp sett is important, notice here, too, how yarns—whether they are thick or thin, smooth or coarse—play a part in determining a fabric's character.

Before moving on to more complex weave structures, I'd like to dwell for awhile longer on some variations of plain weave. And while it is conceivable that an entire book could be written on these weaves, here I'm going to just give you a representative offering of what's possible.

The first variations have to do with weave structure, all of which could be done on two harnesses, though each would require different threadings. All, though, can be done on the same threading on four harnesses with only a need to change the treadling, just as you did when you wove plain weave and twill on your first sample.

You may wonder why I'm starting your four harness lessons with two harness weaves. Partly the answer is that these weaves are the most basic of weave structures and have a lot to offer. Partly the answer has to do with expanding your understanding of drafting (already!) and putting it to work.

Another reason I want to talk about these weaves here is to explore just a sampling of the infinite design possibilities which exist when color and texture are introduced. I'll discuss a few of these variations and hope they inspire you to explore many more.

Structure Variations

Since you have been through the drafting lesson I hope you can look at these drafts and see that first you want to thread your loom just as you did the first time—1, 2, 3, 4, etc.

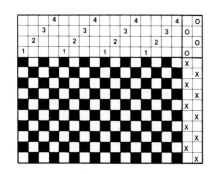

Plain weave or tabby

Tabby

To weave tabby you need to raise harnesses one and three alternately with harnesses two and four. Since you've already done that, it should be old hat by now.

Basket Weave

A basket weave is kind of a doubled tabby, basically the same over/under pattern but with all threads doubled. As you will quickly discover, if you try to weave two shots in the same shed (1 + 2, 1 + 2), your second pass of the shuttle may well serve only to pull out your first weft shot. Wrapping your yarn around a selvedge thread (or two) will secure the end.

If I am going to weave a lot of basket weave then I usually wrap two wefts on one shuttle, eliminating the need for doubling back in the same shed. I was told once that that's cheating and I'm not supposed to do it because the two yarns won't always lie exactly parallel; they will tend to cross over each other. If you are using two colors there will be a marked difference in how those two will look; likewise if you are using very fat weft. Otherwise, the significance of the difference is debatable. Try it both ways, and decide what's acceptable to you for any given project.

For as much similarity as they have, I'm always surprised at how different a basket weave and a plain weave appear. Always one or the other is more appropriate for what I have in mind; I've never found them to be aesthetically interchangeable.

Structurally, there is also a significant difference between the two. When looking at any fabric, and taking into account how tightly or loosely woven it is, the more intersections of warp and weft there are, the stiffer the fabric will be; the fewer intersections, the softer, more pliable the fabric will be. (Intersections are those places where a yarn goes from under to over or over to under, warp or weft.) Therefore, since a basket weave has only half as many intersections as plain weave, basket weave will be much more pliable and drape better than its plain weave counterpart. The same is true with twills and almost all other weaves; pay attention to the frequency of intersections.

There is another effect the difference in numbers of intersections will have. In plain weave, because you have a maximum number of crossovers, the threads will be pushed apart from each other to as great an extent as possible. When threads can draw in together, share space, so to speak, they will. Since basket weave has fewer intersections, more threads will group together. The result of all this space sharing is that the piece will be somewhat narrower and thicker. If you weave 4″ of basket weave, then 1″ of tabby, then another 4″ of basket, the tabby area, being forced apart by many intersections will be wider, and your piece will look like a snake after a large meal. It's fine to combine pliable weaves, but inserting a stiffer tabby will cause a change in fabric quality that you may or may not like. Basket weave, rib weave, and twill all have fairly equivalent drawing in tendencies.

Rib Weave

A rib weave creates another interesting texture. Using one color and a balanced weave you'll get a nice texture, nothing very "ribby". If you pack it a little harder a pronounced vertical rib will begin to appear, wide and narrow stripes alternating. To make it show the most, use two weft colors, one the same as the warp. Use this color when you lift harnesses 2-3-4 together; use the second contrasting color when you lift harness one. What happens is that the second color will cross over three warps and visually begin to build a wide vertical line, while the weft that crosses over only one warp will join with the warp in serving as background. The back side of the rib weave will be the exact opposite, having a narrow rib in contrasting color. How would you

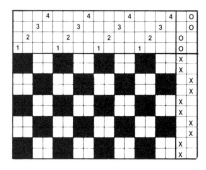

Basket weave

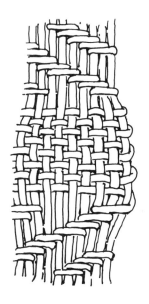

Basket weave, rib weave and twill, when used together with tabby, will draw in more because they have fewer intersections per area than tabby. When threads share space they have a tendency to draw in more which results in a somewhat narrower, thicker fabric.

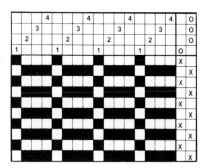

Rib weave

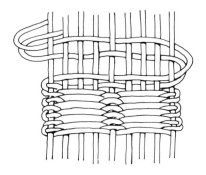

When you use two colors, two shuttles are required. To prevent skips at the selvedge, wrap the shuttles around each other when they are on the same side.

reverse it—bring the narrow contrasting rib to the side facing you?

When you use two colors, you will need two shuttles and for the first time there is another selvedge concern: to prevent skipped warps at the selvedges. When the shuttles are on the same side, wrap them around each other, twisting the wefts together to prevent them from missing the selvedge warp as shown in the illustration. Try it. It's easy to see though tricky to explain.

Aside from these variations in structure, all three of these weaves can have a wide variety of appearances having to do with how close or far apart the warp is set and how much the weft is packed in. A balanced weave, you may recall, has equal ends per inch (e.p.i.) and picks per inch (p.p.i.). If your warp sett is widely spaced, your weft will pack in more, resulting in a weft predominant or even weft-faced fabric, one in which the warp doesn't show at all. If the warp sett is very close then the weft won't be able to pack in as much because the closeness of the warp will put up more resistance. Depending on how close the warp is set the fabric can have a predominance of warp or even be totally warp-faced, the weft showing only where it turns the corner at the selvedge. For those of you familiar with other kinds of weaving, Navajo rugs are weft-faced, inkle bands are warp-faced. I'm not going to tell you more than this because that isn't what I want this lesson to be about, but those are some very basic facts of which you should be aware. Whether we're discussing tabby, basket, or rib weave, altering your warp sett will affect the proportions and appearance to a great degree. (This is true with any weave, not just these three.)

Color variations

Working with color opens up a huge world of possibilities. You probably had an inkling of this when you wove your first piece and noticed how the colors blended together to make a third one when they crossed each other. You probably noticed too that your warp looked different after it had been crossed by weft. If not, take note of this when you weave your next piece. To get a better idea for how color and weave interact take out your sample and look at it up close. You can see the individual colors quite well. Now pin it to the wall and stand on the other side of the room. Notice how your eye blends the two colors together where they cross each other to make a solid-looking color?

Using color can be as simple as crossing a solid color in the warp with a different single weft color, or it can be as complicated as a Scottish tartan with many colors used in warp and weft.

Stripes

In your first piece you put stripes in your warp, so you under-stand how to do that. Any time you have more than one color in either warp or weft, and cross it with a single color, you have stripes. They can be very wide and colorful like awning stripes, or very subtle, tone-on-tone stripes like chalk stripes which resemble chalk lines on a plain background.

Fabrics by: Lisa Budwig, Debbie Redding, Awyn Combs.

Three fabrics with warp stripes. Stripes may be in a regularly repeating sequence as in the two fabrics at left, or in random order as in the fabric at right.

Plaids

Plaids are really only stripes going both ways. They may be balanced or not, seven colors or three, wide or fine, bright or subtle, complex or simple. If you are interested in traditional Scottish tartans there are books with the color formulas given. If not, go look in your closet, choose several plaids and study them, decide what you like and why. Then make up your own. Use crayons or short pieces of yarn, rearranging colors until you get a sequence you like.

Weave structure is a factor to consider in planning either stripes or plaids. A rib weave, where you are weaving three up warps against one down, would affect a plaid quite a lot because of the structural grouping of warps in this weave. Generally speaking it is best to avoid mixing too much color and structural texture in one piece because they compete and create chaos instead of harmony. A plaid rib weave could be very nice, or it could be awful. Try a little at the beginning of a plaid warp and see how it looks.

Plaids can be thought of as stripes going both ways. Consider scale of project and yarn size when planning plaids. As always, weaving a sample first is a good idea.

Fabrics by Ardis Dobrovolny, The Weaving Shop

Color and Weave

Color and weave effect is a phenomenon which happens when color and weave structure interact. Because of the interlacement of color and weave, patterns are set up which can look very complicated even with a weave structure that is very simple.

Log cabin is one kind of color and weave effect which is simple to do and fascinating to look at. It appeals to weavers and weaving fans alike. The structure is plain weave, though what happens to log cabin when woven in twill is lots of fun too. Log cabin requires two colors. If they are highly contrasting, such as black and white, the effect is a kind of op art electric that is exciting. If the colors used are monochromatic or similar in value the effect is more subtle. Choosing two colors between the extremes will, of course, give you an effect in between.

The basic element of log cabin is that the two colors alternate constantly, then shift. For example, a log cabin color sequence would be threaded blue, white, blue, white, then shift, white, blue, white, blue, then shift, blue, white, blue, white. Your weaving would proceed in the same manner, blue, white, blue, white, white, blue, white, blue, etc. It must be a fairly balanced weave to work. If you pack your weft so tightly that it covers the warp you'll probably get something interesting but it won't be log cabin.

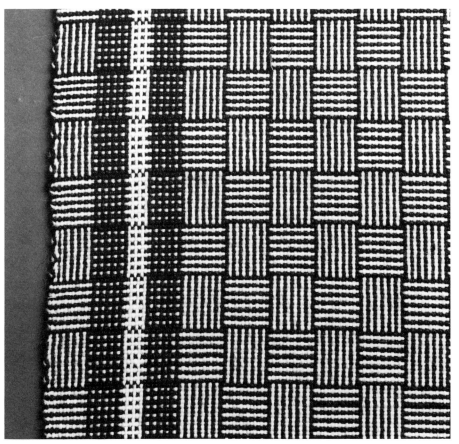

Color and weave fabric by Selena Billington

Log cabin, complex in appearance, is simple in structure. This log cabin piece features borders of solid colored warp stripes. When crossed with two alternating weft colors, dots appear.

Looking at the log cabin shown, what makes it fun is the blocks of design, the changes from horizontal stripes to vertical. To get the blocks to switch you simply switch from bwbw to wbwb in threading and treadling. You can reverse as often as you want, as often as you want the blocks to reverse.

The draft here shows three sequences of a two block log cabin. Remember, *where* the symbol is located tells you what harness to thread. The symbol *b* (blue) or *w* (white) tells you which color to thread on what harness. The draw-down shown here is for the color pattern, instead of for weave structure which we discussed in the lesson on drafting. Color drafting is different from structure drafting and while it's good for you to know there is such a thing, at this point I don't want you to concern yourself with it. If you want to know more about color drafting, see Carol Kurtz's *Designing for Weaving*.

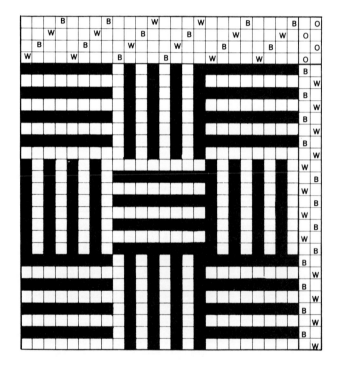

Three sequences of a two block log cabin. The symbols indicate which color to thread on what harness and how two colors should be woven.
W = White
B = Black

Texture

By the very nature of yarn itself, texture in weaving is an obvious consideration. First, keep in mind that everything has texture. Whether it is smooth or rough, cotton or wool, all yarn and all things have texture.

When you think of using texture in weaving you need to consider both the visual and tactile. What do you want your piece to feel like, and texturally how should it look?

The first consideration has to be with choosing yarn. First, think of function. What will the piece be used for? If it's a fabric to be worn against the skin, then you probably won't want a very scratchy yarn. If it's to be a table mat, you won't want anything too fuzzy.

Textural considerations can be purely visual. You can alternate very thick yarns with very thin ones for a striped effect. Crossing these stripes will give you a textured plaid.

Using different kinds of yarn even when they are only one color, can produce interesting results. As you've noticed, some yarns are shiny and others dull. For example, a mercerized cotton is very shiny and will reflect more light because of its smoothness than a fuzzy wool yarn will. By mixing bumpy and looped yarns with fuzzy and smooth ones, you can produce a fascinating fabric with just simple plain weave.

Fabrics by The Weaving Shop, Sharon Alderman, Bethany Thomas

Yarn choice is probably the most important factor in determining the overall tactile result of a fabric. Soft, loopy yarns, loosely set, create an inviting, cuddly-looking fabric in the sample at top left. Similar effects are achieved when a large, bumpy, wooly yarn and a plied wool yarn are set openly to create a squishy blanket-like fabric. Contrasted to these two highly textured fabrics are the two smooth swatches at right. All four swatches are plain weave; notice what a difference yarn choice and sett makes!

In conclusion

This lesson is really a whole lot of lessons in one, and while I won't always give you quite so many options under one heading, know that there are always many to any given weave structure.

The three structural variations, plain, rib and basket weave, can all be done on any straight draw warp you set up. Color variations require separate warps. You can't have both a log cabin and plaid set up on the same warp, though you can use a single weft color for either and have warp stripes.

At the end of this lesson I've given you several ideas for homework. You can use any one or more of these or make up your own. From here on I'm not going to give you exact assignments because I don't know exactly what will appeal to you. I'll make suggestions, you make up your own assignment. If a lesson really turns you on, weave several variations before going on to the next. If it sounds boring, weave one so you'll learn about it. You'll probably find out it has some merit after all. (I have found that any time I'm not interested in a weave, or think I don't like one, the reason is that I don't know enough about it. As soon as I learn more, I get all excited and want to work on just that for awhile.)

I've sometimes pondered the idea of taking a single weave and weaving it with every yarn I could find, and alternating warp setts within each yarn. I'm sure a project like that would be very enlightening. I'm also sure I'd be very sick of that weave before I was done. But once you've had some experience with yarns and how they are transformed, even just thinking about it can give you an idea of the potential that is always present. Just think, after you've used every smooth yarn you can find, in a variety of colors, of course, you can get into novelty yarns, substituting bumps and loops for blues and greens. Now that there are so many yarns available to us, that kind of exploring can go on forever.

Your assignments

1. Set up a one color warp, sleyed for a good balanced weave, and weave plain weave, basket weave, rib weave and twill, each with one color, then again this time alternating two colors. Then pull your warp forward, cut the first sample off, re-sley to a closer sett, and repeat the whole sequence. Then cut that sample off, re-sley the warp looser and weave it all again. To re-sley in the same reed: if you did have one thread per dent, starting in the middle and working your way out to the sides, change to two threads in every even dent and one in every odd dent. That will give you a sley sequence of

1|2|1|2|1| etc. If your warp sett was 12 e.p.i., it will now be 18 e.p.i. Then re-sley looser, maybe one thread every other dent (6 e.p.i., in a 12 dent reed) or skip every third dent, giving 1|1|0|1|1|0|1|1|0| etc. (9 e.p.i.).

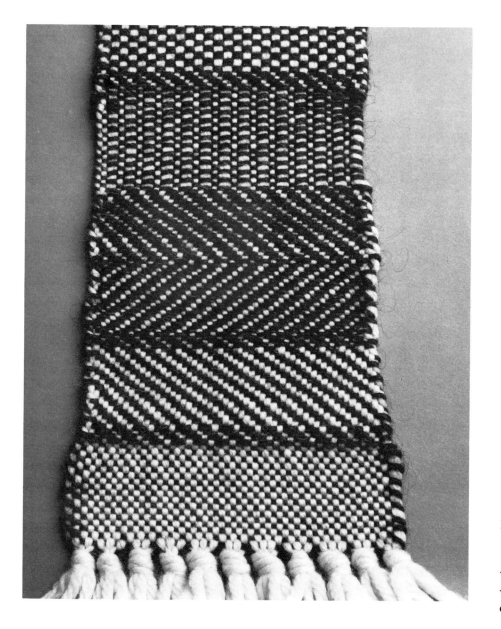

Basket weave

Rib weave

1/3 Twill

2/2 Twill

Plain Weave

Weave sampler: balanced weave, one color in warp, one color in weft.

2. Plan a plaid, weave it in tabby, basket, rib, (and a 2/2 twill if you want to draw from memory of your first piece). If you want your plaid to be symmetrical, be sure that your beat is balanced. You can tell quickly if all is balanced by looking to see if you're getting squares of color along a diagonal line from the corner up. Plaids with an unbalanced color sequence won't necessarily have any squares.

3. Set up a log cabin, maybe trying different color combinations next to each other. You could have 3″ of your warp width in highly contrasting colors, 3″ in mildly contrasting colors, and 3″ in subtle colors, for instance black and white, black and light gray, black and dark gray. Then weave each of those combinations. Log cabin is plain weave, but try other weaves as well just to see what happens.

4. Rib weave variations. Use one color for half of the warp and add a second color on one harness only to the other half. Weave using all one weft color, using two weft colors, using two wefts of different thicknesses, and two wefts with one being a novelty yarn. In all cases try medium beating and hard beating. Then try changing the treadling to raising a different harness by itself, so instead of 1, 234 try 2, 134, then 3, 124, then 4, 123; you can make checks by weaving ½″ to 1″ with one pair, then change to a different pair for a little while.

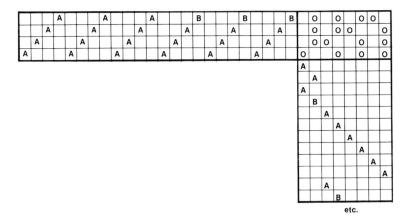

etc.

5. Use different weights and textures of yarn in the warp, and then weave with each one to see how the character of the texture changes. Weave a few inches with each warp yarn used singly, then try alternating two different yarns at a time to see what happens. You could also do this same type of thing with a many colored striped warp to see how the colors of the stripes change when crossed by different colors.

What would you do with all this? Think about a set of placemats or towels, all on the same warp, each having one of these variations. Or two afghans or scarves that for the sake of efficiency you want to weave on one warp but for variety you want to look very different. What changes could you make to achieve that variety?

Lesson 7
Basic Twills

Ratios
The patterns, the drafts
Miscellaneous things to know about twills
    Setts for twills
    Weaving balanced twills
    Using a floating selvedge

Fabrics by: Mary Peterson, Ardis Dobrovolny, Jane Patrick.

Twills, their diagonal lines pointing in one direction or the other, are full of possibilities waiting to be discovered. Even the very simplest straight and point twills have much to offer: set them close for belts; use them for luxurious mohair scarves; try them with lots of color contrast between warp and weft; combine diamonds and straight twill or 1/3 and 2/2 twill treadlings. Mix and match; experiment!

On your first sample you wove some twill, a weave that is identified by its diagonal lines. Other than talking about the problems that may arise on the selvedge (uncaught warp) and giving you the treadling for a 2/2 twill, I didn't discuss twills at all. I just had you weave some. Now I'll tell you more about them so you can begin to understand why it is possibly the most used weave of all, by both handweavers and the textile industry.

There will be three parts to this discussion. First, I'll tell you about proportions, the ratios of warp to weft in four harness twills. Second will be a look at some elementary pattern possibilities and some ways these diagonal lines can be arranged to create interesting designs. And finally, I'll cover some miscellaneous information that relates to twills, things that are useful to know, but don't have anything to do with the drafts themselves.

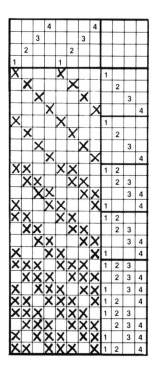 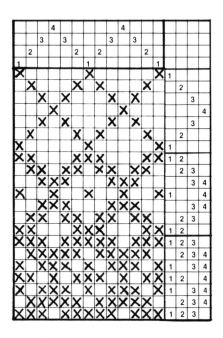

Ratios

As you know already, when weaving with four harnesses you can raise either one, two, or three harnesses at a time to make a shed. A four harness twill can be a 1/3, 2/2, or 3/1. What those numbers represent are warps up and warps down. A 1/3 twill is woven by raising one harness at a time, so the weft goes under one warp and over three. You can also think of these numbers as the visible ratio of warp to weft, i.e., in a 1/3 twill you'll see one part warp for every three parts weft.

What you'll see, therefore, is mostly weft. This is called a weft predominant twill.

A 2/2 twill has two warps up for every two down, thus is balanced.

A 3/1 twill has three harnesses raised for each weft shot, putting more warp on the surface than weft.

If you turn a 3/1 twill fabric over you'll have a 1/3, the two being opposites. One side will show mostly warp, the other mostly weft. So if your warp is blue and your weft is green, one side will be mostly blue, the other mostly green. Likewise, if your warp is striped and your weft is all one color, the 3/1 side will have a very strong stripe, the 1/3 side very subtle stripes. A 2/2 twill will look the same on both sides.

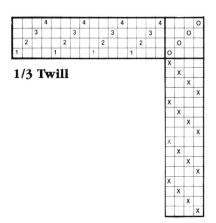

1/3 Twill

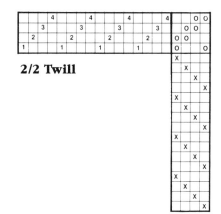

2/2 Twill

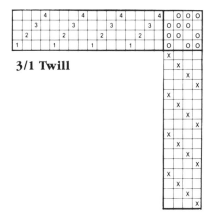

3/1 Twill

The pattern, the drafts

To weave a twill (a diagonal line), each weft float appears slightly to the right or left of the weft before it. As they "climb", the diagonal is built. There are many, many possibilities for varying your threading and treadling to make twill patterns. Discovering these can be a lot of fun.

These four drafts show the most basic of twills. If you reverse the direction of your threading, as in B, then the direction of the twill will reverse horizontally. If you reverse the direction of your treadling, as in C, the twill will change directions vertically. When the twill reverses horizontally this is usually called herringbone; when the twill reverses vertically this is called a reverse twill, or sometimes a vertical herringbone. If you change directions in both the threading and treadling, you'll get diamonds, and that's where the real fun begins. The next twill lesson is almost totally on making diamonds of different sizes, so for now we won't do any more with them.

There are many names for the various twill variations, and often it is difficult to make a distinction as to which is which and why. Therefore I prefer to avoid using names at all. As it is, point twills is a generic and descriptive enough term to cover what I want it to, and beyond that, I talk about specific threadings and treadlings.

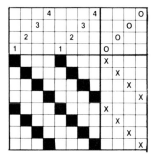

A: Straight Twill

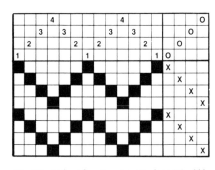

B: Herringbone or Point Twill

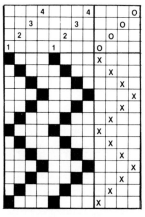

C: Reverse Twill or Vertical Herringbone

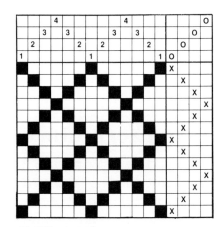

D: Diamonds

When you are threading for a twill, it is not crucial that you end on harness four or one. If you come to your last thread and you've only made it to harness three in the sequence, don't worry about it. If it's a straight twill, it will be impossible to tell because the twill line is the same in all places. If it's a point twill then not finishing a threading sequence will give you an unbalanced pattern, which you may not want. (If you want a balanced pattern you'll want to be sure you've planned for enough threads before you begin measuring your warp.) Structurally, however, the fabric will be fine.

The same is true of the treadling. If there is a changing pattern then you'll probably want to complete a sequence, but if it's a straight treadling, you can stop at any point.

This is enough information for you to embark on basic twills. So far you've threaded the loom in a straight draw (1,2,3,4) every time. Now it's time to open your mind to new threading patterns. After all, there are two reasons the heddles slide back and forth to wherever you want them. One is to accommodate varying thicknesses of yarn and warp setts, the other is so you can use them in whatever order you want.

These drafts are so basic they may seem boring, you may have a sense that you want more than something *so* basic. That's understandable, and you have at least two easy options. One is skip ahead to the next lesson, which is an expansion of the same. A second option is to play around with different yarns, some in the warp, even more in the weft. The assignments at the end will give you some ideas to explore.

Miscellaneous things to know about twills

In the section on basket weave I talked about numbers of intersections and that the more there are the stiffer the fabric is (tabby), the fewer, the more pliable (basket, twill). That rule, and the resulting characteristics of twill fabrics, make twills very desirable for clothing; they flex to respond to body movement. While almost no woven fabric is as stretchy or flexible as a knitted fabric, twills are among the most flexible of woven fabrics. Jeans are woven in a 1/2 twill on three harnesses. Jeans may seem very stiff, and they are, but notice how they bend at the knees, thousands of times, even when they're too tight. Look at your clothing and notice which is twill, which is plain weave, which is knit. Can you tell what difference structure makes in how each feels to wear? How tight or loose can any structure be and still be comfortable?

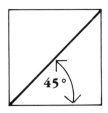

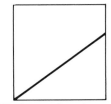

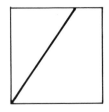

Sharing space will group

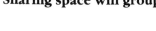

Balanced twill

Weft predominant

Warp predominant

As you may have noticed already, when you wove the twill your weft tended to pack in a little more than when you wove plain weave. That's part of the grouping effect, with the wefts sharing some space and so sliding on top of each other somewhat. (The warps do it too.)

The result is that if the fabric is as solid as your plain weave was, then it's not a balanced weave; it leans toward weft predominant because more weft packed in. For many projects that doesn't matter at all, but sometimes it will. If you have more weft you are very likely to have a fabric that is stiffer across than it is up and down, or not as pliable in one direction. Carried to an extreme, if you wove a scarf that was too weft predominant it would have the characteristics of a collar more than a scarf. It would be too stiff to wear comfortably.

To compensate for the fact that the weft wants to pack in closer, set your warp slightly closer. The resistance it puts up will prevent too much weft from packing in. If you like the balanced tabby you got with a particular yarn set at 10 e.p.i., try twill at 12 e.p.i.; if you liked the tabby at 12 e.p.i., try the twill at 15 e.p.i. This is not an exact science.

As you weave, you can tell immediately whether your twill is balanced or not by the angle of the twill diagonal. A balanced twill has a 45° angle, a weft predominant a smaller angle, a warp predominant a larger angle. Watching that angle is a good way to check your beat, a gauge for its evenness. If the angle has changed, your beat has changed. Visually that's distracting, and it also means that your fabric will be of differing qualities, softer or weaker in some areas, stiffer or tougher in others.

The twill line is a useful tool for checking the consistency of your work, but that is not its primary function. Mostly it's there to provide interesting design. If that is your goal then think about colors. If your warp and weft are both the same color the twill will be there but it won't be easy to see. The more contrasting the two are the easier it will be to see the pattern. Or try a fatter weft, maybe a lot fatter, and see what happens.

When weaving a 1/3 or 3/1 twill most of your weft is on one side, warp on the other. If the weft is a stretchy yarn or if you've laid it into the shed stretched taut and allowed for very little take-up it will relax back into its unstretched state. As it does so it can't help but pull the warp with it. The result is that the selvedges of the piece will curl toward the weft predominant side. This doesn't always happen, but if it does, try allowing for more take-up.

Using a Floating Selvedge

Finally, as promised, I want to tell you about a floating selvedge. When you weave twills you will with regularity have to decide what to do about the fact that the edge warp is not being caught by the weft. We've already discussed some of the alternatives, and the floating selvedge is just one more. (See pages 68-69 for others.) Some people like floating selvedges so much that they use them all the time, even when technically they are unnecessary. Other weavers find them very distracting and use them as little as possible. It is totally a matter of personal preference, so give it a try and see where your preference falls.

As the name implies, we're talking about a selvedge thread, the very edge thread on either or both sides. Floating refers to its position relative to the rest of the warp. Measured, sleyed, and beamed with the rest of the warp, the floating selvedge is not threaded through a heddle. If you look at your warp from the side, with no harnesses raised, the warp should dip an inch or so as it travels from the front to the back beam. The harnesses on a jack loom are set in such a way that if you draw a straight line from front to back beam, the heddle eyes are below that line. Thus, when you raise one set of warps, they will be deflected above the midline the same amount as the rest of the warps are below it. This maintains the same amount of tension on both sets of warps. Counterbalance and countermarche looms pull warps both up and down. So, at rest, with no shed, the warp will go straight from beam to beam. Since the floating selvedge does not go through a heddle eye, it always sits in the middle of the shed, along the imaginery straight line from beam to beam. As you weave, your shuttle will go around the floating selvedge, just as you may have done with your other selvedge threads before.

There are differences, however, that make a floating selvedge preferable to a threaded selvedge thread. First of all, it's easier to use and easier on the yarn. Because the floater is always right there in the middle of the shed, it is easy to pass the shuttle over and under it, cutting down on the degree of stress the edge thread suffers. It speeds weaving too because less manipulation is needed. A floating selvedge is less likely to be stretched or frayed from the constant rubbing of the shuttle. Therefore, it will be both more stable and better looking. Once it's woven you'll never be aware of it; it will look like all the other warps.

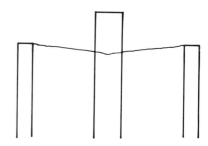

On a jack loom, with no harnesses raised, the warp dips an inch or so as it travels from front to back.

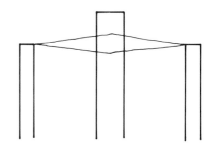

When the shed is opened, the warps on top and bottom are equidistance from an imaginary line traveling from front to back beam.

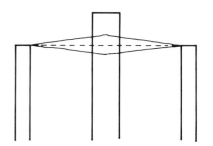

The floating selvedge rests in the middle of the shed.

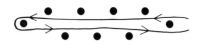

Choose a sequence for going over and under your floating selvedge and use it all the time. Here are a few possibilities.

For efficiency, speed, comfort, rhythm, or simplicity, choose a sequence for going over and under the floaters and use it all the time. You can enter the shed under one floater and exit the shed over the other one, or go over upon entering and under as you exit, or go under both going one direction and over going the other way. Do whichever one feels most comfortable to you.

If you are using a very soft yarn, one that is loosely twisted, it may be weak and not very resistant to abrasion. While that can be fine as warp, the extra rubbing that the floating selvedge gets may be more than it can stand. Consider using two together just to provide the extra strength needed. If you don't want the extra bulk that will give you, choose another strong smooth fine thread, e.g., sewing thread, nylon fishing line, another yarn, and run that with your floating selvedge(s). After you've finished the piece, slide the guest yarn out by pulling from one end; that's why it needs to be smooth and fine.

Conclusion

I've just given you a miniscule amount of information about twills relative to what there is. It is the beginning, a good place to start. The next lesson on altering drafts will begin to expand on this, as will the rest of the lessons in Part II. Twills are one of those things that are so basic that in a way we get bored with them quickly, wanting to go on to more interesting weaves. I'd been weaving several years before it hit me how incredibly versatile twills are and how it would be possible to spend years just exploring their many possibilities. But like so many things, I couldn't recognize or appreciate that until after I'd been out exploring other areas.

So start here, move on quickly, and have fun with starting to make up your own patterns.

Assignments to choose from or expand upon

1. Plan and set up a one color warp that has a point twill threading (i.e., 1,2,3,4,3,2,1, etc.) for a few inches on each side and a straight twill threading (1,2,3,4, etc.) in the center. Use a different color for the weft and weave a 2/2 twill. Treadle a point twill border (i.e., treadle 1-2,2-3,3-4,4-1,3-4,2-3,1-2, etc.) a straight twill center (1-2,2-3,3-4,4-1, repeat), and another point twill border.

    Repeat the whole weaving sequence with a thinner weft, then a thicker one, then a novelty yarn (lots of bumps, slubs, loops, or other textures), then a colored variegated yarn. Record how well each one shows off the pattern. Do the draw-down for this draft, *before* you weave the fabric.

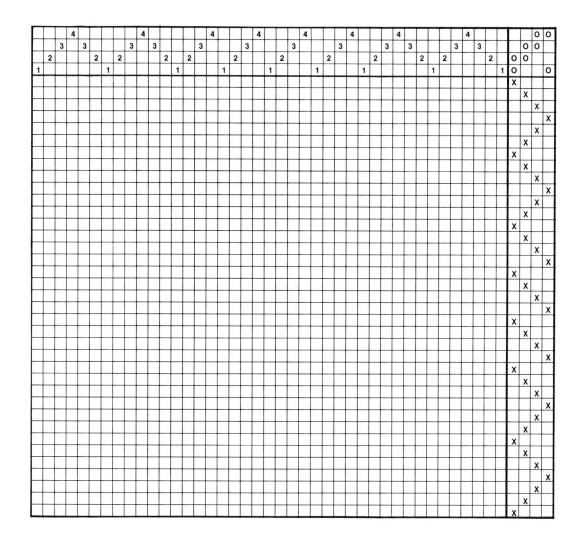

2. Plan and set up a striped warp, part straight twill, part point twill. Weave 1/3, 2/2, and 3/1 twills with one color of weft, then the three again striping your weft. When does it look plaid, when striped, when solid? The colors do not have to coincide with the threading pattern of the point twill, or they can.

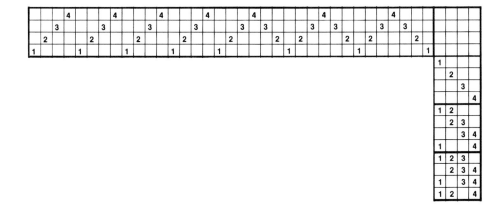

3. Plan your own sampler, trying all of the following in one piece: the two twill threadings, straight and point; the two twill treadlings, straight and point; the three twill ratios, 1/3, 2/2, 3/1; the two color possibilities, same and contrasting. Have it all balance so it looks unified instead of like a conglomeration. You could put a black thread between each section, warp and weft, to designate change, or use two colors alternating in blocks. Below are two threading possibilities.

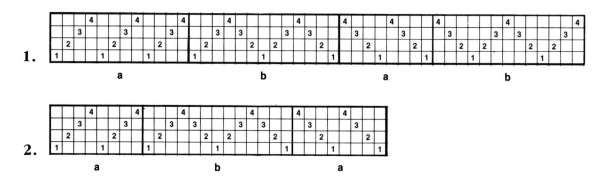

Lesson 8
Altering Drafts

Doing draw-downs to make pattern decisions
More twills, a little less basic
Drafting from cloth diagrams

You know how to read drafts, how to do draw-downs, and how to tell which parts of the draw-down represent which threads in the threading and treadling drafts (straight up, straight across). Some of the drafts you've looked at repeated the same sequence over and over, e.g., 1, 2, 3, 4, 1, 2, 3, 4, , etc., while others gave you only one repeat of the pattern, leaving it to you to repeat it at the loom. For many projects or with many patterns, taking the given draft and repeating it for the width of the warp works fine. For others there is an intermediate step that is very necessary. This step might be the biggest reason for doing draw-downs.

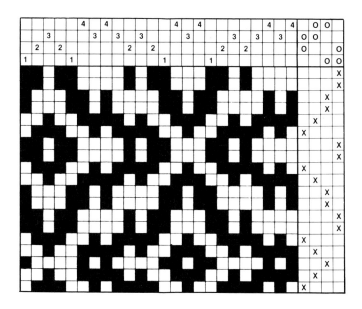

This draft is called "Periwinkle" and comes from page 131 of *A Hand-weaver's Pattern Book* by Marguerite Davison.

This draft is shown just as it is given in the book. It is not centered, probably because the threading sequence is easier to keep track of this way than were it to start where the design looks best. If you were using this pattern to weave a bedspread, whether or not the diamond on the edge ended at its point would probably not be as crucial as it would be on placemats or a table runner. On a bedspread you will see dozens of diamonds all over and almost no one is going to lean over the side of the bed to look at the selvedge. On placemats or a table runner, the selvedges will very definitely show, and it's far more likely that you'll want the diamond to end on the edge.

To decide where you want the pattern to start and stop you need to do a draw-down of two repeats of the pattern, repeating both threading and treadling.

This draft is two full repeats. In the first draft, if you didn't know to look for diamonds you might not have seen one since the two that are there are each dissected into three pieces. Here, however, you can see two whole diamonds and several others that are convincing even if not quite complete. To get your diamond point on your selvedge draw lines through the draw-down and draft where you think the edges should be, then start your threading and treadling from there.

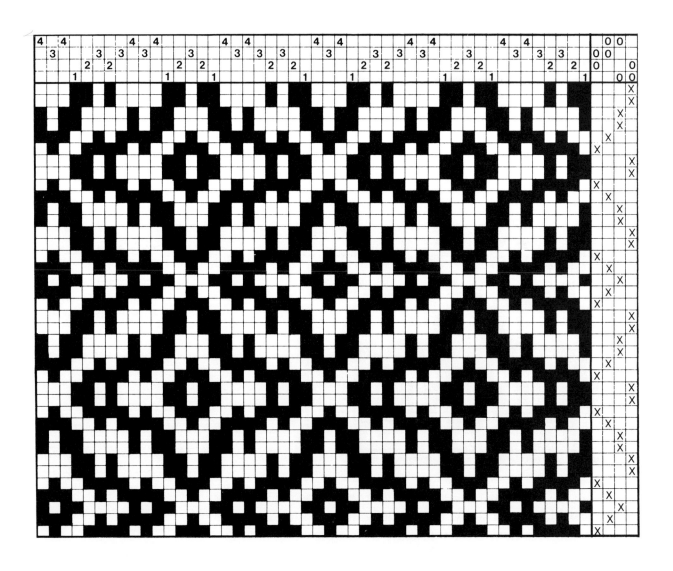

If you want to weave something tiny, you might only use one repeat of the pattern: a bookmark, a tree ornament, gift wrapping decoration, pieces to make a mobile. One single diamond could be very pretty for any of these. In that case, you'd start and stop on the edges of one diamond. Look carefully at the diamonds on the previous page. They are not identical. The diamond whose center is threaded 1, 2, 3, 2, 1 is both taller and wider than the one with the center threaded 4, 3, 4. Look at the centers to see the difference.

Just in case you're considering it, don't weave this pattern until after you've done the lesson on overshot. It might work well for you, but it's more likely not to.

Now let's say you come across a draft that you like only part of. You would treat it the same way as the draft we just worked on. Block off the part you like and use it. This is another occasion for doing a two-repeat draw-down, for the way a pattern looks where it joins when repeated is sometimes a surprise.

In this example notice that the treadling is changed on the second half of the new draft. In the top half I didn't like the opening left between the bottom and top of the diamonds. To close the diamonds at top and bottom I added one more shot in the twill progression before reversing direction. Notice that while the added weft shot changed the outside of the large diamonds it also changed the design in the center of the pattern. The motif changed from a white (weft) cross to a small diamond with a black (warp) dot in the center. Becoming aware of those small changes and how to create them will help you to begin designing your own patterns and make slight alterations in existing drafts to help them suit your desires a little better.

I think that for now that's all I want to say about altering drafts. As you get more comfortable with the whole process of elementary designing, you'll understand how it all works enough to make the drafts do what you want.

More twills, a little less basic

I spent an hour or two drawing out the random assortment of twills on the next two pages, and I hope you have as much fun looking at them as I did making them up. By changing the threading by only a small amount I came up with surprisingly varied effects.

Each treadling follows essentially the same pattern as its threading. The only change is that I started with four instead of one and went in reverse. Had I started with one in the treadling the drawdowns would be varied X's instead of varied diamonds; try a few yourself and see.

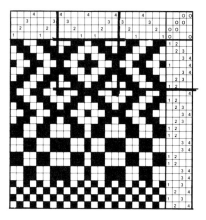

If you want to use only part of a draft, mark off the section you like and then do a two-repeat draw-down.

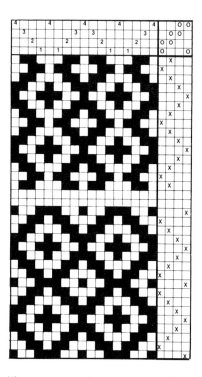

Two-repeat draw-down of the section marked off in the draft above. To close the top and bottom of the diamonds, one more shot in the twill progression was added before reversing direction, as seen in the second half of the draw-down. This not only changes the outside of the large diamonds, the inside of the center pattern is altered as well.

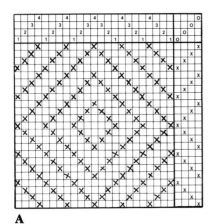

A

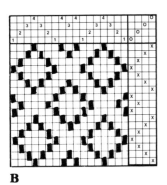

B

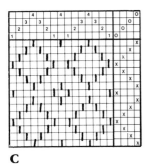

C

While most of these are drawn as a 1/3 twill, they would probably be more practical woven as a 2/2 twill. To change from a 1/3 to 2/2 twill simply treadle 1-2 for every 1, change 2 to 2-3, 3 to 3-4, and 4 to 4-1. My concern for practicality comes from looking at some of the long rows of white space which mean long weft floats (wefts not intersecting warps) on this side, warp floats on the back. Too many floats too long make a fabric unstable and likely to snag. How long any of these floats actually are depends on the warp sett. If a weft is floating over seven warps at 6 e.p.i., that's more than an inch, but at 24 e.p.i., it's about ⅓ of an inch and not very dangerous.

Let's discuss each of these drafts for a moment. Draft A shows you how to get diamonds inside of diamonds, or bigger ones than you did in the last lesson. (I'm going to think of and speak of 1, 2, 3, 4 as forward, 4, 3, 2, 1 as backward.) To get larger diamonds go forward (1, 2, 3, 4, 1, 2, 3, 4, etc.) in your threading several times before reversing. Where you reverse direction will be the point of your twill, and each repeat forward and backward from that center point will be one more concentric diamond. The same is true in the treadling. Use your hand to cover the bottom half of the draft. If you never reversed the direction of your treadling you would have a very large herringbone.

In Draft B you have lots of small diamonds, this time not connected to each other as they were on the preceding page. The diamonds in Draft C also aren't connected; notice that in this draft one diamond is smaller than the others. In an expanded draft of more repeats, you'd see that there are as many smaller diamonds in C as there are larger diamonds. It doesn't look that way now because of where the draft starts and stops, a good case for a larger draw-down.

Draft D combines small and large diamonds, another way to design a pattern with a lot of variety through very simple means. Draft E has a wonderful assortment of diamonds with differing notches and differing centers.

Again, any of these can be woven in a 1/3, 2/2, or 3/1 twill. Depending on your yarn and color choices they can look markedly different from each other.

There is no great secret to making up these designs. All I did was write out a threading that seemed interesting, a treadling that followed the same sequence, and draw the draw-down to find out what I'd concocted. Were I to weave one now, I'd probably pull a section out of E, and then do a two-repeat draw-down of that section. If I still liked what I got I'd try it in a sample.

Notice, too, on these drafts that the pattern of the treadling marks is the mirror image of the pattern created in the draw-down. As

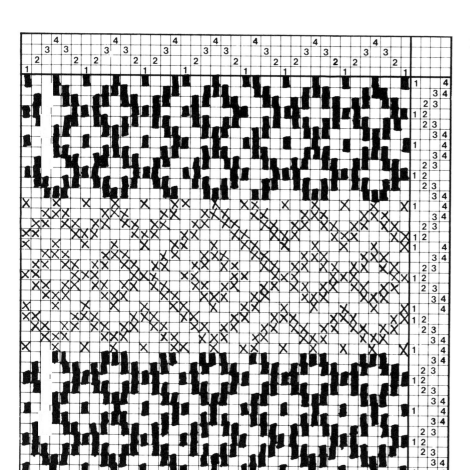

D

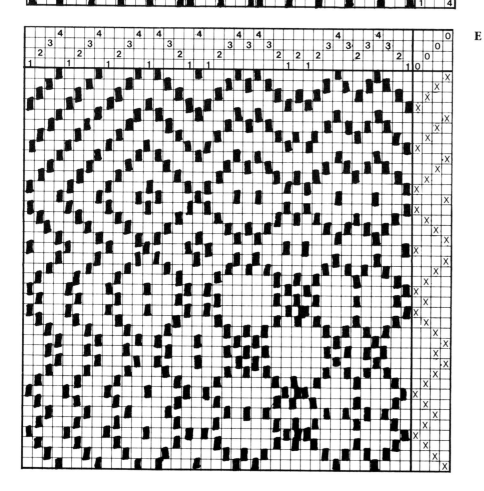

E

you work more with drafts you'll begin to recognize predictable combinations of threading and treadling, knowing in advance what causes what.

In designing twills, the size and number of diamonds you get will be determined by how often you reverse direction in your threading and treadling. What I want you to do is play around with these, make up your own, combine the various threading or pattern units (1,2,3,4—1,2,3,4,3,2,1—1,2,3,4,1,4,3,2,1—1,2,3,4,3,4,3,2,1 etc.) and do draw-downs to see what you'll get. Then weave some. Use a variety of yarns, try different warp setts, experiment with colors if you want. In Marguerite Davison's *A Handweaver's Pattern Book*, the first 54 pages are devoted to straight and point twills. If you have this book take a look, but don't, please don't, decide to copy hers only and forget about making up your own too. Twills are an easy weave to understand and to execute and this is the beginning of some of the fun you can have adding your own personal touch to all you weave.

Your assignments

1. Take one of the drafts at the beginning of the lesson and weave it as is, then again as a 2/2 twill (or 1/3 if you choose D). Remember it needs to be a fairly balanced weave for the pattern to show up well. If you pack your weft in too tight you'll lose the warp and weft visual relationship.

2. Pull a section out of one of the drafts at the beginning of the lesson and do a two-repeat draw-down. Weave it as a 1/3 twill and also as a 2/2 twill.

3. Take the threading from one twill draft and the treadling from a different one and make up a new draw-down. If you like it, weave it using two different colors or textures of weft.

4. Make up your own twill, planning for a particular project. It could be skirt fabric, a border on kitchen or camper curtains, a pillow, a baby blanket. Plan it so that the pattern balances across the warp. You don't have to do a draw-down of the entire warp to know if it balances, just one repeat or a repeat of each section will do.

   A quick design shortcut is to use diagonal lines in place of numbers. Use numbers for the first repeat, lines to get an idea of what the whole piece will look like. Weave it if you like the design.

$$\begin{array}{l} {}_1{}^2{}_{}{}^3{}^4 \quad {}_1{}^2{}^3{}^4{}^3{}_2 \quad {}_1{}^2{}^3{}^4{}^3{}_2 \quad {}_1{}^4{}^3{}_2 \quad = \quad \diagup\diagup\diagup\diagup\diagup\diagup \end{array}$$

$$\begin{array}{l} {}_1{}^2{}^3{}^4 \quad {}^4{}^3{}_2 \quad = \quad \diagup\diagup \end{array}$$

Drafting shorthand: use numbers for first repeat, and then diagonal lines to give an idea of what the whole piece will look like.

$$\begin{array}{l} {}_1{}^2{}^3{}^4 \quad {}_2{} \quad {}^4{}^3{}_2 \quad = \quad \diagup\diagup\diagup \end{array}$$

Drafting from cloth diagrams to threading and treadling

What I want to do this time is approach the draft from the other direction. So far we've started with threading and treadling and then figured out what it would give us. But lots of times you'll have a picture in your mind of how you want a pattern to look. Then what you need to know is how to thread and treadle it to get that particular pattern. To make up threadings and treadlings and then do draw-downs to see if you got what you wanted would be ridiculously time consuming—you could spend days hoping for your pattern to show up. Instead, you can draw a draw-down, now called a cloth diagram, of what you want to weave and determine the threading and treadling from it. Then you only have to do one draft, the one you want.

Actually, you may need to do more than one. The only problem with starting with an original cloth diagram is that until you've done enough of them to understand how they work, you are fairly likely to draw a design that takes more harnesses than you have. When that happens you need to simplify the pattern, maintaining its character while curtailing its flair. If you enjoy doing your own designing and keep practicing and exploring, you'll get to the point where you can count harnesses in your head as you draw and you'll know when to stop adding new ones.

The other reason for knowing how to derive threading and treadling from cloth diagrams is that you will begin to notice fabrics that you want to duplicate. Commercial clothing, upholstery, bedspreads, table linens, often have fabric structures that can be duplicated with four or eight harnesses. You will also come across other handwoven things you'd like to try your own version of, and being able to figure out how they were done makes this possible.

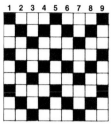

Cloth diagram

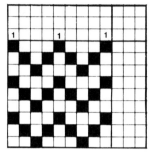

Begin filling in the threading by writing in all the ones.

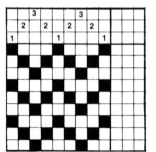

Completed threading for cloth diagram.

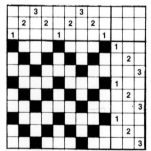

Completed threading and treadling.

This is a cloth diagram, which is a picture of a fabric structure. As before, the black squares represent the warp threads going over the weft threads. From the general design you can see that it is a point twill, but you need to know more than that to weave it. Each column represents one warp thread. So, if our example here were a whole fabric swatch, it would be nine threads wide. *All columns that are identical in pattern represent warp threads on the same harness.* Thus, the first, fifth, and ninth columns/threads are all on the same harness, which we'll label one because it's a convenient place to start. Any column/thread that is different in pattern from those is on a different harness, so the second column/thread, being different from the first, will be on harness two. Identical patterns to column two, all the way up and down the row, are in the fourth, sixth, and eighth columns. These threads are all threaded on harness two. Finally, the two remaining columns/threads are identical, so they can both be labelled three.

The completed threading draft looks like this. You can see that it takes only three harnesses to weave this pattern.

To determine the treadling order is even easier. You know that to weave a shot you need to raise some harnesses, and that the black squares still represent warp on top, or thread/harnesses raised. Each row across still represents one weft shot, and the squares that are filled in show which harnesses are up when that weft shot is thrown. Look above the filled in squares to see what number is at the top of the columns they are in, and write those numbers down at the end of the row. Those are the harnesses you need to raise for that weft shot.

In this draft, for the first weft shot the squares under the ones are filled in, or the threads on harness one are raised. For the second weft shot the number two boxes are filled in, so you will want to raise harness two to weave that weft shot. The boxes below the number threes are filled in in the third row, so harness three is to be raised for the third shot. Etc.

That's really all there is to it. The system is easy, but some drafts are more complex than others. It takes practice and a watchful eye to do this easily.

Let's do a few more, only this time you do more of the work. And remember, just because you have only four harnesses does not mean that the draft will.

Start with the cloth diagram shown at top, opposite. If you begin assigning harnesses with harness number one and count up, then you can go as high as you need to. You could begin with any number, but starting mid-way of an unknown quantity can get confusing. So, we'll say that the first thread is on harness one.

The thread next to it is raised at different times (you know this because the squares are filled in in a different pattern), so it must be on a different harness. We'll assign it to harness two.

How about the next thread? It's different again and should be threaded on harness three. And the fourth thread? The fifth thread is the same as the third, so it's on harness three. You do the rest.

With the threading done, you can easily figure out the treadling. When the first shot was woven, the warps that are filled in in the first row were raised, so look above the filled in boxes to see which harnesses were raised. For the first shot only harness one was raised. For the second weft shot the boxes under the twos are filled in, so harness two was raised. The third shot requires two harnesses to be raised, harnesses one and three. While for most of the weaving you've done so far you have lifted the same number of harnesses for every shot, that is not a rule at all. The rib weave alternated one harness against three, remember? The draft we're working on right now is for a waffle weave, called that because the fabric looks like a waffle, and it will use varying numbers of harnesses for each shot. To weave the fourth shot you need to raise one, two, and four. Now you finish.

All of the following cloth diagrams are that simple, and your biggest problem will be trying to make them too hard. If it's difficult to follow the rows, which it often is, use a ruler or some other straight edge. The answers to all of these begin on page 147, in the next lesson.

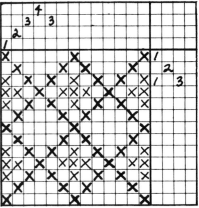

Complete the threading and treadling for this cloth diagram. Check yourself on page 144.

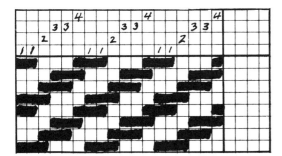

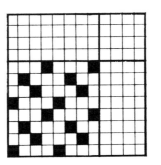

Fill in the threading and treadling for these cloth diagrams.

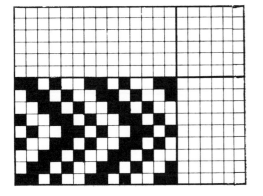

139

I told you that analyzing cloth diagrams is useful if you want to copy an existing fabric. The way to do that is to mark off a section of the fabric with pins and then trace the warp or weft in the swatch. Record on graph paper when the warp covers the weft. Follow one thread, whichever direction is easier, and fill in the squares when the warp is up. Leave them blank when the weft is on top. You are creating a cloth diagram from which you can determine the threading and treadling just as you've done above.

How soon you'll actually use this I can't say. But whether you choose to create your own draft or not, knowing how to alter drafts and work from cloth diagrams will help you to catch errors, your own, a book's, or a loom's.* Generally, you will have a broader base to work from which will make all your weaving easier.

That's an interesting thing I've learned. Most of the techniques and specific information I've learned in weaving have turned out to be most valuable at times that would have seemed unrelated to their subject matter. A bit of information from category A solves some problem in category C. Now I go to learn new things not so much for themselves as for what they will add to my general store of knowledge. It's fun to mix and match, and what you learn about drafting definitely falls under this heading. You'll rarely use one phase of it without incorporating others.

From here on I'm not going to give you anymore "just drafting" lessons. I'll be using drafts to explore other weaves, and I will assume a degree of drafting knowledge on your part. Using drafts will make you more comfortable with them. Later we'll talk some about block theory and block drafting, another segment of drafting. What I've given you here are the basics.

Your assignment

Make up your own cloth diagram and fill in the threading and treadling.

---

*Computers are definitely finding their way into the weaving field, making the mechanics of doing draw-downs and designing lots faster than they could ever be done by hand. Though I'm not going to go into computer drafting here, you should be aware that there are numerous programs available to weavers.

Lesson 9
An Introduction To Other Kinds of Twills

Offset and broken twills
Waffle weave
Combination twills
Weaving on opposites
Twill variations

Fabrics by Debbie Redding, Sharon Alderman, Yvonne Stahl, The Weaving Shop

Treadling variations and combination threadings expand the realm of twills. Here, at far left, is a soft, waffle weave fabric. The threading is an ordinary point twill, and the secret to the waffles, or floats, is in the way the treadling is varied. Compare this waffle weave with the fabric at top right, also a waffle weave, to get an idea of the possibilities and different results which can be achieved when color is an added element. The fine fabric at center combines stripes of point twill and basket weave. It would be suitable for a tailored dress or unstructured jacket. At bottom right is another example of this same combination threading, only done in heavier yarns. Again, this is only a taste of what's possible. As always, note that fiber choice, sett and color usage are important factors to keep in mind when planning projects.

The twills you've done so far have been straight and point. That's only the beginning. In addition to variations of these there are also many other categories of twills, each with its own variations. Steep, low, undulating, satin, mock satin, extended, doublefaced, offset, broken, waffle and combination twills are some of the variations. The vocabulary overlaps and many of these share characteristics even beyond their common twill identity. Some can be done only with more than four harnesses, most have four harness versions as well as others. The drafts that you worked on in the last lesson come from this list, and these plus some others are shown with their threadings, treadlings and names at the end of this lesson. They are there for your reference, to try whenever you feel so inclined. In this lesson I want to talk about only three, offset or broken, waffle and combination.

More twills! At left is an undulating twill; the white warp and the black weft provide lots of contrast for this threading where the optical effects can be played up for electrifying results. Another threading which lends itself well to "op art" interpretation is the extended twill fabric shown at bottom right. Again, highly contrasting colors increase the effect of this threading. Mock satin weave is used for the fabric at top right. On one side the warp predominates; on the other side only specks of warp show. Experiment with one color in the warp and one color in the weft, or cross warp stripes with one color of weft. All three of these threadings invite lots of color-play, whether your color choices are conservative or bold and bright.

Fabrics by Judy Steinkoenig

Offset and broken twills

An offset or broken twill is one in which the twill line is broken. "Offset" is the word applied to straight twills, "broken" refers to point twills.

If you look at the threading of this offset twill you'll see that the 'offset' of the pattern occurs where one harness was left out of the threading sequence. It can be any harness; it can happen at any interval. I recommend you plan your breaks often enough that they look intentional instead of like threading errors.

In a broken twill the harness deletion occurs on one side or the other of the point; thus, instead of threading 1,2,3,4,3,2,1, you'd thread 1,2,3,4,2,1 or 1,2,4,3,2,1. Creating this break is a slight variation that adds new dimension to a point twill, one you might like. While the principle is the same for both, the books I looked in make a distinction between the two, applying offset only to interrupted straight twills and broken to interrupted point twills.

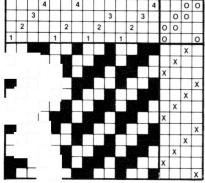

Offset twill

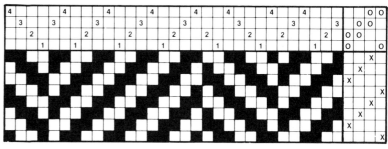

Broken twill

Both of these twills can be created with interruptions in treadling as well as threading. Just leave one shot out of your treadling sequence and you'll have the same kind of interruption. Whether you have a point or straight threading will, of course, affect the design dramatically.*

Waffle weave

I've included waffle weave because it's one of the most fun of all weaves. It has great possibilities for color arranging, and intrigues almost everyone. Waffle weave has a point twill threading. The treadling, which creates an arrangement of warp and weft floats with few intersections, is the key to creating the waffles of waffle weave. This has two significant results to be aware of.

One of the ways to experiment with alterations in drafts or ways of accomplishing patterns is to take a cloth diagram or draw-down and turn it 90°, re-figure the threading and treadling, and see what happens. On simple drafts, such as plain weave or 2/2 twills, there may be no difference. On others there is a tremendous difference in how you would arrive at the same fabric.

Waffle weave

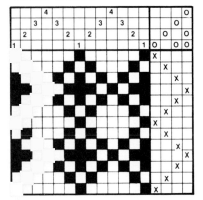

Draw-down

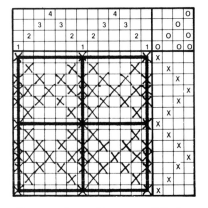

Illustration of woven fabric. Note that the fabric does not look like the draw-down. Squares appear in the fabric although there are diamonds in the draw-down.

First, the fabric does not look like the draft. In the draft you see diamonds; in the fabric you'll see squares. Look at the draft again. Notice where there are warp threads staying up for a relatively long time without intersecting any wefts. Also notice weft floats, rows where there are no warps appearing for awhile. Those warp and weft floats will be the top edge of the waffle. The insides of the square will actually drop in depth just like a waffle does. The stabilizing intersections occur in the centers of the waffles.

Because there are so few intersections it is all too easy to pack the weft in too much. The warp is putting up almost no resistance to the weft and so first-time-waffle-weavers often end up with a weft-faced fabric and no waffles. For the waffles to show you must have a balanced fabric (e.p.i. = p.p.i.) or almost so, so beat lightly, or set your warp half again as close as you normally would, e.g., 18 e.p.i. instead of 12 e.p.i.

One other thing to be aware of is that while the warp is on the loom under tension the waffle will be flat and will have little or no depth. Only when the tension is relaxed will the depth appear. As your fabric acquires more depth, it will draw up a lot in length and width. Depending on your yarn and your beat, the external dimensions of your fabric could shrink as much as 30%, and this is only structural shrinkage; it does not take into account yarn shrinkage from washing. I once wove a four harness waffle weave out of linnay, a linen/rayon yarn that is very nice and shrinks a fair amount. Between the waffles and the yarn shrinkage the piece shrank 47% and was about three times as thick. Do a sample; I didn't on that one and never did figure out what to do with it in its changed state.

Rather than try to explain all the color possibilities that exist for waffles, I'm going to give you some color coded threading drafts. Use the same color sequence in your treadling, and make up more of your own.

The top edge on this side will be the bottom of the waffle on the other side and vice versa. When you start weaving, look on the other side just to see what's happening.

A		B		C			D		E		F		G	
a		b		b		a		d		c		b		b	
a	a	a	a	b	a	a	b	c	c	b	b	b	b	b	b
a	a	b	b	a	a	b	b	b	b	b	b	a	a	b	b
a	a	a	a	a		b		a	a	a	a	a	a	a	a

Some possible color threading sequences.

144

Combination twills

When you have a straight draw on your loom you can treadle to achieve a variety of weaves: plain weave, twill, basket, rib, etc. You can also combine weaves in the threading for vertical, rather than horizontal, patterns. With an unlimited number of harnesses you could combine anything, using a whole new group for each pattern. Since most of us have a limited number of harnesses, however, it is necessary to play around and see what we can and cannot combine.

You've already mixed up straight and point twills. What we're talking about now is combining different weaves. I'll save you some time by telling you that you cannot combine twill and tabby on four harnesses. You can, however, combine twill and basket weave, as in the drafts below. It must be a 2/2 twill, but the twill is not limited in design. Straight, point, broken—try anything you can think of, and remember that by changing colors or textures as you change pattern you can magnify the effects.

This is a perfect opportunity to try out your inventing and designing skills, making drawings of what you want to try and then determining the threading and treadling to see if you can weave them on your loom. At this point you may not do much of that, but as you get more comfortable with the whole process you may begin to. And may really enjoy it.

Combination twills

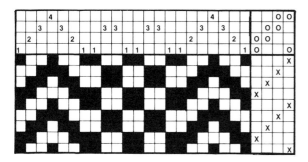

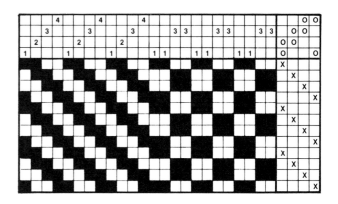

In conclusion

As always, these are the basics. Try what you like, know that there's more if you want it later. In general the things to remember about twills are that they are softer and thicker, may need a closer sett, may benefit from a floating selvedge, may look different on the two sides, are versatile and are easy to weave. You can use any yarn, but a very complex yarn will obscure a small or complex pattern. Any thickness of yarn can work, provided the e.p.i. and p.p.i. are appropriate. And you can go wild with color if you want to.

Weaving on opposites

Weaving on opposites is a term which can be applied to twills. While I'm not going to go into great detail about this here, I do want you to be aware of this technique because twills lend themselves so well to it. Weaving on opposites is a method of treadling rather than a specific weave structure, and can apply to other weave structures, too. Instead of sleying for a balanced weave, to weave twills on opposites, you'll need to space your warp further apart so that a weft-faced fabric can be woven.

Weaving on opposites means just that. After you throw a pick in one shed, the one that follows it will be woven in the previous pick's opposite shed. For example, if you weave shed 1-2, you'll follow it with 3-4; shed 2-3 will be followed by 1-4; shed 3-4 will be followed by 1-2, and so on. In other words, raise whatever harnesses weren't raised the last time. Pack your weft in well so that the warp is completely hidden, and use at least two colors or your pattern won't show. This technique is ideal for rugs, purses, bags and footstools. It may also be used for table mats, runners, belts, or even vests and jackets, if lighter-weight materials are used.

At least two shuttles are needed, one for the "lead" shuttle, the other for the "follower" or "opposite" shuttle. In weaving twills on opposites, all kinds of color possibilities exist. For inspiration take a look at the pillow on page 74.

Assignments

1. Design and weave an offset twill with the breaks coming at regular intervals and one where the intervals are not all the same size, e.g., 1″/2″/1″/3″/repeat or ½″-1″ repeat.

2. Design and weave a broken twill fabric suitable for a winter coat or man's sport jacket. Think of using one color in the warp and another in the weft, with perhaps a single warp end of a third color at the break in the twill.

3. Design and weave a waffle weave using a color sequence that will emphasize the depth of the waffle cells, e.g., light on top, dark on the bottom.

4. Design and weave a waffle weave with one color in the warp with a slightly different color in the weft for more character than all one color would have.

5. Design and weave a waffle weave sample with three color combinations next to each other in the warp, each 3″-4″ wide.

Repeat this sequence in the weft. What happens when color sequence B crosses C?

6. Design and weave a combination twill/basket weave with three colors in the warp, perhaps one as accent only.

7. Design and weave a combination twill other than the one(s) given. You've been making up twills for awhile now, combine some of them in new ways.

8. Choose a point twill draft and weave it on opposites. You might want to label your shuttles 'A' and 'B' to help you keep track of which is which; 'B' always follows 'A'.

Twill variations

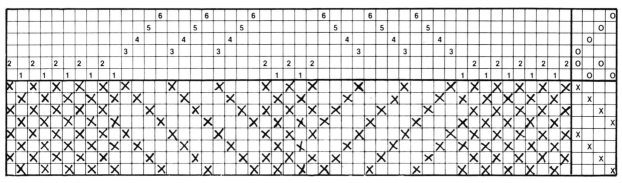

Combination twill

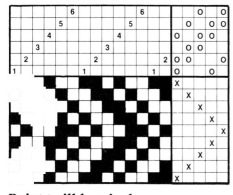

Point twill-herringbone

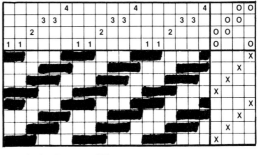

Undulating twill

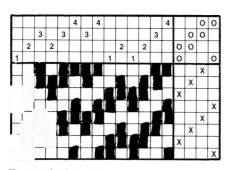

Extended twill

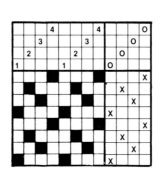

Mock satin

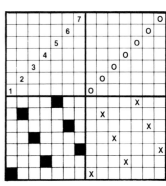

Satin

More twill variations

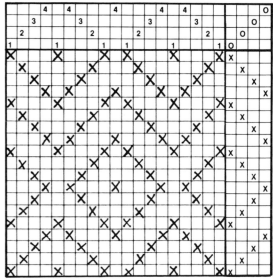

Point twill

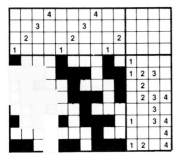

Double faced

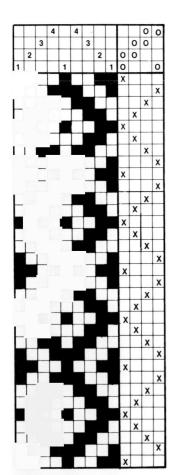

Point twill

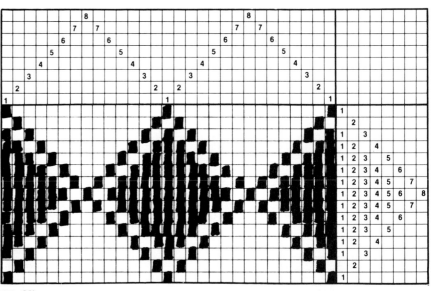

Waffle weave

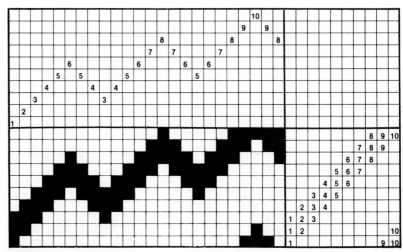

Extended twill

148

Part III: *For Those of You Who Know What You're Doing*

Lesson 10
Double Weave

Setting up
Warp sett considerations
Methods of weaving
Yarns

Threading
Sleying the reed
An alternate threading

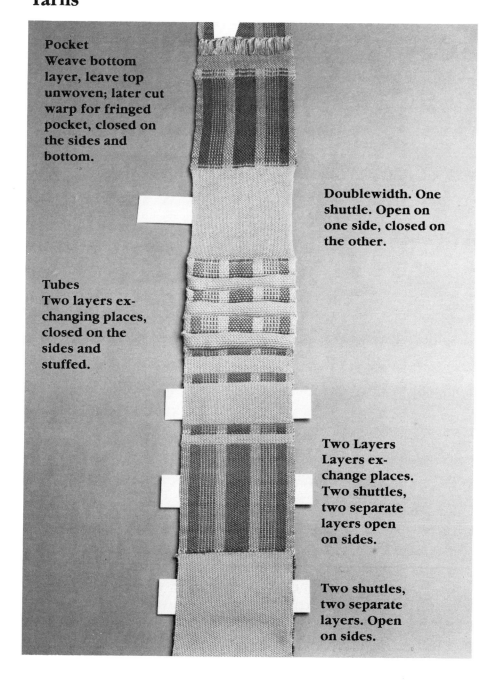

Pocket
Weave bottom layer, leave top unwoven; later cut warp for fringed pocket, closed on the sides and bottom.

Doublewidth. One shuttle. Open on one side, closed on the other.

Tubes
Two layers exchanging places, closed on the sides and stuffed.

Two Layers
Layers exchange places. Two shuttles, two separate layers open on sides.

Two shuttles, two separate layers. Open on sides.

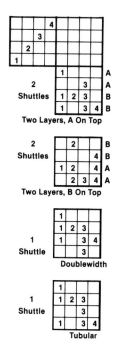

Weaving double weave.

Double weave is a way to weave two layers of fabric at one time. Its versatility lies in how these two layers can be connected. Double weave can be used to create sculptural and three dimensional effects that are great for a wide range of things from toys to contemporary art. In practical ways, double weave allows you to create fabrics twice as wide as your loom: clothing without seams, tubes that can be stuffed and many other possibilities.

Setting up

Double weave is surprisingly simple. You know you can weave one layer of fabric, plain weave or variations of it, on two harnesses. You can then deduce that you can weave two layers of fabric on four harnesses, two harnesses for each layer. Since each layer can be only a two harness weave, no twills or other weaves that take more than two harnesses are possible. (If you have eight harnesses, each layer can use four harnesses, or you can have four layers each using only two harnesses.) But as you know, there are many variations of plain weave, including color arrangements and the use of textured yarns, so the limitations are not terribly restrictive.

The structure of double weave is very simple; what can be done with it can be tremendously complex if you choose to make it so. Let's start at the beginning.

Threading

Double weave can be threaded on a straight draw. (I'll tell you an alternative later on.) The two layers are interspersed. The threads on harnesses one and three form one layer; those on two and four form the other layer. The first time you weave double weave consider alternating two colors in your warp so that one layer is color A, the other layer is color B; if you do that, you cannot possibly raise the wrong harness (wrong layer) without knowing it immediately.

Warp sett considerations

One of the most important things to remember about double weave is the whole subject of warp sett. Each layer needs to have enough warp. So, if you use a yarn that you want set at 12 e.p.i. per layer, you need to have 24 e.p.i. altogether. If you have a warp that is set at 12 e.p.i., each layer will have six e.p.i. You can weave a double weave with a much looser sett (e.g., 6 e.p.i.), but with the warp far apart it is likely that your weft will pack down a lot and you'll end up with a weft-faced fabric on each layer. Again, that's okay if it's what you want, but if it isn't, it's frustrating.

Sleying the reed

Whether or not you'll sley more than one end per dent in your reed depends on the yarn and reed combination you choose. A yarn you want set at 10 e.p.i. per layer, threaded in a 10-dent reed, will need to be double-sleyed to give 20 e.p.i. (Double-sleyed means two threads per dent; you will still thread one thread per heddle.) On the other hand, if you use the same yarn and warp sett and sley it in a 5-dent reed, you'll need to have four threads per dent to make 20 e.p.i. If you want a warp sett of four e.p.i. per layer and you have an 8-dent reed, you could have one thread per dent. How many threads you put in each dent of the reed will depend on the yarn and reed.

Sometimes it is better to have four threads per dent in large dents than two in smaller ones. If the yarn is at all bumpy or fuzzy, it will be less crowded in a reed with large dents. Remember, that as you weave, the warp threads need to pass by each other in the reed, especially if you are changing layers a lot. Rubbing against another yarn which *flexes* is easier on a yarn than rubbing against a steel bar which doesn't flex.

Methods of weaving

So, let's say you've threaded a straight draw using one color for each layer, and set your warp at twice the normal sett for the yarn you've chosen. Now that you're warped up, what can you do with it? The most basic double weave possibilities are described below. Weave several inches of each one before going on to the next.

Two shuttles, two separate layers

The first thing to try is weaving two layers completely separate. You'll need two shuttles, one for each layer. I've given you the treadling in the draft, but I want you to think about the concept of what you are doing also. Each layer is tabby, and tabby has two shots, tabby a and tabby b. (When you first started weaving, tabby a was 1 + 3, tabby b was 2 + 4; that's not what you'll treadle now, but I want to be sure you understand what I mean by tabby a and b because we'll use them a lot in this lesson, and in fact, from now on.)

To weave the top layer, you'll alternate tabbies a and b by raising harnesses one and three alternately. To weave the bottom layer you need to raise all of the top layer to keep it up out of the way, then alternate the a and b tabby shots of the bottom layer, harnesses two and four. So, to weave the bottom layer, you will raise three harnesses, the two top layer harnesses and one for the bottom layer. (1 + 3 + 2, then 1 + 3 + 4) Use the first shuttle for the top layer, the second shuttle for the bottom layer. Be careful not

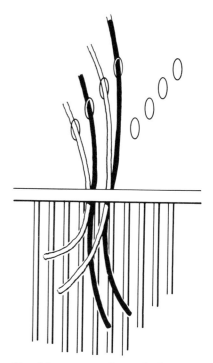

Double weave threaded on straight draw. The threads on harnesses one and three form one layer; those on two and four form another. Here threads on harnesses one and two are threaded through the same dent in the reed; threads on harnesses three and four are threaded through the same dent.

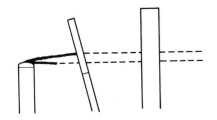

If you weave more than two shots per layer after weaving one layer, the beater will not be able to pack in the weft on the other layer because the shots from the first one will be in the way.

to twist the shuttles around each other on the side, otherwise your layers won't be completely separate.

You can weave two shots on one layer, then two on the other, then back to the first again, etc. The less often you change shuttles the faster and more easily your weaving will go. If you weave more than two shots per layer, after weaving one layer the beater will not be able to pack in the weft on the other layer because the shots from the first one will be in the way.

Next, try weaving two separate layers again, this time with the 2-4 layer on top. The principles are the same, only this time harnesses two and four will make the top layer, one and three the bottom. To weave the top layer you will raise harness two for tabby a, then harness four for tabby b. To weave the bottom layer you'll need to hold up the top layer (harnesses two and four) and raise tabby a of the bottom layer (harness one), then tabby b (harness three).

Weaving two layers completely separate is a good exercise for understanding how double weave works. Practically speaking, however, weaving a whole warp off as two separate pieces has some real drawbacks.

I remember thinking how clever it would be to weave two sets of placemats at one time, one set on each layer. And while it seemed like I was weaving one, when it came off I'd really have two sets. I thought about that for a little while, and I began to realize potential problems. First, you are more likely to have errors in the bottom layer because you can't see it. Therefore, my bottom placemats might need a lot of repair work in order to be nice. Then there is the matter of speed. While weaving two sets off at once might seem very efficient, the constant shuttle exchange consumes more time than you might possibly save. Using one shuttle and weaving off a warp twice as long would be faster. And finally, a warp twice as long would have one set of loom waste, whereas a double weave warp, with twice as many warp ends, would have twice the loom waste. About that point in my pondering I abandoned the idea of weaving off a double weave warp as two entirely separate layers, for placemats or anything else.

There are, however, good uses for two layers woven separately. By weaving an inch or so, then reversing the layers and weaving another inch or so, and continuing to reverse the layers, you can weave a very sturdy fabric. Depending on the yarns used, this can be a great way to weave a rug or saddle blanket. Woven of lighter weight yarns, it can be a beautiful reversible jacket fabric. One of the fun options is to weave a kid's nap mat or grown-up's yoga mat by stuffing the sections with some kind of batting just before you reverse the layers; you can end up with a custom designed padded mat. If the fabric and padding aren't too heavy, you can make you own version of a down vest.

Reversing layers can also be woven with one shuttle in any of the methods below. The advantages would be quicker weaving and the ability to seal the selvedges (to keep the stuffing in). A possible disadvantage would be the loss of exclusively solid colored stripes if your layers were separate colors. One weft could match only the warp. But then, your warp could be one color and the weft in each section a different color. (Any plain weave variation is possible, remember, and color variations may be the easiest to plan and execute.)

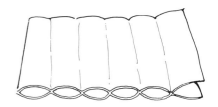
Two layers, woven separately, exchange places to form tubes.

One shuttle

When using one shuttle you cannot keep the layers entirely separate. Stated another way, the various methods of joining the layers are all accomplished using only one shuttle. As the weft proceeds from one layer to the other it connects them. The path of the weft determines whether the resulting piece is double width, tubular, or some other shape.

Doublewidth

The ability to weave blankets, tablecloths, and other projects wider than one's loom is possibly one of the most popular advantages of double weave. There are some special problems that come up, but they are relatively easy to remedy.

To create a piece that will unfold to twice its width, simply connect the two layers on one side. That selvedge then becomes the center of the larger piece.

To join the layers on one side weave tabby a of the top layer, tabby a of the bottom layer, tabby b of the bottom, and then back to the top and its tabby b. The side that is closed will be the side opposite from where you started your shuttle. Which side is closed makes no difference except if you have a particular color plan or your selvedge control is much better on one side than the other. (Make the better selvedge the folded/connected side.)

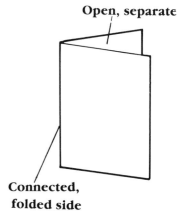
Open, separate

Connected, folded side

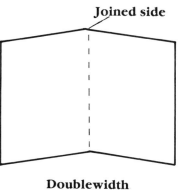
Joined side

Doublewidth

Weaving doublewidth

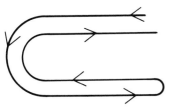
Path of shuttle

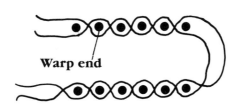
Warp end

If your tension on your closed side is consistent and not too tight or too loose, then the piece will come off looking like one large piece woven the normal way. However, if you get much draw-in, the warp on the center line will be closer together and you'll get a visual line. You would get the same kind of stripe if you sleyed some of your warp closer together in any weaving. If your closed side is woven very loosely and has weft loops extending out, then you'll have a loose center, as if some warps had been pulled out. Either of these problems can be fixed by pulling some warps out or stitching some additional ones in. The biggest aggravation comes when your folded side is inconsistent, sometimes fine, sometimes loose, sometimes tight. To fix that you need to pull some warp out, stitch some in, and try to make it look like it's all the same. And while you're adding and subtracting all these warps (or pieces of warps), you need to maintain the weave structure. For plain weave this means always adding or subtracting two threads, not one.

Repairing the problem is possible; preventing it is even better. If you have pretty good selvedges, you shouldn't have a big problem. Different yarns and setts have different needs, so feel your way accordingly. I'll give you two fairly simple preventive measures for this, and add that there are others as well. Read, talk to other weavers, make up something and then share it.

If you are going to have stripes in your warp, especially bold stripes, plan a color change right on the edge of the warp on the closed side. When the piece is opened out, what will be most obvious is the stripe. A slight variation in the sett will be totally camouflaged, a drastic one obscured.

Another option, especially good for large pieces that you'll be weaving on for a fairly long time, is a separately weighted floating selvedge. Use the strongest yarn or cord you can find. When the loom is all warped and ready to go, tie it to the front apron rod, run it through the reed in the same dent as your selvedge thread, through no heddle, and then hang it over the back beam. Tie to your floater as much weight as it will support, making it much tighter than the rest of your warp. As you weave, have it float inside the fold of the cloth. Go over it when you come from the top layer, under it when you come from the bottom. Because it is so tight you can pull your weft up against it without the selvedge drawing in. Since is will be pulled out later, you can use anything. Fishline is good if you can get the knot to stay tied; seine twine will work if it's fine enough. Or use any very strong yarn. I keep mine so tight that sometimes it breaks. If I repair it immediately I'm fine; if I wait a few shots out of laziness, I'm sorry.

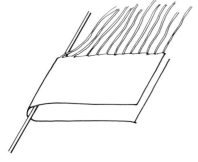

Use a floating selvedge on your closed side to help prevent draw-in on this edge. Use a strong yarn and weight it separately with a lot of weight off the back of the loom.

Weaving a piece of doublewidth is really very easy, and even if you rarely do it, it's nice to know you have the option. A 15″ loom can suddenly go beyond samples, placemats, scarves and neckties.

Weaving tubes

Closing both sides of your weaving will create a tube. People laugh, but one of the biggest kicks in weaving is sticking your fingers down inside a pocket or sack you are weaving to feel the fabric above and below your hand. To weave a tube, weave tabby a across the top, go back with the bottom layer tabby a, back across the top with tabby b, and finally, across the bottom with its tabby b. By going top-bottom-top-bottom your weft will close both sides.

Tubes, in various shapes and sizes, have many uses. The padded mats mentioned earlier can have closed sides to keep the stuffing in. While the tube is then only an inch or two tall and many inches wide, and so doesn't particularly look like tube, it is the same thing.

A narrow warp woven into a long skinny tube can be stuffed and made into a snake. If it's a fairly short tube, you can add ears, legs and a tail to make a bunny or some other animal. You can weave a wall hanging with pockets, closing a section of the tube at one end and leaving it open at the other.

By combining tubes and doublewidth you can make a 'shawl' with sleeves. Sometimes this is called a granny shrug, but you don't have to be a granny to wear it. When worn, the center section will open up and cover your shoulders; the tubes on the ends become the sleeves. They are comfortable, light, quick, something like a fitted afghan.

There are so many other uses for double weave that rather than try to tell you more I'll refer you to the books written on it (see Bibliography). There are at least three books on double weave, and many others that have good sections on it.

Weaving tubes

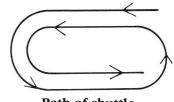

Path of shuttle

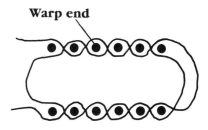

Closing both sides of your weaving will create a tube.

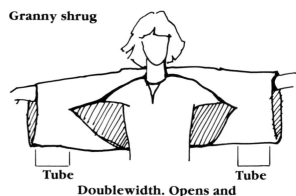
Granny shrug

Tube   Tube

Doublewidth. Opens and drapes over back.

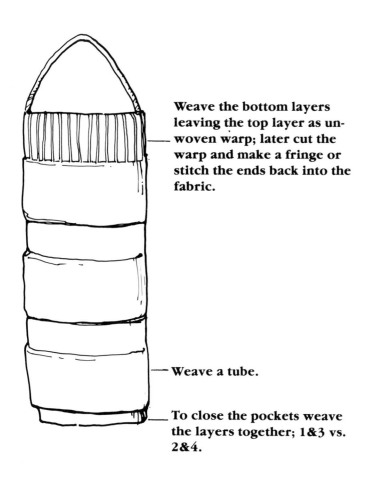

Weave the bottom layers leaving the top layer as unwoven warp; later cut the warp and make a fringe or stitch the ends back into the fabric.

Weave a tube.

To close the pockets weave the layers together; 1&3 vs. 2&4.

One pocket for a weed bag or stick shuttles.

An alternate threading

I told you I'd give you an alternate threading, so here it is. It's at the end so you can consider it when you want to.

A straight draw, which is easiest to thread, puts one layer on harnesses one and three, the other layer on two and four. This alternate threading is slightly more awkward (very slightly) and puts your layers on adjacent harnesses. One layer is now on harnesses one and two, the other one three and four.

For me, it is much easier to think about double weave if the harnesses next to each other work together. On a multiple tie-up floor loom it doesn't really matter much because once you've tied up the treadles, you don't need to think about individual harnesses anymore. But with table or direct tie-up looms you are always aware of individual harnesses. When I think of a layer on harnesses one and three and another on two and four, I feel like my mind is being split up. Thinking of layers on adjacent harnesses is so much more cohesive to me that I almost always use this threading.

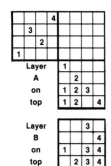

I have a real resistance to trying to keep lots of numbers in my head, probably because I'm not very good at it. For this reason, I plan my double weave projects by drawing very simple pictures or by building models out of paper. I do have a good mechanical sense, and can think of planes and surfaces, three dimensional shapes and how puzzles go together. So, for me, the fun of double weave is planning shapes, layers and connections. Having my layers on harnesses next to each other seems to make this process more unified and neater.

Use whichever threading method makes the most sense to you. Try both and see which you prefer.

Yarns

As always, your weft can be anything; it can change as often as you want a stripe. What to use for warp depends not only on what you're making, but on which form of double weave you'll be doing. If you are going to weave a whole piece as double-width or a tube where the layers are never going to switch places, then you don't need to be concerned with how easily they will pass by each other in the reed. The top layer of warp will always be above the bottom, and the space they share will be vertical which allows plenty of room.

If you plan to change layers, then the warp needs to be able to be crowded and yet be able to free itself again. For this, a smooth warp is far more cooperative than a sticky one. Hairy yarns grab onto each other and don't want to let go. A sticky double weave warp requires constant manual opening of the shed, using your hands to pull the yarn apart. It's a hassle, destroys any rhythm you might develop, and often makes your beat uneven. This doesn't mean not to use wool, but a brushed wool or mohair might spell disaster. If you want a fuzzy piece, use fuzzy weft, instead of warp.

As for color, if you use all one, then your piece will be all one color. If it's going to open out, as a blanket or shawl, then that may be desirable. Just be careful not to raise the wrong harness and weave your layers together; stick your hand in between the layers frequently to check. On your first sample consider using two colors, one for each layer, just to see clearly how it works.

Assignments

1. Put on a narrow warp and try all of the double weave options. Then, weave the rest of your warp off as a tube for a stuffed toy, a snake or a baseball bat.

2. Figure out how to weave a striped or plaid baby blanket doublewidth. Draw what you want to weave, then fold the paper in half.

3. Design a double layer saddle blanket or hanging for shuttles or wooden spoons.

4. What are some options for a shoulder bag? Tubular with no seams? Tubular with pockets woven in, seams necessary? Reversing layers for stripes? Others?

5. Weave a tubular pillow. Tie the two layers of warp together at the ends as a finish.

Notes

Lesson 11
Honeycomb

Size and shape of blocks
Color considerations
Uses for honeycomb

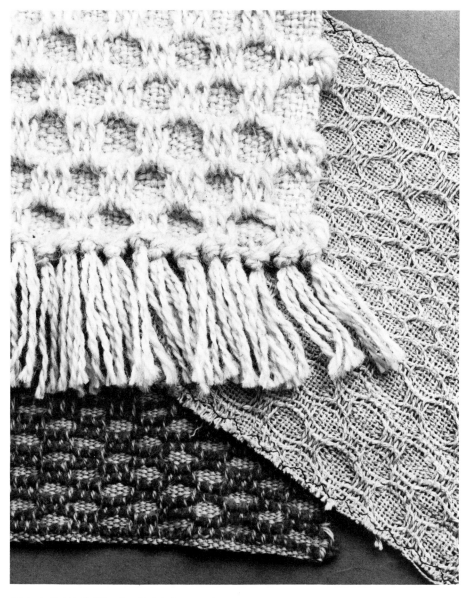

Fabrics by Debbie Redding, Jane Patrick, Betsy Holdsworth

Honeycomb, with its undulating weft, is the epitome of the theory that threads don't want to be woven, that when they can, they will try to escape. For the two-block honeycomb shown here, while one block weaves plain weave, the other block simply floats, so that you have warp floats crossing weft floats. To separate the blocks, and to provide stability, a heavy or outline weft is woven between the blocks. Because the threads need to relax in order for them to shift, most often you won't see the cells until you've removed the fabric from the loom. You can have a lot of fun playing around with color and thick and thin threads. Try different colored warp stripes each time the blocks switch, different colors of wefts for each line of cells, or experiment with very heavy or very thin outline wefts. Try using shiny yarns for the cells and a dull yarn for the outline weft, or vice versa. Keep in mind that understated, solid colored fabrics, in fine threads, can be very effective, too.

Honeycomb derives its name from its cellular structure which resembles a bee's honeycomb. There are many variations, the differences being in size and the patterning of cells. We're going to look at the most basic, a two-block honeycomb.

In the draft shown here it is easy to see that one section of warp will be on the first two harnesses, another section will be on the other two harnesses. These sections are called blocks. Block A is on harnesses one and two, block B on three and four. (Notice the capital letters. Blocks A and B are noted with uppercase letters; tabby a and b are lowercase letters.)

In two-block honeycomb, blocks A and B are alternately woven in plain weave. An outline or heavier weft separates the two blocks. If you look at the treadling and remember the double weave treadling, you'll see some similarities. When block A is being woven, harnesses one and two alternate (weaving tabby) and block B (harnesses three and four) is held up out of the way. When block B is being woven (harnesses three and four alternate) block A is held up. While the principle of lifting threads up out of the way is similar to double weave, the results are completely different. In honeycomb the blocks are threaded next to each other, as opposed to layers above and below each other as in double weave. (The reason I'm pointing this out is that I want you to be aware of how some practices and principles apply to different weaves. The more you understand in generalities the easier it will be to learn new weaves and to adapt what you know to what you want. There are probably no weaving rules that apply in only one case; all of the information gets used in many forms in a kind of mix-and-match that creates new results by rearranging old principles.)

There are two weft shots labelled 'H' in the treadling. The H stands for heavy weft yarn, or honeycomb outline. In the photo of honeycomb you can see cells in the fabric outlined by heavier, curving or flexing weft. Those are H shots. While most of the weft is woven into block A or B, H is woven as a tabby that goes through both blocks. The curving which you see results from the woven cells pushing that weft into the unwoven areas above and below them. Block A pushes H up, block B pushes it down, and the result is a curving around the cells. For this reason honeycomb is one of the weaves in the family called deflected weft weaves.

Many weaves have an added dimension that comes from the threads not being straight all the time, and while most do not flex as much as in honeycomb, the principle is the same. It's another generality to understand. (It was initially taught to me as one of the first principles of weaving: threads don't want to be woven, and when they can escape they will.) Deflected wefts (or warps)

Honeycomb draft.
The 'H' represents the outline or heavier weft.

are straight when woven, but curve when the tension is released, and they can respond to the pushing and pulling of threads around them.

Size and shape of blocks

The blocks of honeycomb can be threaded as wide or narrow as you want, and woven as tall or short as you want. As you are weaving, you need to be sure to throw outline shot(s) between each block to hold the fabric together and to provide stability. It doesn't have to be heavier, but it shows up better if it is. These three elements, block A, block B, and honeycomb outline wefts, work together to make the cellular shapes of honeycomb.

While blocks can be any size, there are some factors you need to be aware of. First, notice in the draft that one block is woven at a time. While one block is being woven in tabby, the other block isn't being woven at all. In this block you simply have warp floats floating over weft floats. The woven block is stable because it's being woven; the block not being woven is very unstable because it's all floats. If your blocks are large, the floats will be long, and the longer they are the weaker your fabric will be. A successful honeycomb needs to be planned around this factor.

On the other hand, if your honeycomb is very small, you won't have the predominant cellular structure which is so characteristic of honeycomb. Also, you want your honeycomb outline weft to be flexible. A heavy, very stiff weft won't have room to curve, especially if the cells are very small. How small is too small depends on the yarns you are using and your warp sett. Experiment with different sized cells and different yarns and see what you like. As a starting point I'll suggest keeping your blocks less than an inch wide, weaving them less than an inch tall. Half an inch cells are quite sufficient. If you are using fat yarns then you'll probably want bigger cells.

Color considerations

How you use color with your honeycomb can be a lot of fun. You can thread block A one color, block B another, weave each block with its own color, and use a third color for your heavy outline weft. Or you can have all your warp one color and weave each new row of blocks with another color. In this case, you could have your honeycomb outline weft match the warp and be more subtle. You could have it change as the blocks do, or use it as an accent color and outline the color changes. On the understated side, some of the most beautiful honeycombs I've seen have been all one color, texture being the focus of those.

Uses for honeycomb

A tightly woven honeycomb can be quite sturdy and can have a wide variety of uses. Pillows, bags, clothing, and blankets can be easily woven in honeycomb. A heavy fabric with heavy outline weft will not have as smooth a surface as you would want for a placemat or tablecloth. Honeycomb with its ridges of outline weft generally make it a poor choice for upholstery because the raised yarns will wear out before the rest of the fabric. Honeycomb can be used to produce a tough or gentle fabric, depending on how tightly you weave it. This is usually more crucial than what yarns you use. Your warp and weft can be the same yarns or different ones, the cells balanced or not, oblong or more circular. Because honeycomb has so much versatility you can use any yarn or fiber; choose according to the project you have in mind.

These are the basics of honeycomb. Variations you'll find will be honeycombs with more blocks which have overlapping cells. Those can be lots of fun, too. You will still need to keep in mind the proportions of tabby areas to float areas appropriate to the degree of stability you want. As you try some honeycomb you'll learn the differences and find out what will work.

Assignments to expand and add to

1. Make a one color warp and use a variety of wefts to weave the cells/blocks. Use several heavy wefts of differing textures to see which curve best. Remember the flexing probably won't happen until you release the tension. You can do this while the warp is still on the loom just by releasing your brake.

2. Try a multi-colored warp. Alternate colors within blocks or make stripes that correspond to blocks.

3. Put on a sample warp that has blocks in ever increasing sizes. For instance, start with four threads per block, then six, eight, and so on up to 20. Weave the sample with the same gradation, and when it's done, study it to see what works and what doesn't and why. Take measurements on the loom, off the loom, and after washing. That flexing outline weft may draw the piece in a lot.

Lesson 12
Harness Controlled Lace Weaves

The lace unit
Blocks
Threading
Tabby
Weaving it
Yarn choices
Sett
Color
Heddles

Lace weaves have a lot to offer. You can use them for a variety of different projects, such as curtains, blankets, placemats, blouse fabrics, or shawls; they are equally suited to heavy- and light-weight fabrics. Lace is effective used all over as in the two bottom fabrics shown here, or in blocks as in the top fabric. Explore texture, color, yarns; experiment with lace stripes, borders and checks.

Fabrics by Lisa Budwig, Bethany Thomas, The Weaving Shop.

A lace weave is one in which there are open spaces in the fabric. There are many ways to achieve such an effect, including finger manipulation of the warp, leaving empty dents in the reed, and weaving a pattern that causes some threads to group together, leaving gaps where they were before they grouped. The last of these is what this lesson is about.

Swedish lace, Atwater-Bronson lace, mock leno, huck-a-buck, barleycorn and canvas weave are names of weaves in the lace weave family. Some of these are identical, some have only slight differences, some can be distinguished very easily. One pattern may have different names in different books, and the same name may have a different pattern in different books. When you want more information on lace, look in books under all these names.

The one we're going to learn goes by three names that I know of: Atwater-Bronson lace, Swedish lace, and 5/1/5 mock leno. In the more traditional books it is called Atwater-Bronson lace because of the threading we're going to use, but the structure of all three is virtually the same.

1 Unit
A single unit of lace structure takes three harnesses.

The lace unit

Atwater-Bronson lace is a two-block weave which is structured in such a way that some threads group together, leaving spaces or windows in the fabric. The combination of threads grouping and spaces being left is what creates the lace. This is the same escape principle which we found in honeycomb: when a thread is allowed to escape, it will.

One unit of lace is six threads and takes three harnesses. It looks like a tic-tac-toe game plus one thread on the side. In this drawing there is still one more thread drawn in just to balance the draft. If you have only one isolated unit you won't get the lacey effect characteristic of this weave, you'll get a "spot". Lace appears where there are several units together, separated by only one thread, a dividing or tie-down thread.

Blocks

Lace is formed when there are several units together.

At left are two units of block A (one unit of block A = 1,3,1,3,1,2). What's so neat about this weave is that if you wanted to, you could thread this same block over and over, across your whole warp width, and weave it for your entire warp length. If you did this you could have lace all over. On the other hand, if you wanted to have blocks of lace, you could thread a second block, block B (one unit of block B = 1,4,1,4,1,2). Block B will look exactly like block A; the only difference is that they will weave at different times.

The threading for block B is the same as block A, except that where you used harness three in block A, you use harness four in block B.

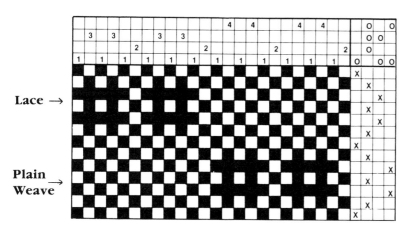

By using two blocks you can get lace in some areas, plain weave in others.

Threading

What makes this lace so simple to comprehend and design is that no matter where you want the lace to appear, harnesses one and two are always doing the same thing. Harness one is called the ground harness, harness two the tie down harness.

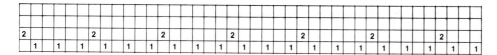

Every other thread across the entire warp is on harness one; it provides the ground or stabilizing factor for all else going on. The threads between each unit of lace are all on harness two. Look at the previous lace drafts again and notice that the horizontal lines of the tic tac toe pattern represent five adjacent warps raised at once. That tells you that there is a weft float on the other side floating under/across those five warps. The dividing thread, the thread on harness two, serves to tie those floats down. It is the only time those wefts quit floating. Thus harness two is called the tie down harness, and every sixth thread needs to be on it.

Harnesses three and four (and any more you have) are your pattern harnesses. Remember that each unit must be six threads wide, or is composed of the threads between those threaded on harness two. You can put your lace blocks in any pattern you want. Just fill in the rest of the draft with threes and fours. How many you use before changing is determined by how wide you want your blocks to be.

														4	4			4	4											
3		3			3		3			3		3										3		3				3		3
			2					2					2				2				2					2				2
1		1		1		1		1		1		1		1		1		1		1		1		1		1		1		

Tabby

Up to now, most of the time when you've wanted to weave tabby, you did so by raising harnesses one and three, then two and four. That was because regardless of the actual sequence you were threading, you went from an odd numbered harness to an even numbered harness. Raising all the odds (one and three) gave you every other thread, the evens (two and four) every other thread. Look at these threading sequences if that's not quite clear.

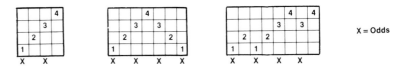

X = Odds

This time, however, you are not threading odd-even-odd-even. Since every other thread is on harness one, tabby a will come by raising harness one alone, tabby b by raising all of the other harnesses at once.

Weaving it

Now look at the large draft showing both blocks and two sides of the lace. As we've talked about before, when there are warp floats on one side, there are weft floats on the other side. While it is the spaces or openings between the lace units that give the lace effect, the presence of warp or weft floats is very much a part of the overall look of this weave. Not always, but on most pieces you'll like one side or the other better. And if your warp is one color, your weft a second color, the two sides will have different colors predominating. You can weave with either the warp or the weft floats toward you, or some of each; just change your treadling according to which you want.

Look at the treadling on the draft. To a great extent it's as regular as the threading. Harnesses one and two are being raised alternately the whole time, regardless of what the pattern harnesses are doing. When you want a lace block woven with warp floats, keep its pattern harness up for five shots, the height of the lace unit. When you want a lace block woven with weft floats, keep the appropriate pattern harness(es) down for five shots. The pattern harness not being used for lace is raised with harness two, and by that, all areas that are not lace are tabby, a good, solid, inconspicuous background.

You can weave block A alone, block B alone, both blocks at the same time, or neither. With this draft, if you want a vertical area to be tabby all of the time with no lace at all in it, you can thread this block on harnesses one and two, no pattern harnesses required. Because your treadling is always alternating harnesses one and two, it can't help but have tabby all of the time. (Remember though, this works on this draft, not on other lace drafts; you cannot combine two threadings and expect only one result. When in doubt, do a draw-down.)

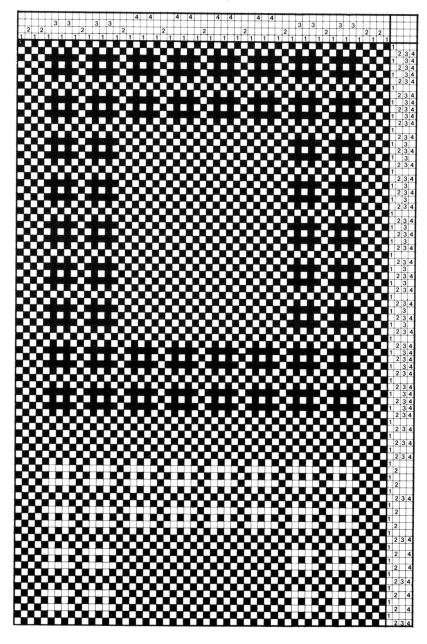

Some lace designs

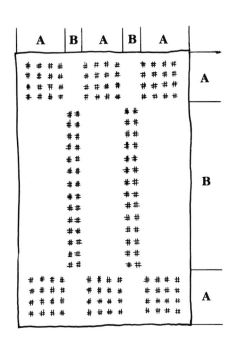

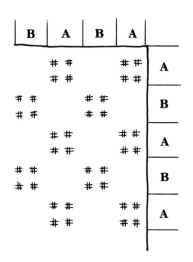

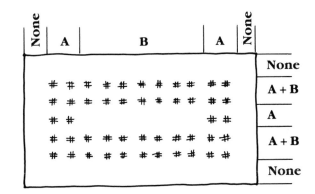

Lace Threading:
Block A 1,3,1,3,1,2
Block B 1,4,1,4,1,2

Yarn choices

Because you are trying to create openings, and the openings occur when the yarns slide together, the harder, crisper, and smoother your yarn, the more the lace will open up. If you're weaving a scarf or shawl, you won't want a hard yarn, so go with a smooth soft yarn. (One of the prettiest lace pieces I've seen was woven with alpaca, about as far from crisp as you can get.) The texture of the weave is pretty, and most of the time the openness of the lace actually is not important. Curtains are a nice way to use lace, for they let in lots of light but still afford privacy. In this case you will want the openings to be open. About the only yarns that will really defeat lace are very hairy or very bumpy yarns, e.g., brushed wool or mohair, heavily textured novelties.

Sett

Your warp sett is at least as important as your yarn choice. Often a major portion of a lace weave is actually tabby, and that is what to gauge your sett by. A balanced tabby will give a balanced lace as well, which is definitely desirable—weft-faced lace weaves won't be lacey. But, you can weave a balanced tabby very tightly or very loosely or somewhere in between. If you want your lace to be fairly open, aim for a looser tabby. If you have only one reed, one that gives you a nice medium balanced tabby with the yarn you've chosen, but you want a little more openness in your lace, leave an empty dent between each threading unit, i.e., to the right or left of each tie down thread (thread on harness two). That will give a little more space where you want it.

Color

Lace weaves have a wide range of color options even without getting complicated. When the warp and the weft are the same the lace structure itself is what is most visible, for nothing about the color pulls your attention away. Using a slightly different shade for one will add some depth without being distracting. Likewise, a heathery yarn will have depth where solid colored yarns look flat.

If you want to use more than one color you can thread each block with its own color, then weave with one and get warp stripes or with two and get a more checkered effect. Or you can have the threads on harness two, those dividing the lace units, be a contrasting color from all of the rest. The result will be a kind of overall check with the lace units bordered by the contrasting thread. As you weave, use your base color for most of your weft, your contrasting thread for the weft shot that divides the units vertically (harness one by itself, between blocks).

How you plan your colors will be determined in part by how you plan your blocks and overall design. Draw out a simple sketch of where you want your lace to appear on your piece, then plan your colors accordingly. The drawings on the previous page will show you more how to do that. If your colors change in the middle of your lace units, they will compete with each other and the lace will be obscured.

Heddles

One last thing, or first, to remember. Half of your warp is threaded on harness one. That means you'll need a lot of heddles on that harness. Usually heddles are divided evenly, with each harness having the same number. And usually you have more than you need. You may have enough heddles on harness one for whatever you plan, especially if you have a wide loom and a narrow project. But count before you start threading because it's much easier to move heddles before you've begun threading. If you must move some heddles, and it seems like a major hassle, turn to page 209 to get some ideas for making it easy.

Assignments

1. Plan and weave a lace sample with three monochromatic colors, each for approximately ⅓ of the width. Weave it using the same three colors, the idea being to see which color combinations you like best and why. Have warp floats on top, then weft floats on top. If you have both types on the same side of the sample, you don't have to flip it back and forth to see the differences, which is nice if you mount it on a record sheet or bulletin board.

2. Plan (and weave?) a set of placemats all using lace but each with a different arrangement of blocks.

3. I once wove a set of curtains for a living room that had just been carpeted. I planned carefully, wove samples, matched the colors with the new carpet, and when they were done they looked magnificent on the carpet. Unfortunately they were hanging next to the wall and against the wall they almost disappeared because the colors were so close. See if you can plan a set of curtains better than I did. The lace, by the way, worked very well for letting the light in.

4. Design a summer top, with lace sleeves or lace across the bodice. Draw pictures of pattern pieces as you'll weave them to plan where your lace areas need to fall.

5. Do you like sets of things? A set of things for the kitchen, all in lace weaves, could include curtains, dishtowels, dishrags, placemats, table runners, tablecloths, napkins, aprons, a wall hanging and a bread basket cover. For the living room you could weave an afghan, pillows, curtains, cabinet scarves or a wall hanging. Some projects would require different yarns than others, but a feeling of unity can easily be maintained if the colors and patterns are similar. Plan two warps that will give you related products, both in lace weaves, of course.

Lesson 13
Block Theory

Block patterns
Profile drafts

Fabrics by Audrey Kick, Jane Patrick, Judy Steinkoenig, Yvonne Stahl

Blocks apply to many weave structures. Here are a few examples of some of the possibilities. From the top, working clockwise, are samples of lace weave, double weave, double binding and overshot. One exercise which you might find instructive, as well as intriguing, is to make up a block pattern and try to weave it in a couple of weave structures. Up to this point you've woven one block weave which lends itself to this kind of interpretation; summer and winter, in the next lesson, is another one.

In the last two lessons you planned your threading partly according to how wide you wanted blocks A and B to be. In honeycomb the threading unit for block A is 1,2, repeated as many times as desired. For block B the threading unit is 3,4, repeated. In Atwater-Bronson lace, the threading unit for block A is 1,3,1,3,1,2; for block B it's 1,4,1,4,1,2. Every weave has its own threading unit, and units may be repeated as often or for as wide as you want a block to be. Threads combine to make up units, units combine to make up blocks, blocks combine to make up overall patterns.

Let me give you some more examples, which you don't need to understand yet.

Threading Units				
Weave	Block A	Block B	Block C	Block D
2-Block honeycomb	1,2	3,4	——	——
4-Block honeycomb	1,2	2,3	3,4	4,1
Atwater-Bronson lace	1,3,1,3,1,2	1,4,1,4,1,2	1,5,1,5,1,2	1,6,1,6,1,2
Summer and winter	1,3,2,3	1,4,2,4	1,5,2,5	1,6,2,6
Overshot	1,2	2,3	3,4	4,1
Twill blocks	1,2,3,4	5,6,7,8	9,10,11,12	13,14,15,16
Double weave blocks	1,2,3,4	5,6,7,8	9,10,11,12	13,14,15,16
Ripsmatta	1,2	3,4	5,6	7,8

As you can see, each weave above has its own threading unit. Sometimes some harnesses are shared as in Atwater-Bronson lace, summer and winter, and overshot. Sometimes each block gets all its own harnesses. The point is, when you are designing block patterns you are not yet concerned with how many harnesses are needed or whether or not you can weave something. For the time being forget about harnesses, threading, treadling and weaving. It's cut and paste time.

Block patterns

Think about the overall pattern you'd see in a fabric if you were standing far enough away that you couldn't see the weave structure. These illustrations can be thought of as block patterns. Some are balanced or squared in that they look the same no matter which way you turn them.

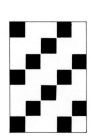
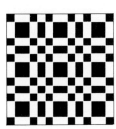

From these illustrations or block patterns, it is a simple matter to determine how many blocks a given pattern has. In the same way you determined how many harnesses a cloth diagram used, you can now determine the number of blocks used. Each vertical column is a block, and each one that has pattern areas filled in in the same places is the same block. Each one that is different is another block. The pattern of the column is of no significance at this point, only its similarity to other columns. Look at these illustrations and trace the columns to remind yourself how this works.

Block Patterns

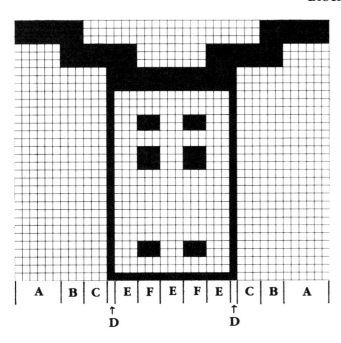

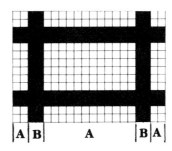

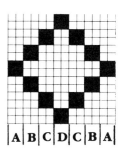

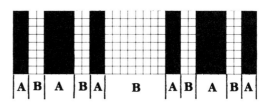

To find out which blocks to combine to build a pattern you'll do the same as you did to find out how to treadle a particular cloth diagram. Consider the black areas as the pattern being created on a white background. To create the pattern at right you'll need to first weave block B alone, then A and B together, then B alone again, then A and B, then finish up with B alone. Remember that we are not yet concerned with whether or not it is possible to weave this, rather how to create the design.

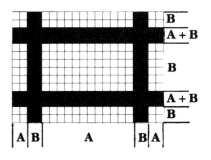

Combine blocks to build a pattern

Profile drafts

A profile draft can be called the threading draft of a block diagram. This moose, which is different from the first moose, requires eight blocks, seven for the moose and one more for the borders on the sides. The profile draft underneath the moose shows the block sequence, including both changes and width of blocks. To thread from a profile draft you insert the chosen threading unit for the block shown, repeating it as many times as necessary for the block's width. Let's translate part of the moose's profile draft into a couple of threadings, just to see how it works.

Block A is four squares wide, so whatever weave structure's threading unit you choose it needs to be repeated four times. For simplicity let's use Atwater-Bronson lace, since you know how it works, and summer and winter since it's the next lesson.

As you know, to thread block A in Atwater-Bronson lace you thread 1,3,1,3,1,2. In summer and winter you thread 1,3,2,3. Block A is four squares wide, so the threading unit needs to be repeated four times. Block B is two squares wide, so you'd need to repeat the threading sequence twice; 1,4,1,4,1,2 for lace, 1,4,2,4 for summer and winter. Look at the threadings below.

Profile draft of the moose above.

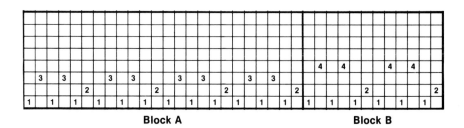

Block A   Block B

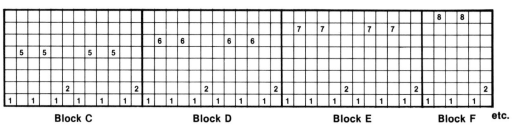

Block C   Block D   Block E   Block F   etc.

Atwater-Bronson Lace

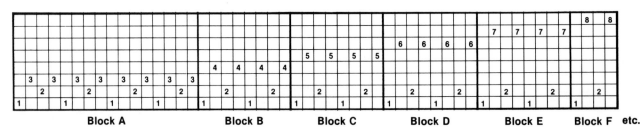

Block A   Block B   Block C   Block D   Block E   Block F   etc.

Summer & Winter

174

You can insert any threading unit into any block pattern that easily. These two happen to be very similar and require the same number of harnesses; not all will. Also, not all weaves work well with all patterns.

The honeycomb you wove relies on alternating A and B blocks in order for the honeycomb pattern to show. You can't weave two blocks together in a two block honeycomb and still get honeycomb; you'd have plain weave instead. With lace, however, that's no problem; you can weave as many or as few blocks together as you want.

This is a very basic discussion of block theory. You'll understand it more as you learn more weaves and see how blocks apply. I will give you the next stages of this in small doses, within the following lessons, as they apply.

For your reference, now and later, here is a two block design shown in profile draft, block diagram, and full thread-by-thread drafts and draw-downs for both Atwater-Bronson lace and summer and winter.

Profile Draft

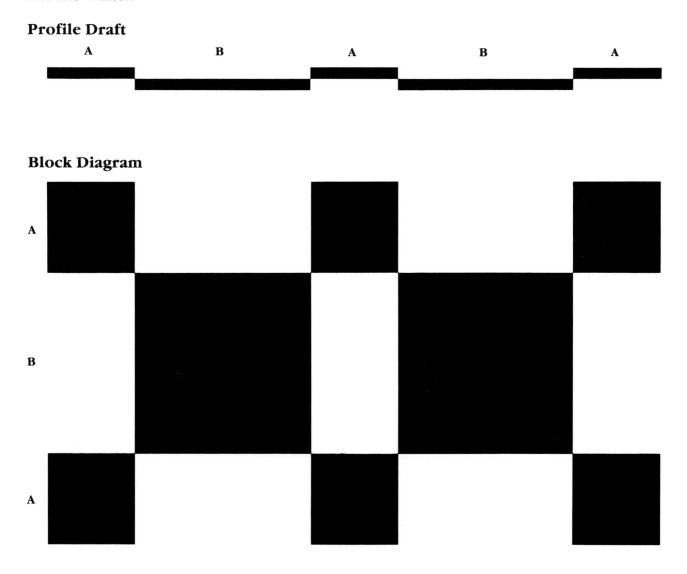

Block Diagram

Atwater-Bronson Lace

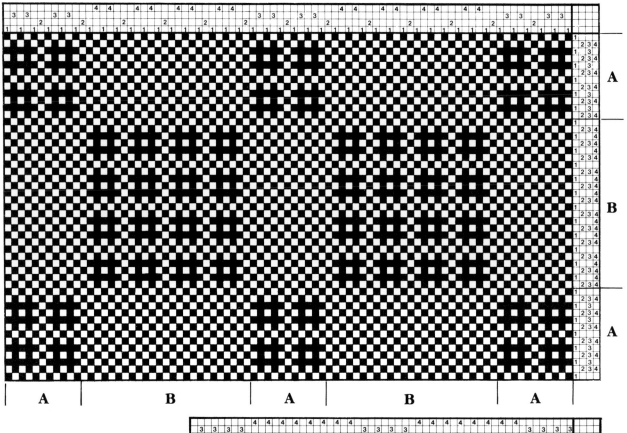

Summer & Winter

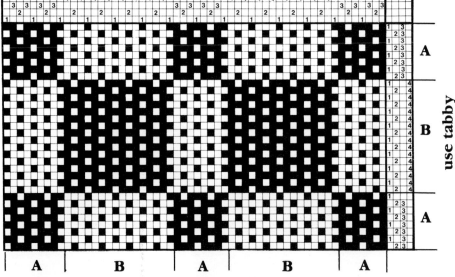

Your assignments

1. Using graph paper draw some block designs you find interesting and then make a profile draft from your block pattern. Using the chart at the beginning of the section, which weaves could you do in the design you've drawn with the number of harnesses you have? (For now don't be concerned with which ones would actually work.)

2. Design a block pattern and weave it in Atwater-Bronson lace. Would your design work for a two block honeycomb?

Lesson 14
Summer and Winter

The basics of summer and winter
Using two wefts
Yarn and color choices
Treadling summer and winter
Variations
Uses

Fabrics by Lisa Budwig, Bethany Thomas, The Weaving Shop.

Summer and winter is a versatile block weave. As in Atwater-Bronson lace, the blocks can be as wide and long as you wish to make them. Two wefts (requiring two shuttles), a pattern weft and a tabby or background weft, are needed to weave summer and winter. Notice in the samples shown here that both the background weft and pattern weft are integral parts of the pattern. That is, the pattern weft predominates in some blocks, the background weft in others. This allows much for the imagination!

Top threading draft:

				4	4	4	4				4	4	4	4					
3	3	3	3						3	3					3	3	3	3	3
2		2		2		2		2		2		2		2		2		2	
1		1		1		1		1		1		1		1		1		1	

Summer & winter

The basics of summer and winter

'Summer and winter is one of my favorite weaves because it is easy to design and the fabric has great versatility. It is both stable and durable. Once you've woven one summer and winter (from here on s&w) piece, you'll find it's easy to understand, and it has so many variations it's unlikely that you'll ever exhaust the possibilities. As always, I'm going to give you the basics, and if you decide you like this weave, you can get more information from numerous other books.

Like the lace weave you just learned, s&w has two harnesses whose threading remains constant from block to block, and two harnesses that take care of the pattern blocks. In s&w every other thread is alternately threaded on harnesses one and two, consequently they are called ground harnesses, each acting as a tie down harness. Like the lace, you can start a draft by drawing in the ones and twos because they are always the same, and after that, you can add the threes and fours where you want your pattern blocks to be.

In summer & winter the ground harnesses are threaded on harnesses 1 & 2. They remain constant from block to block.

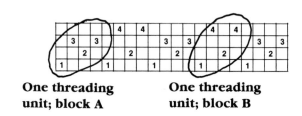

One threading unit; block A   **One threading unit; block B**

A threading unit for s&w is 1,3,2,3 or 1,4,2,4. Your blocks can be any width from one unit on up. Again, you can weave any two-block pattern. And now that you already have some experience with block drafting and how to use block diagrams, here is an assortment of two-block patterns which will work for s&w, as well as other block weaves.

Some two-block diagrams

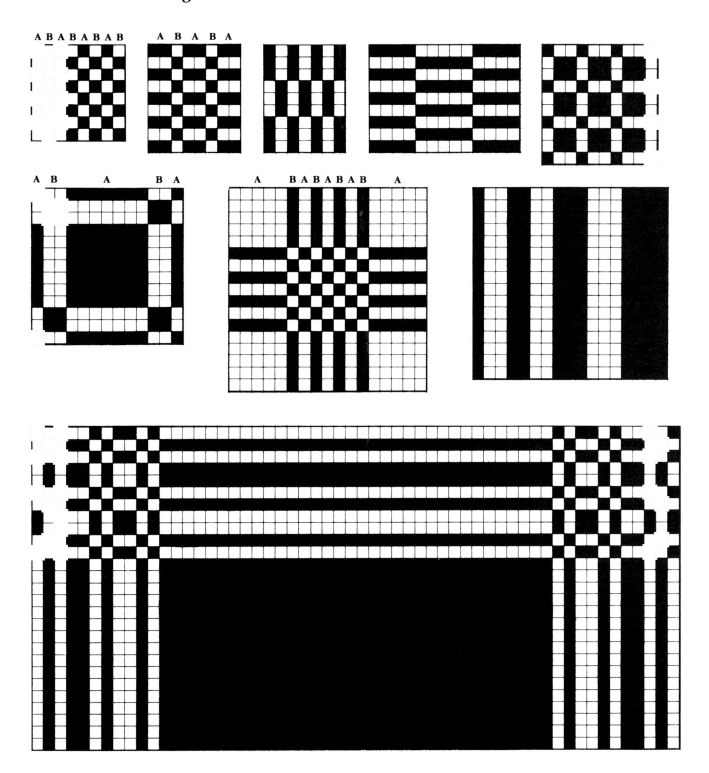

Using two wefts

The treadling for s&w is where we begin to get into the new things for you to learn.

Summer and winter uses two wefts, a pattern weft and a tabby weft. The two are used alternately throughout the whole piece: tabby, pattern, tabby, pattern, etc. The pattern treadling will vary according to which blocks you are weaving. The tabby weft *always* weaves tabby, regardless of what the pattern is doing. In most books the draft gives only the treadling for the pattern weft because that is what changes. For tabby it will only say "use tabby". It may not even say that, just expecting you to know you are supposed to.

As you know, to weave tabby you alternately raise every other thread. Look at the threading draft. Every other thread is on harnesses one and two, and all the others are on three and four. Therefore, you can raise harnesses one and two for tabby a, three and four for tabby b. Put in your mind that your tabby a weft will always go through shed 1-2, then a pattern weft, then tabby b (3-4), pattern, tabby a, pattern, tabby b, pattern, etc. With two shuttles going and a constantly changing pattern weft, it is practically impossible to remember which tabby shot you threw last. So, determine which shed is open when the shuttle is going right to left and know that the other needs to be open when the shuttle goes left to right. From then on the direction the shuttle is going will tell you which shed to open.

The purpose of weaving tabby is to provide a ground fabric under the pattern that makes the whole fabric stable. By using a tabby ground, consecutive pattern shots can change or repeat in the same shed, depending on the pattern desired. If tabby is not used, weaving a lot of shots into the same shed over and over can make a weak fabric structure since there are few intersections of warp and weft.

Yarn and color choice

In s&w the tabby is also an integral part of the design. When you raise the harnesses to have block A be an area with the pattern weft predominating, block B will be an area with the tabby background as the strong design element. For this reason, color is very important. You have three yarn elements in s&w: warp, tabby weft, and pattern weft. For the pattern to show off to its maximum, the warp and tabby weft should be the same color (and often the same yarn); the pattern weft should be another color and a somewhat fatter yarn. How much fatter depends on the quality or style of the yarn you choose. If the yarn is soft and fluffy, it can be as much as three or four times fatter; if it's a hard twist yarn, it would probably be better if it is only twice as fat. Try several wefts on your first sample so you can see and feel the differences yourself.

For a softer visual effect use a tabby weft of a color that falls between the other two. If you use three very contrasting colors, you are likely to lose a lot of your pattern. The tabby is meant to be background, and several strong color choices will compete and obscure all the work you're doing. That can be okay, but what do you want it to look like?

As long as we're talking about yarn now, let's discuss warp sett. When a s&w piece is done, if you pulled all of the pattern wefts out you would (ideally) have a balanced tabby fabric left. In order to do this, you would need to weave your fabric in such a way that you are actually putting in twice as many wefts per inch as you have warps per inch. For instance, if you set up a cotton carpet warp at 12 e.p.i., you'll weave in 12 pattern wefts and 12 tabby wefts per inch, 24 shots altogether. Sometimes it seems hard to believe that you can get all that in there, but the pattern weft doesn't take up as much space as it would seem because it is sliding on top of the tabby weft next to it most of the time. So pick a warp sett that is approximately what you would for a balanced tabby, or maybe slightly looser.

Treadling

In terms of durability, one of the big advantages of s&w is that no weft ever passes over more than three warps before it is tied down again. (This is perhaps the greatest difference between s&w and overshot, which are often confused because both are traditional coverlet weaves. With overshot, however, weft floats can be very long and can snag easily. More on this in the next lesson.) In s&w the even distribution of the warps threaded on harnesses one and two, which act as tie down threads, is the reason the pattern floats aren't longer. To weave a pattern shot one of the ground harnesses is raised plus whichever pattern harnesses are desired. Harnesses one and two are raised alternately, and a full treadling unit (comparable to a threading unit) consists of harness one plus pattern(s), tabby a, harness two plus pattern(s), tabby b. For a block to show up at all the pattern harness(es) raised throughout the treadling unit need to be the same. With this information you can now make up any treadling you want to try. Look at the draft.

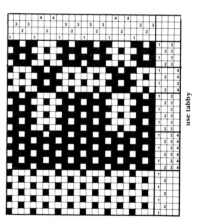

A full treadling unit is: harness one plus pattern(s), tabby a, harness two plus pattern(s), and tabby b.
Tabby a = harnesses one and two.
Tabby b = harnesses three and four.

Here's a summary of all we've talked about with regard to treadling. Only the pattern shot treadlings are noted. Part of the reason for this is with just the pattern shots drawn in, it will look more like what the fabric will actually look like than if the tabby shots were drawn in also. Since the tabby shots are relatively obscure in the actual fabric, drawing them in will throw the proportions of the draw-down way off.

Remember that the draw-down shows warps as *filled in boxes*, so the blackest areas are those in which the warp is mostly raised. The pattern weft will predominate in the blocks where the draw-down looks whiter.

Harnesses one and two alternate with every pattern shot; three and four are raised as needed for pattern blocks.

Summer and winter may be so named because the two sides look opposite from each other. What appears black on one side, is white on the other side, and vice versa. If your pattern is evenly divided between blocks A and B, then the two sides will be fairly balanced. Block A predominates on one side, block B on the other. One of the stories that goes with summer and winter weave is that the dark side of a summer and winter bedspread faces out in the winter, the light side in the summer. To have a significant difference in sides, your blocks need to be unbalanced. Look at the assortment of two block patterns at the beginning of the chapter again, and think about which would look approximately the same on both sides. Which ones would have two sides that appeared as different colors?

For the basics of s&w, that's about it. In summary then, choose a warp yarn that will make a good visual background (smooth and solid colored). Set it for a balanced tabby, perhaps slightly looser than normal. Thread your warp according to one of the drafts shown or one you make up from your own block pattern. You'll have two wefts, one the same as the warp (or close to it) to use as tabby weft, the other fatter and of another color or texture to use as your pattern weft. You can use a treadling from a draft or make up your own. The tabby shots will always intersperse the pattern shots, alternating one and two vs. three and four. (You'll know which one to throw by looking at the direction the shuttle is going.)

Variations

The lesson up to this point has been for what is called "weaving singly". You can also weave s&w "in pairs", a phrase referring to the pattern shots. You will still alternate tabby, pattern, tabby, pattern, but this time, instead of alternating the ground harnesses with each pattern shot, you'll repeat them once. For example, instead of weaving 1-4, 2-4, 1-4, 2-4, you'd weave 1-4, 1-4, 2-4,

2-4, 1-4, 1-4, 2-4, 2-4, alternating tabbies a and b between each pattern pick. The effect is a blockier pattern and stronger color. It

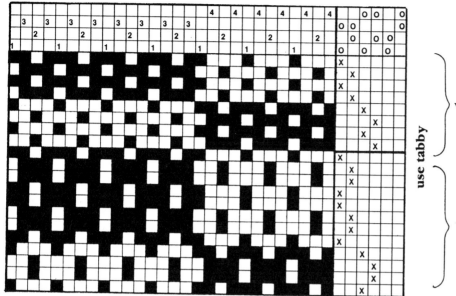

weaving singly

use tabby

weaving in pairs

The point at which you change blocks in your treadling will alter the appearance of your pattern as illustrated here.

also changes the background design. Look at the draft for how it works, then try it on your sample.

The other thing I want you to know is that you can start and stop your treadling units at any point, and which treadlings you choose will affect what the pattern looks like on the corners where the blocks connect. The differences can be quite surprising, so try them all. Some examples are at right. Look at the treadling changes and block corners. Woven in pairs, these will have even more variations.

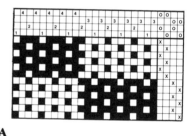

A

B

C

Uses

I've said repeatedly that s&w is versatile, but I've not mentioned many uses. For a lightweight fabric it could be used for a whole piece of clothing; more often s&w is used as a border design with most of the garment being tabby. As a border, s&w can be a beautiful accent on elegant towels, table linens, cheery curtains, scarves, shawls, blankets, etc. As a border or the whole fabric it is sturdy enough for pillows, shoulder bags, backpacks, upholstery. It made a durable coverlet fabric during our colonial days and still does.

I must admit that part of why I like s&w so much is that I have eight harnesses, and like lace, with two harnesses for ground harnesses I then have six for pattern blocks. With six pattern blocks I can make many, many designs: stars, animals, letters, flowers, and many others. I try hard not to make anyone think they *need* eight harnesses, for there are thousands of things possible with four. But it is also true that if you like drafting and making up patterns, you are likely to enjoy having eight harnesses. Lace and s&w are perfect weaves to show how easy it is to use the other four.

Assignments

1. Put on a sample with blocks of varying widths. Treadle to get block A alone, block B alone, blocks A and B together, and no blocks on the surface. Go through this sequence with at least two different pattern wefts, woven singly and in pairs. Then, alternate from block A to B and back again, trying each of the corner variations shown on page 183.

2. Set up a warp with blocks one threading unit wide, and repeat these for several inches. Surround these by wider blocks. Then, treadle a variety of patterns, including a sequence to match the threading sequence.

   In older books you'll find only the profile draft given for s&w, nothing else. It may be called a "short draft". The intent is for you to treadle according to the threading pattern. This is called "tromp as writ" or "weave as drawn in". To do so, weave as many pattern shots as there are warp threads in the block, throwing 1-3, 2-3, etc. for the pattern block on harness three, 1-4, 2-4 for the block threaded on harness four.

3. Try using pattern wefts of varying thicknesses. If you use a very fat pattern weft, try using a skinnier tabby weft to balance it. See how it affects the look of the pattern. Then, try a slightly fatter tabby weft, and see what that does.

4. Plan a bedspread. Weave a sample or two (or more) to find out if the fabric you are thinking of would be a good weight for a bedspread you'd like. Will your bedspread be primarily for decoration, or is it intended to keep you warm? (Do you live in Bangor or Atlanta?) Does it need to be machine washable, dog or kid proof? Do you want a design with seams down the middle or down the sides where it is likely to be inconspicuous? How big does your sample need to be to get an accurate idea of weight and drape? Do you want something subtle or flashy?

5. Design a set of s&w pillows that are all woven on the same warp, but which have different treadlings so that each pillow has a different design.

Lesson 15
Overshot

The pattern blocks and threading
Tying up the treadles for tabby
Yarns and related information
Miscellaneous notes
Wrap up

Overshot, with its overlapping blocks, brings curves and circles to your weaving repertoire. Try it for borders on skirts, placemats, or dishtowels; use it all over for pillows, seat cushions or table runners. This is a good one for exploring pattern and color.

Fabrics by Lynda Short, The Weaving Shop

This is the last lesson in this book, and it is a compilation of many of the things you've learned already. A few things will be new, but mostly you'll be drawing on previous lessons. The patterns of overshot intrigue people because they look so complicated, but in fact, the ingredients are all very basic. You should have little or no problem understanding what's going on.

Overshot is a twill derivative where the blocks often follow a twill sequence. Part of the fun of overshot is that now you have four blocks to design with instead of only two. The treadling is the same as that for a 2/2 twill, but with even more variations available. Like summer and winter, overshot requires two shuttles, one for tabby and another for pattern. Therefore, it has the same considerations for relative yarn weights, sett and beat, and color choice. Let's start at the beginning.

The pattern blocks and threading

On four harnesses, overshot has four blocks available. The threading unit for block A is 1,2 for block B it's 2,3, block C it's 3,4, block D it's 4,1. Notice that blocks share harnesses, but not in the same way that lace and summer and winter did. There are no separate ground harnesses in overshot; all harnesses work as both ground and pattern harnesses. The sharing of harnesses from block to block causes a slight overlapping, which makes it possible to have curves in patterns. Whereas most summer and winter designs are fairly geometric, many overshot patterns utilize circles and curves.

Let's look at some block patterns first, then translate them into threading.

This is a very simple block pattern, one in which it is easy to see that overshot is related to twill. Not all overshot patterns are this twill-like, but many are.

In order for overshot to work, the threading must always go from odd to even or even to odd harnesses (this is necessary to be able to weave tabby, which we'll discuss more later). So, to get from block A (thread 1,2) to block B (thread 2,3), requires the addition or subtraction of one thread to break the 2,2 (two evens together) pairing that would exist otherwise. So, the transition threading from block A to block B would *not* be 1,2,2,3 but rather, 1,2,1,2,3, or just 1,2,3, depending on whether

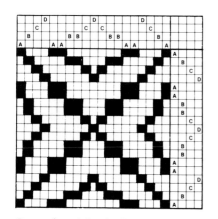

Overshot block diagram

you add or drop a thread. If you consistently add a thread all the
way across, the threading for the above draft will be:

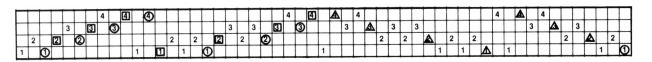

O = extra thread   □ = shared thread   △ = both shared and extra threads.
                                                          Works where they overlap.

If you consistently drop a thread the threading will be:

Here is a second block diagram and its thread by thread draft.

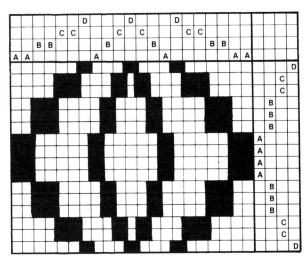 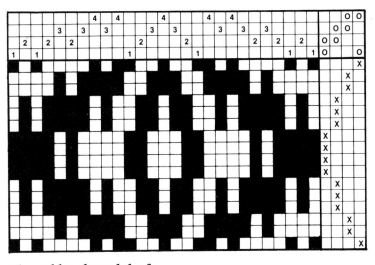

Block diagram   **Thread by thread draft**

Remember that the filled in squares in the draw-down represent
raised warps, so the white areas are where your pattern weft will
show. Like summer and winter, the tabby shots in overshot are
not noted, and for the same reasons. "Use tabby", written at the
side of the treadling, is your clue that you are to use tabby. Other
signals are the large areas of black or white that could be dangerously long floats if there were no tabby in between. The possi-
bility of long floats may be the most fundamental difference between summer and winter and overshot. When you are making
up a pattern, you can plan blocks as wide as you want them. The
problem is that wide blocks make long weft floats. If they are
very long, they will snag easily. If you need a wide block, but
want a good structure, put an occasional thread on the odd or
even harness not being used. For instance, a wide block of
1,2,1,2,1,2,1,2,1,2,1,2 would be much safer threaded
1,2,1,2,1,4,1,2,1,2,1,4; the fours will tie down the float without
disturbing the pattern a great deal.

To determine treadling is very simple. I said before that the pattern shot treadling is the same as for a 2/2 twill, and that there are two wefts, tabby and pattern. The harness combinations for a 2/2 twill are 1 + 2, 2 + 3, 3 + 4, and 4 + 1; the same combinations are used for overshot. The primary difference is that when you are weaving a twill you need to change the harnesses raised every time or your fabric will get mushy and not be structurally sound. With overshot, because you'll have a tabby shot between every pattern shot, you can repeat a harness combination as many times as you want. Having more and fewer shots in various blocks is what determines the angles, curves, squares, and other shapes that make up the patterns. There is some explanation and exploration of this in your assignments.

Tying up the treadles for tabby

We also need to look at the tabby shots. As in summer and winter, it will be much easier to remember whether you want tabby a or tabby b if you determine at the start which goes to the right, which to the left. If you are using a loom with multiple tie-up treadles there are at least four places you can tie up your tabby treadles. Which you choose should depend entirely on what is most comfortable for you.

Tie up the pattern treadles in the same sequence as they appear in the tie-up of the draft, then step on them in the order given.

As for what harnesses to raise to get tabby, think back to the threading. Overshot requires you to always go from an odd to an even harness and vice versa, so your threads will always be odd-even-odd-even. To weave tabby, simply raise the odds, one and three, and then the evens, two and four.

Yarns and related information

Your choice of yarn for overshot is very important in that it will affect the dimensions of the pattern and how much the pattern actually shows. In overshot structure, the pattern weft is "shooting over" most of the warp. You can think of the pattern weft passing through the fabric from one side to the other, producing weft floats over and under the tabby background. (Occasionally you'll find areas called halftones where, instead of floating above or below the rest of the fabric, the pattern weft is woven in just as the tabby shots are.)

This is part of why it's fairly easy to get twice as many wefts into each inch as would seem to make sense. For a balanced or squared pattern, you need to have the same p.p.i. of your tabby weft as you have e.p.i. in your warp. This is as it is in summer

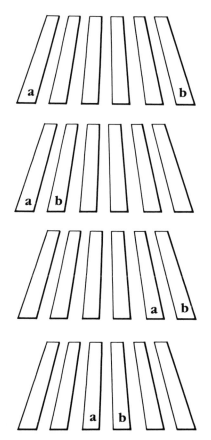

On multiple tie-up looms, there are at least four places you can tie up your tabby treadles, as shown here. Which way you choose depends solely on what feels most comfortable.

and winter, and your yarn choices for overshot could be the same as you'd chose for summer and winter.

Overshot is different from summer and winter in that with overshot the tabby background is not as integral a part of the design, and so you want to choose a weft that will, in a sense, hide the background. Fluffy, soft, squeezable yarns add fullness to your design, helping you see the pattern instead of the yarn. When the pattern weft goes from the front to the back of the fabric, it is pinched between the threads so it can fit through; where the pattern weft is part of the design, it fills out again, covering the tabby shots around it. The more loft your yarn has, the more successfully it will do this.

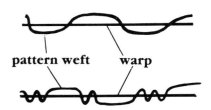

In overshot, the pattern weft is "shooting over" most of the warp as it passes through the fabric from one side to the other, producing weft floats over and under the tabby background.

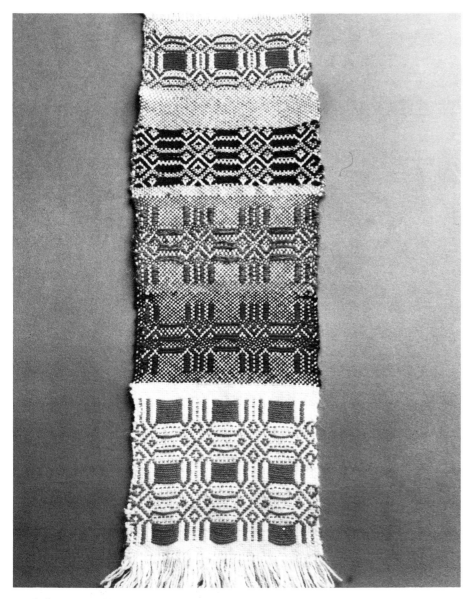

Sampler by Yvonne Stahl.

Overshot sampler. Try experimenting with different tabby colors, pattern yarns and treadlings. Explore dark colors of pattern weft on a light colored background; see what happens when a dark tabby crosses a light colored background; try several colors of pattern wefts for different parts of your pattern; repeat over and over certain parts of your treadling, skip parts of your treadling pattern, or make up your own.

Thickness of the pattern weft is also important. If the yarn you first try is so thin that your pattern looks sparse, unconvincing, try doubling or tripling it. If your chosen weft is so fat that your pattern is coming out much taller than you anticipated, try switching to a thinner tabby weft. Of course, you can alter the height of your pattern somewhat by how hard you pack your weft in, though this is more of a fine tuning. Yarn choice will be your primary determining factor.

You can also make some difference by how closely you set your warp. If it's closer, you won't be able to pack as much weft in, and your design will be taller. You can change the number of pattern shots in each block, adding or subtracting as necessary to make the design taller or shorter.

How balanced, tall, or short your design is, is of importance only to you and the project. If it's pleasing to look at or matches whatever else you want it to match, then it's the right height. It does not have to be balanced unless that is what you want.

Color choice depends on how strong you want the pattern to be. A warp and tabby weft of one color, used with pattern weft of another highly contrasting color, will show the pattern the most. You can vary from this any amount you want, knowing that the greater your divergence, the less the pattern itself will dominate. Some of the most beautiful overshots I've ever seen had striped warps; the pattern was very secondary to the overall effect. Try whatever comes to mind and find out if you like it. You could stumble onto something wonderful.

Miscellaneous notes

As you weave, you will need to twist the two wefts around each other to be sure that your pattern weft stays all the way out at the selvedge. When your shuttles are both on the same side, lay one down in front of the other; if the wefts don't cross over automatically as you use the shuttles, lay them down in the opposite order. The one that needs to be in front on the right will need to be in back on the left. In lieu of this, you could also use a floating selvedge.

In both threading and treadling your blocks can be in any order; you can go from block A to block C to block D, back to block A, for instance.

There are many, many overshot patterns in books. The single most popular source is probably Marguerite Davison's *A Handweaver's Pattern Book*. Don't forget to do draw-downs; the threading drafts are not necessarily centered. Also don't forget sinking vs. rising sheds. The pattern Periwinkle, in the drafting lesson on page 131, is an overshot pattern. If you use tabby, you can now weave it.

Assignments

1. Choose any overshot pattern (make one up or use one of those given at the end of this lesson) and try the treadlings shown here. When there is a number greater than one in the treadling, it means to throw that many shots in that shed, with tabby in between, as always.

2. Again, on any overshot warp, raise pairs of harnesses until you find the pair that will allow the pattern weft to show on the block closest to the left edge. Weave that block for however many shots it takes to have a square block. Then find the next block and weave it to square. Then find the third block and weave it to square. Continue in this manner all the way across the warp. You'll end up with square blocks running in a diagonal line from the bottom left corner to the top right, with all kinds of interesting things happening everywhere else.

3. Take an overshot draft and weave it once with the pattern on top, again with the pattern on the bottom. To do this, keep your treadling the same, and change from a rising to a sinking shed tie-up. Tie up the empty boxes in the tie-up instead of the ones with O's in them.

4. Weave the same pattern with at least four different pattern wefts. Try different textures, sizes and colors.

5. On one threading, weave four placemats, towels, scarves, pillows, or samples, each with a different treadling. This will give you four different patterns on one warp.

6. Choose one overshot pattern you really like and weave something glorious for yourself!

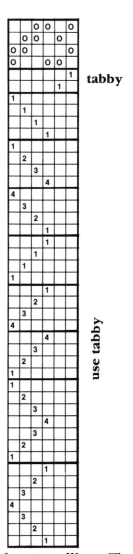

tabby

use tabby

Try these treadlings. The numbers in the treadling tell you how many pattern shots to throw in that shed. Use tabby in between each pattern shot. Repeat each section several times before going on to the next.

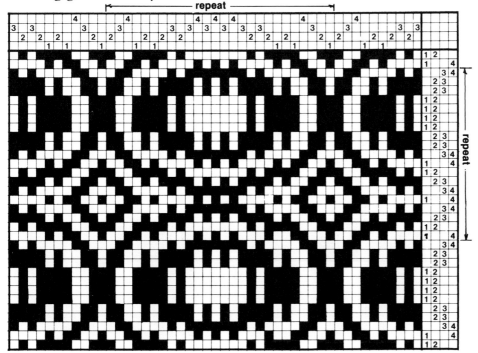

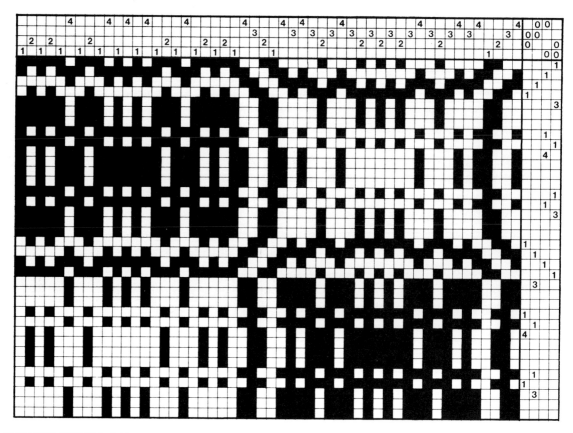

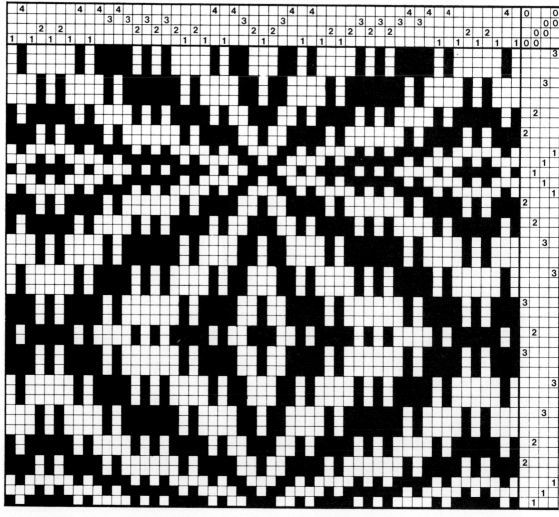

Wrap up

At the end of our classes we always have a party to celebrate. Everybody brings munchies, and we talk about what everyone has learned and where to go from here including books, looms, guilds, suppliers, magazines and other resources. You and I can't have a party together, but if you've used this book with friends you can have one with them. If you've used this book alone, invite over your best friends to show them what you've accomplished. They'll love it!

The most important thing is to look at what you've done, to appreciate how much you've learned. How long ago was it that you didn't know anything?! Now you are literate in weaving: you can plan and weave projects, read drafts and maybe make up some of your own. You have a whole new vocabulary, which, even if you can't easily speak it yet, you probably can read it reasonably well. You've come a long way—congratulate yourself!

Where to go from here is a good question. Certainly, while this is the end of your beginning lessons, it is only the beginning of your weaving. The toughest part of teaching a beginning class, in person or through this book, is wanting to give you everything all at once; the problem with that is it overwhelms instead of informs. I'm sending this course out to you knowing that there is much more you need to learn. I guess I mostly want you to know that you will continually discover more about every subject than what I've told you, and that's how it should be. No one can ever tell all there is to know on a subject, and I haven't even tried. Rather, I've attempted to give you a sound foundation, an understanding that will make it easy for you to learn more from all of the other sources of information that will come your way. We've only "scratched the surface", as they say. You will read and hear lots of different philosophies on weaving; my philosophy is that there are no rights or wrongs, only personal preferences. If you read or hear something you don't understand or don't like, ask for an explanation or ignore it.

Where next? What do you want to know more about? Are you drawn toward clothing or rugs, or toward drafting and experimenting? Do you want more books or can you now take a workshop or class from someone? Maybe it's time to start over with this book and do it all again, this time learning a whole lot more because you're starting out way ahead of where you were before. You only need to plan your weaving future one warp at a time. What do you want to weave next?

If there have been any glaring omissions or errors in these lessons, I hope you'll write and tell me so they can be corrected before we reprint. I want the book to work for you and those who come later.

Now it's time to close, except, of course, for Part IV. In some ways, Part IV may be one of the most valuable parts of this book, certainly as a reference over the long haul. Look through it all; read what is interesting now. I hope you've been using it all along. It doesn't contain everything you need to know by any means, but it should cover a lot of the most basic stuff. Your own notes to yourself will teach you a lot more.

I guess it's time to say goodbye. There are dozens of reasons people want to weave, and for most of us the reasons change as we do. I hope that you are getting some of the satisfaction you were seeking, and that you will continue to. Thanks for including me on your weaving journey for a little while.

Debbie

Part IV
Other Useful Things to Know

People To People

Is it one of the drawbacks of weaving that it is an isolating activity, or is it a craft chosen by people who prefer to be alone? Whichever your perspective, even the most reclusive weaver gets a welcome charge from contact with other weavers, and most weavers find the camaraderie of other weavers a real plus to their total weaving experience.

Weavers gather in several ways, each with its own characteristics and advantages. In the U.S. and Canada there are at present approximately 650 guilds devoted to weaving and/or spinning. They range in size from five to 500, with the nature of their activities varying according to local needs and desires. Projects may include weaving shows, sales of members' work, educational fairs, classes and workshops, programs, demonstrations, etc., and of course, annual picnics and parties. Many guilds publish newsletters, which may include swatches of members' experiments and discoveries. Most guilds meet once a month (some take the summer months off) and may have special interest group meetings in addition to general guild meetings. Dues are nominal considering what you get. Since most guilds do not have phone book listings, the easiest way to track them down is to ask area weavers or call the closest weaving shop and ask them.

There are dozens of summer craft schools across the country, some large permanent institutions, others small, existing-at-the-time-only. Some offer only fiber courses, others a whole range of subjects. Class lengths vary from a weekend to three weeks. Living accommodations may or may not be provided. A few offer college credit, work-study programs, even scholarships. All include inspiration, fun, new friendships. Many have beginning level classes, so don't feel that you can't go yet—you can go as soon as you want to. On the other end, some of the most exciting and famous teachers in the world enjoy spending all or part of their summers at these schools, and by looking around you can learn from people you've admired from afar. To find these schools, read the ads in weaving and other craft magazines.

Conferences are also a real shot of energy, usually enough to keep one going for a year. What makes conferences so special is the diversity of what they offer. Workshops and seminars may be considered the main course, complemented by generous and equally important side dishes. There will be numerous weaving shows, each on a different theme. Through them you may be inspired, and can see how your work compares to others (it's usually better than you thought). The commercial exhibits provide an unparalleled opportunity to see, feel, and experience a vast array of yarns, equipment, books, and other weaving related goodies—far more than you'd ever see in one store or even several. Lectures by the "big names" in the field will give you new ideas to ponder. And you will meet weavers from a wide geographic distribution with an equally wide range of experiences and aspirations. It's almost guaranteed you won't get enough sleep, and you won't get to see and do all you want to. What *will* happen is you'll have a wonderful time. There are approximately ten conferences per year, mostly May through September, scattered around the country. Again, read magazine ads, ask at shops, talk with other weavers.

You already know that I'm in favor of attending classes whenever possible. It's not because I think teachers are so great (I wish they all were) but because I think students are (they are). What you can learn from your peers, from other people's interpretations of the same information, is beyond description. Instead of learning just what you're learning every week, say three or four things, you will benefit from what five or seven people have learned—dozens of things. Just as you can learn not to jump off a cliff from someone else's experience, so can you avoid weaving mistakes, thanks to others. Likewise, you can be moved and inspired by others' successes as well. And they will learn from you; your presence is a gift to them.

Contact with other weavers, in any of the settings listed above (or any other) is part of the means to your weaving enrichment. Sharing ideas, celebrating successes, bemoaning (and then letting go of) disasters, appreciating discoveries, even telling bad jokes—those and much more are what are available to you in the weaving community, whether your participation is perpetual or occasional.

Choosing Yarns

Now that I'm comfortable with choosing yarns for my projects, I have mostly blocked from memory the horrors I went through in the beginning. I do, however, have a vivid recollection of being confused and frustrated by constantly taking beautiful yarns and weaving ugly projects and never understanding what was happening. When I see and hear beginning students feeling overwhelmed by the variety of yarns available to choose from, I realize once again that while eventually all these choices represent opportunity for individual expression, at first the options are paralyzing. Experience will be your best teacher. The more you weave and begin to keep track of how particular yarns behave in particular projects, the more you'll begin to see relationships, rules, cause and effect.

Yarn can be an inspiration. A fuzzy mohair may provide inspiration for a soft, cuddly scarf or throw; a fine linen may be just the thing for a dishtowel or tablecloth; a bumpy cotton novelty yarn may invoke visions of a casual loom-shaped top. Ask yourself questions about your project before choosing a yarn: what will its function be, how should it look and feel, how will you plan to wash it.

Yarn is the raw material of fabric; fiber is the raw material of yarn. Every yarn has been designed with a specific purpose in mind, and being able to recognize characteristics of intended use will greatly aid you in making successful choices. You won't always use a yarn for the same thing as the manufacturer had in mind, so the more you understand, the more easily you'll be able to make substitutions.

There are at least three different ways to think about yarn suitability. One is to think about the yarns themselves: how does wool differ from cotton, a singles from a plied yarn, etc.? A second perspective comes from project considerations: what yarns work for shawls, for rugs? And finally, from the standpoint of weaving requirements: what makes a good warp that will hold up well during weaving?

Fiber content

Yarn is usually divided into five categories, of which four are source and one is process. Animal, vegetable, and mineral are all natural fiber sources. Synthetics are processed from petroleum which starts out as a liquid and is made into fiber. Manmade yarns are those made from natural fibers, but processed as synthetics, i.e., made into a pulp and then extruded into yarn instead of being spun directly from the fibers.

Animal fibers include hair, fur, down, fleece, and silk cocoons. Wool, the fleece of a sheep, is probably the most commonly used. Weavers also enjoy the gifts of camels, goats (mohair, cashmere, others), llamas (and their cousins, alpacas and vicunas), dogs, musk oxen, rabbits (angora), silkworms, and numerous other critters.

Vegetable fibers come from many different plant parts and include cotton, linen, jute, ramie, hemp, sisal, raffia, coir, and others even more obscure. Mineral fibers include asbestos, which comes from a rock, and metallics such as gold, silver, copper, etc. Synthetics are too numerous to list; they include such families as nylon, polyester, and acrylic. (For an extensive booklet on synthetics send $1.50 to the Education Department, Manmade Fiber Producers Association, Inc., 1150 Seventeenth Street NW, Washington, D.C. 20036 and ask for the Manmade Fibers Fact Book.) Some manmade fibers are made from a cellulose base, e.g., wood chips and cotton linters, and include rayons and acetates.

Animal

Wool

I'll tell you a little about wool as representative of the group, with the added statement that the others (except silk) are not exactly the same, but have the same tendencies.

One wool fiber is a hollow cylinder with scales growing up the outside. The scales open or close depending on what is happening to the fiber, and are responsible for the insulative and elastic qualities that make wool such a joy to use and wear. In an acid solution the scales close up, holding close to the core. In an alkaline solution the scales open out, and in the process tangle into the scales of the fibers near by; once the fibers have entangled with each other they can't let go. Soap makes an alkaline (or basic) solution, so when wool is washed the fibers tend to merge into each other to some degree. Sudden, extreme temperature change, serious agitation, and the shock of a stream of water hitting the fibers also encourage this process, called fulling when it's mild, felting when it's severe. Felted fibers don't need to have been spun into yarn and woven or knitted to create a sturdy fabric; the fibers lock together so securely and permanently that they form a fabric, felt, on their own. (Feltmaking is both an industry and an art form, not only an accident of the over-zealous.) Fulling is desirable for many handwoven fabrics, especially yardage for clothing, for it helps stabilize the fabric and gives it a more unified appearance. Remember, it is not reversible, so use caution and don't carry the process too far.

Wool will hold up to 30% of its weight in moisture and still feel dry and warm, one of the reasons it is so good for winter clothing. Because wool is a protein fiber, as our hair is, rinsing woolen fabrics with a dose of creme rinse or hair conditioner can add a nice softness.

Silk

Unlike the other protein fibers, silk is an extrusion, not a growing hair. The fiber is still hollow but has no scales. It looks like a glass rod. The cocoon of the silk worm is made of a fine filament that is actually stronger than a steel filament of the same diameter. The finest, most lustrous silk yarns are made from reeled silk, obtained by unwinding cocoons. Other silks, some shiny and some with a relatively coarse looking finish, are spun from broken or cut pieces, coming from cocoons that the silk worm ate its way out of or that were damaged in some other way.

In its natural state, silk comes in basically two colors, white and golden. White silk, called *Bombyx mori,* is finer and softer. Tussah, the blond variety, is coarser, stronger, and less expensive.

The difference comes from the different species of worms and what they eat, and within the two main categories there are numerous gradations.

Silk is stronger and warmer than most people expect, and more durable. It's really very practical as well as being spectacularly beautiful (that's only slightly subjective), and is growing in popularity as people discover that it is well worth the price.

Vegetable

Cotton

Cotton grows on a bushy plant that produces dozens of cotton bolls, each yielding less than one-half ounce of cotton even before the husk and seeds are removed. Remember Eli Whitney* and his cotton gin? I didn't appreciate this until I discovered that a cotton seed hangs onto its cotton the same way a cling peach pit clings to its peach, only tighter; trying to pick these seeds out by hand had to have been very slow and difficult.

A cotton fiber is also hollow, but when it is picked it wilts, as plants do, and the tube collapses. While the space inside is now more or less gone, the fiber also curls and shrivels, as wilted plants do, and those convolutions provide the air pockets that contribute to cotton's warmth and softness. The mercerization process, which will be discussed later, restores the fiber to its original form, bringing back the hollowness of the fiber and straightening out the curling.

Cotton is a good conductor of heat, taking it from your body and releasing it into the air; that's why it is a favorite fiber for summer clothing. It is also very sturdy, able to withstand tough treatment in use and washing.

Linen

The flax plant, from which linen is made, has a tall stalk, some of which becomes linen yarn. Flax has very little elasticity, is famous for absorbency (though I find this to be more true after years of use), and usually produces a fabric that is somewhat stiff and always classy looking.

Linen has many of the properties of cotton, both being cellulose fibers, especially with regard to summer coolness. Linen is stronger when it's wet than when it's dry, giving it particular value for projects that expect to live wet lives.

---

*To set the record straight: though Eli Whitney has the patent and is credited with its invention, Catherine Greene was really the first inventor.

Construction

As important as fiber content is how a yarn is made. Short fibers are twisted together, spun into yarns. Continuous filaments, be they silk or nylon, are run together and barely twisted, deriving their strength from their inherent qualities.

A yarn can have a lot of twist and be harder and stronger, or it can have very little twist, making it softer and weaker. One spun yarn is called a single or singles; two singles twisted together form a two-ply yarn. While most yarns used by handweavers are two-, three-, or four-ply, yarn may have as many as 24 plies. The number of plies does not necessarily tell how thick a yarn is, for this depends on the size the singles were in the first place.

Generally speaking, a plied yarn is stronger than a singles for it has more total twist and is also more abrasion resistant because of the twist and plying. However, a tightly twisted singles will be stronger than a loosely spun plied yarn. So, look at all factors, and feel the yarn, rather than making any decisions based on gross generalities.

Before yarns are spun they go through a variety of preparation procedures. Of greatest concern to us is the carding/combing sequence. While each fiber is handled differently, there are some consistencies that make it all easy to understand.

Carding is the process that takes fibers, be they locks of wool or bolls of cotton, and pulls them apart, fluffs them up, so that they will be evenly distributed and can be drawn consistently out of the mass into a form called roving. Combing comes after carding, if it's done at all, and is the process that combs out the fibers so they are all parallel; the longest fibers emerge from the combs in a ribbon-like strand called top, the shorter ones fall out, often going back to the carder.

Wool spun from roving, carded only, is called woolen spun and is loftier and warmer due to its ability to trap more air. Combed wool, top, becomes worsted yarn; the parallel fibers allow less air to be trapped, which results in a denser yarn, one that is slicker and smoother to the touch, and usually stronger and shinier.

Cotton may also be carded or combed, and in clothing you may find a label indicating that the fabric is combed cotton, a finer quality. Combed cottons are used for mercerization, so while you will not find a mercerized cotton that is not combed, you may find a combed cotton that is not mercerized. When cotton is mercerized it is put through a caustic soda bath, causing it to swell and straighten; mercerized cottons are stronger and usually shiny, which is how to recognize them immediately. Unmercerized cottons are usually softer, loftier. Mercerized cottons will shrink very little, unmercerized cottons may shrink quite a lot (25%).

When flax is processed it is not carded, only combed. The long fibers that create top are spun, with moisture, into line linen, a strong, smooth, lustrous yarn that is elegant. The short fibers that are combed out are then carded and spun in a dry process into tow linen, an earthy, grassy looking yarn that is still linen, but with a whole different appearance.

Sizes

A pound of clean fiber will make a pound of yarn; how many yards that is varies. If it is spun skinny, then the pound will last longer and will make more yards. Conversely, a fatter yarn will have fewer yards per pound. Yarns are assigned numbers to indicate their sizes, based on yardage per pound. The higher the number the more yards, and therefore, the skinnier the yarn. Thus, a size 20 is thinner than a size 10, and a size 3 is fatter still. If a yarn is plied, this will, of course, affect the relative weight and yardage, and so the number of plies is also given. Common yarn sizes are 20/2, 16/2, 10/2, 8/2, 7/2, 5/2, 3/2, 12/3, 8/3, 5/3, 8/4, 16/1, etc. A 20/2 has twice the yardage of a 10/2; a 16/1 has twice the yardage of a 16/2, which is twice as thick being two 16/1's plied together.

Because each fiber has a different density, and even worsted and woolen spun yarns have different densities, a 20/2 wool does not have the same yardage as a 20/2 cotton. Both are skinny though, and in the beginning that's all you really need to know. For some yardage comparisons, see page 208.

Novelty yarns

Novelty yarns are fun to use, add interest to some pieces, or make others really special. Using novelty yarns in the weft is always an option; and as you come to understand them better, more often in the warp.

There are several basic constructions that most novelties fall into. Some are simply a single ply yarn spun with thicker and thinner places. Some have a core yarn with other fibers or yarns spun or wrapped around them. And some are one or two plies, possibly looped or bumped, with a thin binding thread twisted around to hold everything in place.

In considering a novelty for warp, what you need to look at is whether or not the yarn is stable. Do the bumps or loops slide around? How strong is the strongest element? Consider how easy it will be to weave with and how successfully it will maintain its texture. A large dent reed and large eye heddles will usually prevent stripping. Hairy yarns, brushed mohair, etc. are strong and stable but need to be kept out of reach of each other so that the hairs from one will not grab the hairs of the next causing them to lock together, giving no shed or immobilizing the beater.

If you're trying novelty yarns in the warp for the first time, consider starting by using them in conjunction with other smoother yarns, interspersed evenly across the warp. As your confidence and experience grow, try more. Gradually, you'll learn what will work for you and what won't.

One last word on novelty yarns. If you're weaving a fancy pattern use a plain yarn; save the fancy yarns for plain patterns. Trying to mix fancy yarns and fancy patterns often results in chaos and competition, where neither shows to good advantage.

Yarn packaging and conversions

Yarn comes in a variety of packages or shapes, called put-ups. Skeins, balls, pull skeins, cones, and tubes are all different kinds of put-ups; the style does not indicate quantity or quality. Skeins need to be made into balls before using to prevent tangles, or may be used directly if mounted on and pulled from an umbrella swift or its equivalent. The other put-ups are made so that you can pull the yarn directly from them without problems. The reason regular skeins still exist, and will continue to, is that they are the healthiest for yarn storage (no tension) and look the prettiest.

Below are some of the more common quantities that yarn comes in, along with their metric equivalencies. Since I'm not yet accustomed to thinking in meters, I usually figure that a skein with 400 meters has about 400 yards plus a cushion, in this case an extra 33 yards, ample but not excessive.

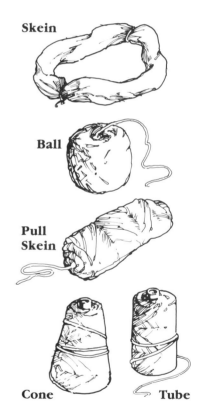

Skein

Ball

Pull Skein

Cone   **Tube**

almost ⅓ oz.	10 grams	1 yard = 36 inches
1 oz.	28 grams	1 meter = 39 inches
1¾ oz.	50 grams	
2 oz.	57 grams	
3½ oz.	100 grams	
4 oz.	113 grams	
8 oz.	227 grams	
1 pound	454 grams	
2.2 lb.	1 kilogram	

Project perspective

There are too many projects and too many yarns to be able to tell you all the combinations, so instead I'll say ask questions. Think about the life the project will live, the kind of abuse it will take, the needs it will have, and then try to pick yarns accordingly. Use common sense in thinking about the project's requirements, then add to this your understanding of the basic yarn properties. Softness, durability, washability, abrasion resistance . . . which are important to the project?

Coarser fibers are usually tougher, less likely to break. Consequently, rug wools are spun from coarser wools, not softer, finer ones. In most cases, abrasion is a bigger concern than out and out strength. Coarser fibers are less likely to break, but longer, finer fibers will be twisted into the yarn more times and will be less likely to pull out, pill or get fuzzy.

A yarn that is too expensive or in too short supply to be used for a whole project can be mixed with another yarn to cut down on the cost and consumption. How to mix them and in what proportions depends on the pattern, how much you have and what effect you want.

If you have questions about the suitability of a yarn for a certain project, now is the time to ask questions of the person selling you yarn. Keeping your own records is important too, but unless a piece is being used in your own house, you won't know how it holds up over time. Taking a sample and abusing it as much as possible can be something of an aging equivalency, and you can ask the people you give things to to let you know how well they wear, in the interests of education—yours.

Read the section on Project Considerations, page 216 and ask questions, keep records, and all will begin to make sense pretty soon.

Warp requirements

Possibly the most useful thing to remember about warp is that you're never pulling on only one thread—you're pulling on many at the same time. A group is stronger than an individual, so don't rule out a yarn as warp because one thread will break easily; test a bunch together. Many yarns that are soft and loosely twisted are fine for warp; just keep your tension as even as possible and don't tighten it more than necessary.

You'll have the most freedom of choice if you assume that any yarn can be warp until you find out it can't. By using reasonable care, I've come across less than half a dozen yarns I could not use for warp, some of which I didn't try a sample with first and regretted it.

Abrasion is probably the greatest warp killer; the friction of the reed or the yarns grabbing onto each other create fuzz and eventually rub through the yarn. Any yarn that looks to have low resistance to abrasion (scratch it with your fingernails, see how much fuzz appears) will do better if it's double sleyed in a wider reed. If you are having trouble getting the shed open, and the sticking is hard on both the yarn and you, raise your harnesses one at a time instead of two, e.g., to raise one and three, raise one alone, then three to join it. It's easier to lift out one fourth of the threads than one half. Also be sure your beater is pulled forward so the warp is trading places with as little restriction as possible.

If you are mixing yarns in the warp, using some that are stiff with some that are stretchy, be sure to blend them as homogeneously as possible. Avoid wide stripes. Sometimes even good mixing won't do enough to make some yarns work together, as some will be dangerously tight while others are too loose to weave. Mixing yarns of similar elasticity will prevent many problems. To determine differences in elasticity, stretch each yarn taut and cut off a piece one yard long. When they are all relaxed see how long they are; the shorter they are the more elastic they are. If you are using a very stretchy yarn for your warp, measure it longer and weave it looser so that when the tension is released and the warp draws up, it's as long as you wanted and the weft is packed in at the density you wanted, not tighter.

In general

Perhaps the single most important thing to remember about yarn choices and about weaving in general, is that it's only yarn. The world is not going to stand still if some project is a total disaster. You can afford to make mistakes, first because most of them can be fixed, second because it's one way to learn. Don't be afraid to try something new, whether you are reading it somewhere or making it up yourself. If it works, you'll feel creative and satisfied and encouraged. If it doesn't, figure out why, so you don't need to make the same mistake again.

Experienced weavers make mistakes, have disasters, get surprised, and I'm always amazed when a beginning student thinks that teachers' weavings always work. The only way to avoid surprises is to never try anything new; always playing safe is boring, a fate far worse than disaster in my book. Experienced weavers don't make the same mistakes as beginners, mostly, we make bigger ones!

One of the truisms about weaving, the textile arts, is that you can never know it all. There's just too much. Some days this is overwhelming. Eventually it's a relief, for since you can't know everything, you don't need to feel obligated to. If you keep this in mind, it's easier to pick and choose—to say, ''This is what I want to learn next; that one doesn't interest me now.''

If you want to know how a particular yarn is going to behave, take a skein home and try it. Weave three different samples, wash them all, and see how the yarn acts in each one. Then write down what you've learned. Teach yourself, for then you'll really know.

Reeds And Warp Setts

There are two ways to approach matching up reeds and yarns. If you have only one reed, then you must choose yarns that will fit in that reed. If you own a variety of reeds, you can use any yarn you want and choose the appropriate reed for it. Clearly, there is more freedom with the second method, but reeds are expensive enough that a full set is a luxury most people work into only gradually.

Reeds come in a wide range of spacings, most often with four, five, six, eight, 10, 12, or 15 dents per inch. Frequently you will sley more or less than one thread per dent. The change in sequence depends on the size of the yarn, how closely set you want the warp to be, etc. By sleying two threads in each dent, a 12-dent reed yields a warp sett of 24 e.p.i.; sleying one thread in every other dent results in six e.p.i. To get 18 e.p.i. you'd sley one thread in the first dent, two in the next dent, then one again, then two, etc.

While it is mathematically possible to get a sett of 10 e.p.i. in a 12-dent reed (sley five dents, skip one, sley five, skip one), it is not a practical thing to do. If you have a fairly consistent sleying pattern, e.g., 1/0/1/0 or 2/2/2/2 or even 1/1/2/1/1/2, the warp threads will slide into an even distribution quite successfully, if not immediately, then after washing. If your doubling up or spacings, such as 1/1/1/1/0, are irregular or very far apart, your threads are unlikely to shift enough to result in an even sett. Just because it is possible, doesn't mean that it is practical. So, try whatever you think you need, and learn whether it will work or not. It may work with some yarns and not others. Always wash your sample as you plan to wash your finished piece to see for sure that your warps will even out. Often you'll have reed marks after removing your fabric from your loom that will go away with the first washing.

That fat yarns must go through widely spaced reeds is immediately obvious. Novelty yarns, with their bumps, loops, hairiness, slubs, and other protrusions, catch in narrow places and so need relatively widely spaced reeds, too. They need to be able to pass through freely so as not to get stripped by the reed. For a closer sett, double sley in a wider reed. This works well, for the yarns will rest on top of each other and move about without too much abrasion.

Choosing a warp sett for any given yarn is not really as mysterious as it seems at first. A standard trick that will give you a ballpark idea of sett is to take your warp yarn and wrap it around a ruler, compacting it tightly for an inch. Wrap the yarn as densely as you want your fabric to be, remembering that the fabric will be half warp and half weft. Your warp sett will therefore be half of the number of wraps in one inch. If the yarn you've chosen wraps around the ruler 20 times in one inch, it needs a warp sett of 10 e.p.i. to weave a balanced fabric with the same density as the wrapping.

How precise this is depends on you, the yarn, and what fabric you'll be weaving. For myself, I usually prefer a warp sett slightly closer than the number I get from dividing by two; for someone else it could be a number slightly lower. It's a good starting point, from which you can learn your own divergence.

As you weave more samples and projects, label sheets of paper with the warp setts you use, e.g., 5, 8, 10, 12, 20, 30 e.p.i. Then, as you try a new yarn, stick a piece of it onto the page for the sett you used (or decided you should have used). As the sheets fill with samples you'll begin to see which sizes work at which setts, and eventually you'll be able to pick a good sett just by looking at the yarn.

Remember that you'll use different setts for different patterns, and for different projects. The same yarn you set at 18 e.p.i. for a soft skirt fabric, you might set at 24 e.p.i. for a tablecloth. Likewise, if you were weaving lace curtains out of this same yarn, you might set it at 16 e.p.i. for a more open fabric. Remember that for a twill weave structure, you'll generally want to set your yarn closer than you would for a plain weave structure. There are no "right" setts, which is another reason samples are so useful.

All the above applies to balanced warp setts in particular. But, what about setts for warp-faced and weft-faced fabrics? Again, type of fabric and weave structure are important factors, and using what you know about figuring setts for balanced weaves will give you a place to work from. You know, for instance, that for a fabric to be weft-faced, the warp must be completely covered by weft; and yet, you want your warp to be set close enough so that the fabric is not unstable. A yarn with a lot of loft will pack in easier than a tightly spun, hard yarn; this needs to be an element in determining sett. Figuring a sett for a warp-faced fabric works similarly, though here you need to think of warp completely covering weft. Again, yarns will be a factor. As a warp-faced fabric has warp ends set very closely together, you'll need to be sure that they are not too close together or you won't be able to make a clean shed, for your warp yarns will be sticking together.

A rule of thumb is that for a warp-faced fabric multiply the number of warp ends in one inch by 1.5 or two (two or three times your normal balanced sett). For a sett for a weft-faced fabric, again wrap your ruler, this time using one warp yarn and two weft yarns. Then, count only the warp ends in this inch to find your sett. These are only starting places. Too much depends on your materials and the intended use of your fabric for these to be hard and fast rules.

Sett Chart

Yarn Size	Yd/Lb	Tabby	Twill
20/2 cotton	8,400	24-30	32-36
10/2 cotton	4,200	24-28	30
5/2 cotton	2,100	15-18	20
3/2 cotton	1,260	10-12	15
20/2 linen	3,000	20-24	30
12/1 linen	3,600	22-25	30-32
4/1 linen	1,400	12-15	15-18
20/2 worsted	5,600	20-24	28
12/3 worsted	2,160	15-18	20
6.5/1 wool	3,200	18-20	22-25
12/2 wool	3,000	18-20	22-25
7/2 wool	1,640	12-15	15-18
6.5/2 wool	1,600	10-12	12-15
1.3/1 wool	600	8-10	10-12
2.2/2 wool	550	8-10	10-12
22/2 cottolin	3,250	15-20	20
mohair loop	1,000	6-8	6-8
brushed mohair	800	4-8	4-8
linnay	1,200	10-12	15

Reed Substitution Chart

Order of Sley in Reed	5	6	8	9	10	12	14	15	16	18	20	24
0-0-1	2	2	3	3	3	4	5	5	5	6	7	8
0-1	2½	3	4	4½	5	6	7	7½	8	9	10	12
0-1-1	3	4	5	6	7	8	9	10	11	12	13	16
0-1-1-1	4	4½	6	7	7½	9	10½	11½	12	13½	15	18
1	5	6	8	9	10	12	14	15	16	18	20	24
1-1-1-2	6	7½	10	11	12½	15	17½	19	20	22½	25	30
1-1-2	7	8	11	12	13	16	19	20	21	24	27	32
1-2	7½	9	12	13½	15	18	21	22½	24	27	30	36
1-2-2	8	10	13	15	17	20	23	25	27	30	33	40
1-2-2-2	9	10½	14	16	17½	21	24½	26	28	31½	35	42
2	10	21	16	18	20	24	28	30	32	36	40	48
2-2-2-3	11	13½	18	20	22½	27	31½	34	36	40½	45	54
2-2-3	12	14	19	21	23	28	33	35	37	42	47	56
2-3	12½	15	20	22½	25	30	35	37½	40	45	50	60
2-3-3	13	16	21	24	27	32	37	40	43	48	53	64
2-3-3-3	14	16½	22	25	27½	33	38½	41	44	49½	55	66
3	15	18	24	27	30	36	42	45	48	54	60	72
3-3-3-4	16	19½	26	29	32½	39	45½	49	52	58½	65	78
3-3-4	17	20	27	30	33	40	47	50	53	60	67	80
3-4	17½	21	28	31½	35	42	49	52½	56	63	70	84
3-4-4	18	22	29	33	37	44	51	55	59	66	73	88
4	20	24	32	36	40	48	56	60	64	72	80	96
4-4-5	22	26	35	39	43	52	61	65	69	78	87	104
4-5-5	23	28	37	42	47	56	65	70	75	84	93	112
5	25	30	40	45	50	60	70	75	80	90	100	120

Warp Sett (ends per inch)

About Heddles

There are four kinds of heddles readily available to weavers. String heddles are the traditional heddles which were used for centuries before flat steel, wire and inserted eye heddles became available. String heddles are just that, string, though there are new improved versions made from nylon. These nylon heddles feature braided areas that hold the eyes open for ease of threading. String heddles are very lightweight and are quieter than metal heddles; they are flexible and will forgive a knot or a bumpy warp yarn. They make for slower threading because they don't slide along the heddle bars as easily as metal heddles will. Most jack looms need the extra weight of wire heddles to prevent the harnesses from floating, therefore, string heddles are not always desireable for these types of looms. You'll find string heddles on most countermarche and counterbalance looms. Ask your loom manufacturer for more information on this.

The metal heddles, flat steel, wire and inserted eye, are self adjusting in that they will space themselves out on the heddle bars after they've been threaded; string heddles need to be placed into position. Wire heddles are made from twisted wire and weigh the least of these three. Inserted eye heddles are wire heddles with a smooth ring soldered into the eye for added smoothness; flat steel heddles are flat pieces of metal with slightly twisted eyes. Wire and inserted eye heddles are more forgiving of knots and bumpy warps than are flat steel, though these two are more prone to bending around each other. All three styles of heddles have a directional twist to the eye which you need to be aware of when threading. You will notice that when you twist your heddles either toward you or away from you, the heddle eye appears to be more open one way than the other. (This is most apparent with flat steel heddles.) The twist is made in the heddle so that when your warp is inserted, it will make a straight line through it from front to back. If you thread your warp from the other side you should be able to see a bend in your warp thread; this will cause undo wear on your warp end and possibly cause your ends to break. Because of this directional twist, your heddles will be a lot easier to thread if they are on the heddle bars in the same direction. Notice how, when your heddles are next to each other, they nest inside each other. Try threading a warp end through a heddle from both sides of the eye. You'll notice that when the warp is being threaded in a straight line, it is easier to thread through the heddle.

Moving heddles

If you need to move heddles from one harness to the next, *do not* just slide the heddles off the heddle bar. If your heddle bar has holes in the ends, tie a strong string through the hole. If there are no holes, tape a string to the end of the bars. Then slide the heddles onto the strings, tie them securely, and then slide them onto the harness where you need them. Even if you don't expect to ever put the heddles back on, put them onto strings anyway. Some day someone will want to use them again, and it will be a whole lot easier if they are strung. It doesn't hurt to mark the bundles with how many heddles they contain.

To avoid moving heddles after you've started threading, check to see that you have enough heddles on each harness before you begin to thread. However, if you have an eight harness loom and are using only four of the harnesses, and find that you've run out of heddles, you can simply start using the unused harnesses. Think of harness five as harness one, six as two, etc. When tying up your treadles just add the extra harness where appropriate. This is one of the less renowned but valuable advantages of having more harnesses.

Repair heddles

If you have made a mistake in your threading and have the right number of threads but no heddle on the harness you want the thread to be on, you can do either of two things. Tie a string heddle onto the proper harness, striving to get the heddle eye even with all the other heddle eyes. Or take a pair of wire cutters (not scissors, please, they don't heal) and cut a heddle off the loom. Bend the wire to get the heddle off, put it where you need a new heddle, and bend the wire back into place. Save it for when you might need it again.

Marking heddles

If you have dyslexia or depth perception problems, use paint or fingernail polish and paint your lower heddle bars (or heddles if you can) different colors. If you have string heddles, dye them. Then it's easy to see which harness you need to pull heddles from. That's especially useful when you have more harnesses; with twelve or sixteen it's almost essential, whether you have eye problems or not.

Heddle distribution

If you have more heddles than you need and you are putting on a full width warp, leaving the extra heddles on the sides may cause damage to the selvedge warp trying to go around them. To prevent this, simply space the extras amidst your warp as you thread. Thread a couple of inches, then leave a few empty heddles next to those threaded, then thread some more, then leave more empties.

On Buying a Loom

There are a lot of good looms available and while there are, of course, differences in all of them, there are really more similarities.

Choosing a company

To some extent it doesn't matter which one you buy because they all work. I would suggest you look at the company, find out how long they've been in business and/or how long they expect to be. While looms don't break down very often, you may want to replace parts broken in moving or add accessories later. That's difficult to do if the company no longer exists. There are well over 20 stable, reputable loom companies in the U.S. so you have plenty of good choices. At least seven of those sell only directly, so you can't see them at your local weaving shop. This does not make them less reliable, but may make them less accessible to you. So if you plan to buy through the mail then look at all of the companies equally, see who responds to you the best, feels right to you.

Decide what kind of loom you need

The first thing you need to do is decide what you want to weave. Are you going to weave only tapestries, only rugs? Is clothing of all kinds your interest, or coverlets? Probably most American weavers have a wide range of interests, settling into a single focus for periods of time perhaps, but not forever. It's probably easier to choose a loom for one thing only—a tapestry loom, a rug loom—but if you're versatile then you need a loom that is. Make a list of the first ten things you want to weave. The first two or three are easy, those have been on your mind for a long time. Getting to ten may take more effort, and that's good. By then you'll see if there is a pattern. Is everything on the list less than

25″ wide? More than 40″ wide? If it's all small stuff don't buy a 60″ wide loom. If it's all rugs don't buy a lightweight loom. Clothing has a surprise to it. While commercial fabric is a set width, pattern pieces are rarely over 25″ wide. Because you are custom weaving your fabric you can weave it longer and narrower; you don't need a wide loom to weave fabric for clothing.

After width the most significant question is complexity. Two, four, eight, or more harnesses? A rigid heddle loom (two harnesses) will weave a tremendous variety of projects, from shawls to blankets, wall hangings to rugs. And it costs a lot less. If you learn to use multiple heddles, or even just one pickup stick, you can do a lot of pattern playing as well. For speed and patterns combined, a four or more harness loom is more appropriate. One of the most often asked questions is, "Four or eight harnesses?" There are a number of looms that come with expansion possibilities, four harnesses in place, the option of adding more later. One gauge for yourself is if you like puzzles, figuring things out, you'll probably like more harnesses. If color and textured yarns are what get you excited then you probably won't need more. If you are one of those unfortunate souls who is intimidated by harnesses being there that you don't know what to do with, then by all means don't buy them— they'll spoil your enjoyment of the ones you do know what to do with.

Years ago I was in a community where the local practice was to buy looms by weight. Whichever loom weighed the most was the one people bought. It was a novel approach. I think that the idea was an outgrowth of "looms need to be sturdy", which comes from rug weaving. Yes, of course a rug loom needs to be sturdy, as do all looms. But rug weaving puts a lot of strain on a loom that most weaving does not. If you expect to weave one or two rugs a year and mostly much lighter fabrics, then go ahead and buy a light loom and tighten the bolts after you've woven your rug. (Once a year or more you should clean and tighten everything anyway.)

Consider your warping method

There are many different ways to warp a loom. Ask what features a loom has to accommodate your method. If you don't have a method yet, ask the question in general terms. Do the beams lift off, does the back fold up or drop down out of the way, is a sectional beam available, can the loom be warped in a folded or partly folded position, how close can you sit to the castle on whichever side you want to thread from?

Loom types

Probably the last thing I'd include in the "very important" category is the type of lifting mechanism the loom has: jack, counterbalance, or countermarche. A jack loom has separate lifts for each harness, each operating totally independently. You can raise whatever harness(es) you want and the others just sit there, allowing total freedom of design. A counterbalance loom has harnesses hanging over rollers opposite each other, one opposite two, three across from four, and one and two together opposite three and four together. When one and three go up, two and four go down. Any two harnesses can be raised or lowered, but they must work in pairs, not one against three. (While this is the theory, some counterbalance looms will give an unbalanced shed; it's not supposed to work that way but sometimes it does.) The rollers make the treadling action easy on the weaver's legs, and the raising vs. lowering of the harnesses is useful in separating sticky warps. A countermarche loom is one in which each harness is counterweighted opposite the treadles. That means you can raise/lower whichever harness(es) you want, giving you infinite design possibilities, and because the harnesses have a counter-action, the ease and anti-stick advantages of the counterbalanced system have been maintained. Theoretically, therefore, the countermarche loom, having the best elements of both of the other two types, should be the best loom. In truth, however, each of the three types of looms has many other features that are not necessary to the style but are traditionally connected to it, features that must be taken into account as well. With a few exceptions, jack looms have a bottom mounted beater, countermarche looms have an overhead beater. They feel entirely different and you may have a strong preference for one or the other.

Tie-up system

Every loom has its own tie up system, the means for tying the treadles to the lamms. Cords of any kind are subject to stretching, only interesting when they stretch different amounts. Wire connections don't stretch but they may get bent or fall out of their holes. Whichever you get you will get used to, know which quirks to watch for. If you're interested in speed, then ask about the tie-up system as some are substantially faster or slower than others.

Brakes

There are two kinds of brakes, friction and ratchet. The purpose of the brake is to hold the beam firm so your warp won't unroll as you weave. I've heard of only one loom with a front friction brake; most others have a ratchet and dog or pawl, a piece that falls into the notches of the ratchet to hold it in place. There are a few looms which have worm gears. On the back beam there might be another ratchet or a friction brake, a drum with a cable wrapped around it. The beam won't move when the cable is holding tight, will move when it is released slightly. The advantage of the friction brake is that your warp tension can be adjusted infinitely, you are not limited to the increments of the ratchet teeth. The disadvantage of the friction brake is that if the cable gets bent, (can happen in moving, not likely under normal circumstances) it won't work and must be replaced. Most friction brakes have a break-in period, ratchets don't. Occasionally a friction brake won't release properly; without proper precautions a ratchet will release too quickly. Some weavers prefer one, others the other; generally they prefer the one they have, having learned its idiosyncracies and how to work with them.

There are basically three kinds of heddles, flat steel, wire and string. As with everything else there are weavers with strong preferences for each. The advantage of flat steel is speed in threading and sliding around; the disadvantage is weight, not significant if you have fewer than 1000 and healthy legs. The advantages of wire are flexibility—they'll flex around a snag in a yarn rather than hold firm and force the yarn to give way—and price, being the least expensive of the three. Looms come with heddles so price is no object until you buy more. String heddles are quiet and very light weight. They can be purchased or tied by you. As of now there are several commercial varities, those from Texsolv rapidly taking over the field. Unlike the olden days, string heddles now come with an open eye, eliminating their major disadvantage; if you come across some that have eyes that stand closed, avoid them—it takes two hands and four or five fingers to thread them. (If you tie your own, use square knots to get open eyes.) The other disadvantage of string heddles is that they don't slide easily across the harness frame or heddle bar, important to some, irrelevant to others. A big advantage for people with eye problems is that they can be dyed, a different color for each harness. (Also useful when you have many harnesses.) Most looms come with one type of heddle standard but substitutes can be made in most cases.

Other than heddles, what comes with looms varies considerably. One comes with a bench but no reed; most come with a reed but no bench. Shuttles, books and threading hooks are those things manufacturers do or don't include; dealers may throw in other equipment, lessons or shipping costs. If money is of major concern for you then be sure to find out what's included and what else you'll need to acquire to get started. Because many, if not most, looms are sold to existing weavers, those who already own warping boards, etc., looms do not come complete with everything you'll need to start weaving. It would increase the cost with things you may not want.

Price

Remember when comparing prices that all looms are not created equal. There are a number of looms designed as good starting looms, lighter weight, less expensive, some coming as kits for you to assemble. It is not appropriate to compare those looms in price with those that are more substantial, designed for years of prolonged use. The latter will cost two-three times as much, as well they should. Decide which kind of investment you want to make, then look at the options within that range. Resale on most looms is good. The market is ever growing so there is a strong demand for good used looms. The very small and very large are harder to sell, the mid-range easy. (Four harness 36"-48" is probably the most sought-after.)

Aesthetics

Do you like what the loom looks like? To some people this is very important, to others it hardly matters. If it does matter to you then honor that. If you buy a loom you think isn't pretty, or worse, is ugly, you'll rarely look at it without that coming to mind. On the other hand, if you buy one that you think is beautiful it will add a warm sparkle to your day every time you look at it. Listen to your insides, they are you and they do need your attention.

What is your space situation?

How crowded are you willing to be? Obviously basic dimensions of loom and room are the factors here, but there is one other less tangible thing to be aware of. A loom with a low castle *appears* to take less room because it doesn't block vision across a room. A high castle loom that takes exactly the same floor space will look bigger because it really is, but it is using up otherwise unused air space. Against a wall it doesn't matter, in a room alone it doesn't, but in the middle of a room a tall loom will act as a room divider, something you may or may not want.

Other considerations

There are numerous other factors to consider when choosing a loom: size of shed, lamm system, type of wood, noise level, height of beams if you are tall, style of bench, spacing of treadles, portability, and more. Read loom catalogs. Each will tell of its own strengths, and from that you'll know what questions to ask about other looms. What one company calls a strength another may see as of no importance; the question is how important is it to you?

I haven't given you any hard core this-over-that information for several reasons. First, I don't work that way. While I will express my own preferences in a face to face conversation, I don't want you to buy the loom I like, I want you to buy the one you like. I think that in this context it is best for me to tell you some of the things to look for, questions to ask, factors to consider, and then based on your needs you decide what the "right" answer is for you.

Second, this is a small industry. We all know each other. Everyone is doing his or her best to give weavers something they need. While we all need to make a living, none of us is doing this to get rich, so no one is cutting corners to increase shareholders' profits. There is little danger that you'll be ripped off. The worst that can happen is that you'll encounter a personality you'd rather not be around. Your loom may well last you the rest of your life, so take the time you need to be happy with your purchase. At the same time remember that the loom doesn't *have* to be a lifetime commitment, you can sell it and buy a different one if you change your mind later. Since I've been weaving seriously I've sold three looms because they no longer suited my needs for various reasons. I love the loom I have now, have every expectation of buying another when I again live in a bigger place.

I've had students ask, half seriously, "Why don't they just make one loom, the best one, and save us all this confusion?" I suppose they could, the same as they could make just one car, one breakfast cereal, one house design.

Whichever loom you buy, the odds are it will be the right one for you. You'll learn to use it, understand its traits and quirks, and the two of you will develop a strong bond.

This section "On Buying Looms" first appeared in Handwoven, *November-December 1983, page 18.*

Project Considerations

There are some basic questions to ask before you begin any project, and the planning stage is when to ask them. Take the needs of the project into consideration. How sturdy does it need to be, or how delicate? Soft? What kind of wear will it get—pulling or rubbing? Will it be washed often? Is sun rot a potential problem? Does it matter how heavy or light the fabric is? Warmth? Etc.

Rugs

Heavy or light traffic—front door or bedside? Will it get wet a lot—bath mat, kitchen rug or mudroom foot scraper? Will it lay on linoleum which is slippery, or on another rug where sliding won't be a problem? What is its first purpose: decoration, warmth, absorbency of wetness, absorbency of sound, to cover an ugly place, to unify a decor, to be a gift? How much can it cost? Is your loom small enough or light enough that you are limited in what kind of rug you can weave? (Any loom can weave some kind of rug.)

There are many, many different ways to weave rugs, from rag to rya. Some are very heavy, some light. High traffic rugs, such as those in hallways, near doorways, need to be durable. Rugs that go under tables, next to beds, or in other low traffic areas probably need to be more pretty and/or warm, but don't need to be as indestructible.

Some rugs are sturdy because of the yarn used, others because of the weave structure. A softly twisted yarn is not sturdy, but a sturdy weave may sufficiently compensate. Weft-faced weaves are most often used for rugs, but there are also plenty of sturdy rugs with warp showing. Most rag rugs, for instance, which seem to last forever, are neither very heavy nor totally weft-faced.

A few things to be aware of: some kind of padding under a rug will add years to its life as it won't get ground so hard when it's stepped on. If the rug is located where it will be in the sun a lot, it will deteriorate faster; of the natural fibers, linen and cotton resist sun rot better, wool and silk are most susceptible. There are rubber cement-like backings available to help prevent dangerous sliding. It's okay to walk on a handwoven rug.

Good rug books: Peter Collingwood's *The Techniques of Rug Weaving;* Interweave Press's *A Rug Weaver's Sourcebook.*

Clothing

There are so many kinds of clothing that it would be hard to make very many generalizations. The two things that come to mind are: be careful not to weave a fabric too heavy or stiff to be comfortable to wear, and yes, you can cut handwoven fabric just like you cut "real" fabric.

Basically, handwoven clothing falls into two categories: loom shaped and tailored. Loom-shaped garments require very little cutting. They are mostly made of rectangles and squares and are more ethnic-type garments. Tailored clothing refers to fitted garments, those cut and sewn from sewing patterns. Handwoven fabric does need some care taken with it that commercial fabric may not require, but care and common sense are the rule.

Things to consider in advance: when you weave your samples, make them big enough to feel how the fabric drapes, at least 8″ square. Wash and full your fabric before you finish your garment, not after it's done and can't be replanned.

Books: *Fashions From the Loom* by Betty Beard; *Handwoven, Tailormade* by Sharon Alderman and Katherine Wertenberger; *Clothing From the Hands That Weave* by Anita Luvera Mayer.

Towels, placemats, napkins, etc.

I loved it when weaving dishtowels suddenly became not only respectable but almost a fad; I just hope it continues. Even if it doesn't, weaving table runners, placemats, and other table linens will always be a favorite activity of weavers. They can be practically anything, so provide opportunity for a wide range of tastes in color, texture, pattern, weight, fiber, etc. Conservative or outrageous, casual or elegant, delicate or sturdy, expensive or not, there is tremendous freedom of design in weaving for your dining room or kitchen.

So, what are the limits? Washability is pretty important, whether it's by hand or machine. This means not only appropriate fibers, but not too loose or sleazy a weave. Your piece needs to be able to withstand agitation, maybe even abuse. If you are thinking about towels, absorbency is desirable, as is reasonably quick drying time (though that may depend more on your climate than on your towel). Placemats and table runners need to be a pretty smooth fabric or glasses and salt shakers may tip over. If you don't mind hand washing, then wool placemats are fine, and many people prefer them. If you want to just toss them in with the rest of the laundry, then a non-felting fiber—cotton, linen, rayon, nylon, etc.—would be better.

Books: There is a whole series of beautiful books from Sweden that have table linen projects, available from Glimakra Looms 'n Yarns dealers; *Handwoven's Design Collection #2, Table Linens,* and *Design Collection #5, Dishtowels.*

Wall hangings

About the only functional thing I want to say here is, that over a period of time, a heavy piece may stretch, hang out of shape. Be sure you mount it in such a way that it is well supported. If it's weft-faced, consider having the design work sideways as there are many more wefts to provide strength than warps.

From a design standpoint, a wall hanging can be anything you can think of, any size, any shape. I admit I've been turned off by so many people taking a piece or sample that didn't quite work out and for lack of an alternative, hanging it on the wall and calling it a wall hanging. This practice as much as says wall hangings are those pieces that weren't anything. If they weren't much else, they probably aren't much as wall hangings either. On the other hand, a piece designed for a particular place can be a real plus to a room, a great enhancer of the environment. Wall hangings conceived and born to be wall hangings, and well finished, are fine art at its best.

Books: Go for inspiration. Fiberarts' *Design Books; Beyond Craft: The Art Fabric* and *Mainstream* by Jack Lenor Larsen and Mildred Constantine; *Woven Works* by John and Susan Hamamura.

Curtains

Here you have a combination of considerations from above. How much sun, how well will they drape, will they support themselves hanging over a long period of time? For small north windows these are not critical problems, but for large south windows they are. Wool drapes getting a lot of sun may not last a year. If the weft is stiff the curtains may not curve and fold well when open. I knew a woman who wove drapes for her sliding glass doors; she hadn't done a sample, and when she hung them the weft slid to the floor.

Lining drapes protects them from sun rot. There are numerous ways to attach curtains to curtain rods, some simple, some fancy; choose according to your fabric and your window. And plan carefully so your curtain will be long enough; don't forget to add take-up into your warp length.

Lace weaves let in light and sun, are cheery. Double weaves, especially stuffed or with thin insulative material (like space blankets) placed between the layers, can be real heat savers. Waffle weaves are also good insulators, but don't use too many harnesses or your fabric will be unstable for hanging.

How often do you want to clean them, and by what means? What do they need to match in the room? What qualities in the curtains already there do you want to keep, and what do you want to improve on? What makes a good set of curtains or drapes good?

Book: *Fabrics for Interiors* by Jack Lenor Larsen and Jeanne Weeks.

Blankets, bedspreads, afghans, baby blankets

These might be my favorite things to weave. Because they are large, they are enormously satisfying. They are almost always much faster to weave than it seems like they're going to be. (My first bedspread took two months and five days—two months dreading the time it would take and five days to actually get it done.) They can be heavy or light, colorful or conservative, any of dozens of patterns. Depending on the size of your loom, afghans and baby blankets may be woven in one piece; blankets and bedspreads probably need seams. There are even lots of ways to make seams, some strictly functional, some decorative: sewing by machine, sewing by hand with yarn instead of thread, crocheting, or weaving narrow bands as joining strips, to name a few.

Is this blanket for warmth or decoration? Is it going to North Dakota or Florida? Will it be slept under or pulled back for the night? What will happen to it during the day? Is the house full of kids (age 2-90) and animals who will play on the bed, sit on it to tie shoes, shed all over it, take naps on it as often as under it, etc., or will it be looked at but never abused? Abrasion resistance, the snaggability of long floats in some patterns and how easily it can be cleaned, all need to be considered in light of the lifestyle it will support.

As for baby blankets, is this for sleeping, grocery shopping, or dress-up? The most frequent concern seems to be washability; after this comes softness. I'd like to toss in flamability, a bigger threat with synthetics which flare and melt and cause far more severe burns than natural fibers which burn up and off; wool is self-extinguishing, the safest of all. Little babies can't push irritations away, and a fuzzy or fringey blanket could be a real tickler.

There are some very soft and washable wools and wool blends. There are more and more cottons available all the time, functional, fun, elegant. Consider silk, which may seem extravagant but is actually very practical—it's durable, washable, warm, light, and beautiful.

In general

If I were to make one recommendation about planning projects, it would be to ask questions. Think about what you are planning to make, and question its purpose, requirements, freedoms, limitations. Study existing similar goods and decide what are their strengths and weaknesses, what you want to reproduce and what you want to do away with. Common sense is a major part of such planning, combined with your growing knowledge of yarns and weave structures and how they work together.

One of the most valuable resources you can have is Bette Hochberg's book, *Fibre Facts*. It is small, easy to understand, and contains a wealth of information about fibers that we all can benefit from knowing.

Finishes

In most cases, in order to keep the weft from coming out at the ends of your weaving, it will need to be secured, finished, in some way. What finish you choose is one of the first things you need to consider during the planning stages of your project. Some of the questions you'll want to ask are: Do you want your piece to have fringe? If so, how long should it be and what kind of edge or end finish do you want to give it? Will your piece have a hem? If so, how deep will it be? Whether you decide on fringe or hems, you will need to allow for your finishing method in your weaving plan.

There are a few other things to consider when deciding upon a finish. What kind of yarn you use is one of them. Linen, for example, when used as a fringe, disintegrates quickly and will look untidy after a few washings. Some novelty yarns, especially slick ones, have a tendency to untwist; experiment with your yarns before you begin to weave to see how they might behave as fringe.

Should you want fringe, but are using a yarn which you feel might not hold up with wear and washing, there are many techniques for braiding, twisting and knotting which will yield a stable and neat fringe. (See *Finishes in the Ethnic Tradition.*)

The overall design of your piece should also be taken into consideration during the planning stages of your project. Will the fringe or finish be a focal point? Should the finish be fancy or plain? How will the finish work with the whole of your design?

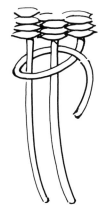 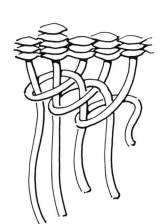 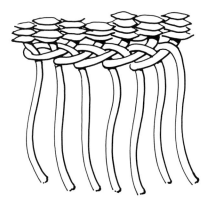

Phillipine Edge utilizes the fringe itself and is done after the piece is removed from the loom.

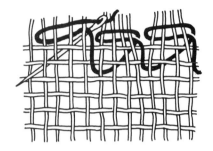

Hemstitching uses a needle and a new piece of yarn for sewing. It is easiest to do if done while the piece is still on the loom, under tension.

What you are making will often determine what kind of finish you choose. Keep in mind function, design and wearability. For example, a very long fringe could be stylish on a shawl, but impractical and untidy for a dishtowel. Blankets, shawls and scarves all lend themselves well to fringe; placemats, runners, napkins and tablecloths might have fringe or hems depending on your design and the yarns you choose. In weaving garments, again consider the total garment design and the yarns you will use. Current styles and your own body type should play a part, too.

Though there are dozens of edge finishes, and you'll want to experiment and try many of them, I've included just three of my favorite ones here. An excellent resource which I highly recommend is *Finishes in the Ethnic Tradition* by Karen Searle and Suzanne Baizerman. It's a wonderful and inexpensive book showing many finishing techniques in easy, clear drawings.

Twining is done on the loom. It forms the first and last wefts.

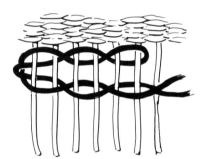 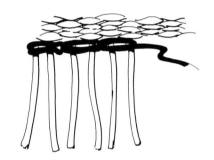

Further Reading

I have some hesitation about giving you a list of good books because by the time you read this there will be more available. With this as a disclaimer, I will go ahead and list those books I like to recommend to new weavers, as well as some others you will find useful for exploring further the techniques and weave structures discussed in this book. There are dozens more, many very good ones, and I hope you'll look at all of them. I apologize for any great ones I've left out, and I know there will be some.

Alderman, Sharon and Kathryn Wertenberger. *Handwoven, Tailormade: A tandem guide to fabric designing, weaving, sewing and tailoring.* Loveland, Colorado: Interweave Press, 1982.

Baizerman, Suzanne and Karen Searle. *Finishes in the Ethnic Tradition.* St. Paul, Minnesota: Dos Tejedoras, 1978.

Beard, Betty. *Fashions From the Loom.* Loveland, Colorado: Interweave Press, Inc., 1980.

Black, Mary E. *Key to Weaving.* New York: The Macmillan Publishing Co., Inc., 1957.

Davison, Marguerite Porter. *A Handweaver's Pattern Book.* Swarthmore, Pennsylvania: Marguerite Porter Davison, publisher, 1944.

Drooker, Penelope B. *Samplers You Can Use: A handweaver's guide to creative exploration.* Loveland, Colorado: Interweave Press, Inc., 1984.

Garrett, Cay. *Warping All by Yourself.* Sonoma, California: The Handweaver Press, 1974. Interweave Press, distributor.

Hochberg, Bette. *Fibre Facts.* Santa Cruz, California: Bette and Bernard Hochberg, publishers, 1976.

Guagliumi, Susan. *Drafting Primer.* Rockville, Maryland: The Unicorn, 1978.

Held, Shirley, E. *Weaving: A Handbook of Fiber Arts.* New York: Holt, Rinehart and Winston, 1978.

Kurtz, Carol S. *Designing for Weaving, A Study Guide for Drafting, Design and Color.* Loveland, Colorado: Interweave Press, Inc., 1985.

Moorman, Theo. *Weaving as an Art Form, A Personal Statement.* New York: Van Nostrand Reinhold Co., 1975.

Regensteiner, Else. *The Art of Weaving.* New York: Van Nostrand Reinhold Co., 1970.

-----. *Weaving Sourcebook.* New York: Van Nostrand Reinhold Co., 1983.

Sutton, Ann. *The Structure of Weaving.* Asheville, North Carolina: Lark Communications, 1982.

Tidball, Harriett. *The Handloom Weaves.* A Shuttle Craft Guild Monograph. Santa Ana, California: HTH Publishers, 1957.

Further reading by subject
Drafting
Frey, Berta. *Designing and Drafting for Handweavers: Basic Principles of Cloth Construction.* New York: The Macmillan Publishing Co., Inc., 1958.

Guagliumi, Susan. *Drafting Primer.* Rockville, Maryland: The Unicorn, 1978.

Kurtz, Carol S. *Designing for Weaving, A Study Guide for Drafting, Design and Color.* Loveland, Colorado: Interweave Press, Inc., 1985

Doubleweave
Beard, Betty. *Fashions From the Loom.* Loveland, Colorado: Interweave Press, Inc., 1980.

Brostoff, Laya. *Double Weave: Theory and Practice.* Loveland, Colorado: Interweave Press, Inc., 1979.

Regensteiner, Else. *The Art of Weaving.* New York: Van Nostrand Reinhold Co., 1970.

Tidball, Harriet. *The Double Weave, Plain and Patterned.* Shuttle Craft Guild Monograph 1. Santa Ana, California: HTH Publishers, 1960.

Weigle, Palmy. *Double Weave.* New York: Watson-Guptill Publications, 1978.

Honeycomb

Black, Mary E. *Key to Weaving.* New York: The Macmillan Publishing Co., Inc., 1957.

Davison, Marguerite Porter. *A Handweaver's Pattern Book.* Swarthmore, Pennsylvania: Marguerite Porter Davison, publisher, 1944.

Tovey, John. *Weaves and Pattern Drafting.* London/New York: Brastsford/Reinhold, 1969.

Lace Weaves

Black, Mary E. *Key to Weaving.* New York: The Macmillan Publishing Co., Inc., 1957.

Davison, Marguerite Porter. *A Handweaver's Pattern Book.* Swarthmore, Pennsylvania: Marguerite Porter Davison, publisher, 1944.

Drooker, Penelope B. *Samplers You Can Use: A handweaver's guide to creative exploration.* Loveland, Colorado: Interweave Press, Inc., 1984.

Frey, Berta. *Designing and Drafting for Handweavers: Basic Principles of Cloth Construction.* New York: The Macmillan Publishing Co., Inc., 1958.

Snyder, Mary E. *Lace and Lacey Weaves.* Pasadena, California, 1960.

Tovey, John. *Weaves and Pattern Drafting.* London/New York: Brastsford/Reinhold, 1969.

Tidball, Harriet. *Loom Controlled Lace Weaves.* Shuttle Craft Guild Monograph. Santa Ana, California: HTH Publishers, N.D.

Summer and Winter

Atwater, Mary Meigs. *The Shuttle-Craft Book of American Hand-Weaving.* New York: The Macmillan Publishing Co., Inc., 1951.

Barrett, Clotilde. *Summer and Winter and Beyond.* Boulder, Colorado: The Colorado Fiber Center, Inc., 1982.

Black, Mary E. *Key to Weaving.* New York: The Macmillan Publishing Co., Inc., 1957.

Burnham, Harold B., and Dorothy K. Burnham. *Keep Me Warm One Night, Early Handweaving in Eastern Canada.* Toronto: University of Toronto Press, 1972.

Davison, Marguerite Porter. *A Handweaver's Pattern Book.* Swarthmore, Pennsylvania: Marguerite Porter Davison, publisher, 1944.

Frey, Berta. *Designing and Drafting for Handweavers: Basic Principles of Cloth Construction.* New York: Collier Books, 1958.

Tidball, Harriet. *Summer and Winter and Other Two-Tie Unit Weaves.* Shuttle Craft Guild Monograph 19. Santa Ana, California: HTH Publishers, 1966.

Overshot

Black, Mary E. *Key to Weaving.* New York: The Macmillan Publishing Co., Inc., 1957.

Bress, Helene. *The Weaving Book: Patterns and Ideas.* New York: Charles Scribner's Sons, 1981.

Burnham, Harold B., and Dorothy K. Burnham. *Keep Me Warm One Night, Early Handweaving in Eastern Canada.* Toronto: University of Toronto Press, 1972.

Davison, Marguerite Porter. *A Handweaver's Pattern Book.* Swarthmore, Pennsylvania: Marguerite Porter Davison, publisher, 1944.

Frey, Berta. *Designing and Drafting for Handweavers: Basic Principles of Cloth Construction.* New York: The Macmillan Publishing Co., Inc., 1958.

Tovey, John. *Weaves and Pattern Drafting.* London/New York: Brastsford/Reinhold, 1969.

Fibers, Finishes and Finishing

Baizerman, Suzanne and Karen Searle. *Finishes in the Ethnic Tradition.* St. Paul, Minnesota: Dos Tejedoras, 1978.

Gordon, Beverly. *The Final Steps: Traditional Methods and Contemporary Applications for Finishing Cloth by Hand.* Loveland, Colorado: Interweave Press, Inc., 1982.

Hochberg, Bette. *Fibre Facts.* Santa Cruz, California: Textile Artists' Supply, Berkeley, California (distributor), 1981.

West, Virginia M. *Finishing Touches for the Handweaver.* Newton, Massachusetts: Charles T. Branford Company, 1968.

Wilson, Jean. *Joinings, Edges and Trims. . .Finishing Details for Handcrafted Products.* New York: Van Nostrand Reinhold Company, 1983.

Suppliers and Magazines

I've decided not to put in a list of suppliers for several reasons. First, I've never read one yet that wasn't already out of date by the time the book was in print. Second, I'm wholeheartedly dedicated to local retailers as I feel they are readily able to support you with products, information and service. Mail order suppliers do most of this too, but it's not the same as a friendly smile greeting you as you walk through the door.

I know you need information, however, so what I'll say instead is read the ads in weaving magazines. They are always up to date with the information and addresses you need. Below is a list of current weaving or heavily fiber-related magazines and their publishers. Each has a very different slant, so try to look at copies of each to decide which is best for you.

Handwoven—Interweave Press, 306 North Washington Avenue, Loveland, CO 80537.

Spin·Off—Interweave Press.

Fiberarts—Lark Communications, 50 College Street, Asheville, NC 28801.

Prairie Wool Companion—126 Phillips Avenue, Sioux Falls, SD 57102.

Shuttle, Spindle, and Dyepot—Handweavers Guild of America, 65 LaSalle, West Hartford, CT 06107.

Weaver's Journal—P.O. Box 14-238, St. Paul, MN 55114.

Threads—The Taunton Press, P.O. Box 355, Newtown, CT 06470.

9/86 cor

Trouble Shooting

Problem	Possible Causes	Solutions
Breaking selvedge threads.	Too much draw-in, beating is exerting too much pressure.	Leave more weft in shed.
	Large group of extra heddles is causing longer path, strain on sides of warp.	This time, remove heddles; next time space heddles as you thread.
Broken warp.	Uneven tension—broken threads were too tight.	Cut new one, replace broken one and pin into weaving until woven securely or weave without it until you can pin old one to web; after piece is off loom stitch in repair thread.
	Knot that didn't fit through reed or heddle.	
	Weak place in yarn.	
Warp fraying and breaking.	Sett too close.	Re-sley into larger dent reed.
	Sett okay, but in too fine a reed.	Open and close shed with beater forward.
	Yarn too softly spun for use as warp (see below for solution to this).	Sprinkle with oil to keep fuzziness contained. If linen, sprinkle with water.
Sagging warp making design error and interfering with clean shed.	Uneven tension—floating threads too loose.	Hang some kind of weight on loose threads between back and warp beams to take up slack—fishing sinkers, washers, shuttles, etc.
Whole section goes loose.	Knot on apron rod loosened, or one section messed up during beaming.	Even warp tension by padding the loose section with anything from a pencil to a dish towel into the roll of warp, depending on how much slack needs to be taken up.
	With a multi-yarn warp, yarn elasticity varies.	Next time blend yarns more.
	You could have too wide a stripe of one kind of yarn.	Mix warps better.
When shed is open, bottom warps are slack, tops tight, making it hard to get shuttle through without catching loose ones.	Jack loom problem. Harnesses are sitting too close to neutral when at rest— heddle eyes need to be *below* a straight line drawn from beam to beam.	Adjust harnesses so that those not raised have heddle eyes as far below beams as the heddle eyes of the raised harnesses are above the beams.
Weft not beating in straight.	Uneven tension.	Pad loose areas or hang weights off back to even up tension.
	Beater not quite straight due to floor not being level.	Put a shim under one corner to straighten beater.
Can't beat enough weft in.	Warp sett too close; if selvedges are closer than main body, they alone can stop weft.	Re-sley looser.
		Try a different weight of weft, or a softer weft.
Too much weft packing in.	Warp sett too loose.	Re-sley warp tighter.
	Too much muscle in beating.	Don't beat so hard; use fatter weft.
Warp grabbing around beater; beater won't move. Hairy yarns refusing to allow open shed.	Hairy warp sett too close.	Re-sley with hairy warps far enough apart so they won't stick to each other. To get a good shed, place hairy yarns on same harness—then they don't have to separate.

Problem	Possible Causes	Solutions
Need just a few more inches of warp to finish—it's there but out of reach.	Measured warp too short.	Loosen tension for better shed.
	Figured too closely.	Lift reed out of beater, slide it back to castle.
		Extend your warp length by untying warp knots on your apron rod and running a cord through the warp knots and around apron rod, adjusting for even tension when done. In extreme cases, tie new warps to old warps so that old warp can continue forward on through heddles and reed. That's desperate.
Can't get a shed.	You forgot to go over the back beam— warp goes from heddles down to warp beam.	Remove back beam and slide it under warp, loosen tension on warp, lift and replace back beam.
Can't get a clean shed.	Crossed warps.	Untie, straighten, and re-sley from front.
	If it's a countermarche loom the cause may have to do with adjustment of harness heights.	See loom owner's manual.
	Uneven tension.	Re-tie front knots.
	Tie-up cords for treadles vary in length too much.	Put cords of same length on same treadles.
Grease marks on warp.	New reeds have machine oil protecting them from moisture.	Wipe off new reeds before beginning to weave. These marks usually wash out.
Threading errors—minor.	Inattention during threading.	Tie string heddles where you need them—untie wrong warp in front, pull out of reed and heddles, re-thread, re-sley, re-tie.
	Pattern has error.	
Thread errors—major.	Inattention during threading.	Hopefully you discover this right after you finished threading, before beaming. Sometimes a bunch of repair heddles will solve it, sometimes you must re-thread half your warp, depending on the error. If you must rethread a lot from the front, first open a shed, put a lease stick into it behind the castle, do the same with a second shed (tabby if you can get it). The sticks will give you back your cross so you can easily thread the proper threads. Since it's already beamed you don't want a lot of crossing over—this screws up tension. This is a no fun experience; usually once is enough to prevent it from ever happening again.
	Pattern has error.	
Pattern doesn't look right.	Proportions are off. Colors are interfering.	Change warp sett, beat, or yarns.
	Treadling error.	Check tie ups.
		Check treadling draft.
		Check sinking or rising shed.

Problem	Possible Causes	Solutions
Finished piece is too short.	Wrong warp calculation due to arithmetic or error in warp take-up or shrinkage.	Sometimes the piece can be salvaged or lived with. Other times it's just a good learning experience.
Desired yarn is too expensive or too weak to use as desired.	Expensiveness has too many causes. Weak—designed to be soft instead of strong.	Dilute use. Support as warp with plainer, stronger yarn every other thread, or use it for weft only.
Finished piece is ugly.	Didn't do a sample first. Perspective, pre-conceived notion. You tried to put too many ideas into one piece so they fought each other instead of complementing each other.	Often what you think is ugly really isn't, it's just not what you expected. Put it away for a month, then take it out and look as if as a new piece, without expectations. It may look a lot better. If you still don't like it, you have at least two alternatives—give it to someone whose taste is different from yours, over-dye it so it's monochromatic, a new color range that looks good.
Too many ideas.	Enthusiasm, excitement. You're an interesting person with more energy than time.	Keep notes on all ideas; otherwise, by the time you get time, you won't remember them all. Also some will later be abandoned because others were better. Also some will join together and you can use up two or three in one piece.
Not enough ideas.	All of the above is true, but you've hit a dry spell—we all do.	Subscribe to a weaving magazine, go to an art show, ask friends what presents they would like, consider what clothing or other fabric item you are going to buy next and think about weaving it instead. Think of who in town would appreciate a handwoven donation—blankets for people in nursing homes, wall hangings for your church, banners for the football team bus, matching saddle blankets for the 4H club riding group, etc. Or just take a rest, knowing you'll weave again when the time is right.
Lack of motivation.	It's not as much fun to weave alone as to talk about it with someone interested.	Join or start a guild. Teach a friend to weave.
Tired back.	Leaning over too much.	Find a lower stool for threading, a weaving seat that's a better height.
Your kids are too helpful.	They're interested in you and in weaving.	Help them start their own project, on a frame, inkle, rigid heddle, other loom good for their age and interest.
Puppies or kittens destroyed your warp.	Puppies and kittens are like that.	Close the door next time.
Not enough time for weaving.	Organization and scheduling of priorities.	Read *The Creative Woman's Getting It All Together at Home Handbook* by Jean Ray Laury, published by Van Nostrand, Rinehold.

Index

Apron, 50

Apron rods, 49-53; bent, 52-53; kinds of, 50, 94; position over back beam, 49-50; tying on to back, 51-52; tying on to front, 58-60; types of attachment, 50

Atwater-Bronson lace, 164-168, 176; threading, 165; using tabby, 166

Back beam, 15; removing, 43-44, 50

Balanced weave, 20, 64, 97, 109, 112

Ball winder, 19, 27

Basket weave, 110-111

Beaming, 21, 53-57; errors in, 53; tension during, 56

Beams, back, 15; breast or front, 15; cloth or fabric, 15; sectional warp, 20; warp, 15

Beater, 14, 16, 43; not straight, 227; securing for threading, 37

Beating, 64, 65; problems, 227; sequence of, 69-70

Bibliography, 222-225; magazines, 226

Blocks, 172-176; Atwater-Bronson, 164-167, 176; diagrams, 175, 179; overshot, 181, 186-189; patterns, 172-173; profile draft, 174-175; summer & winter, 176, 177-184; threading units, 172; two-block diagram, 179

Bobbin winder, 18, 66; electric, 18

Bobbins, 19; winding, 66

Brakes, 15; friction, 55, 70, 71, 214; ratchet and dog or pawl, 55, 70, 71, 213

Calculations, warp, 93-95, 97, 99, 232; weft, 96-97, 98, 99, 232

Castle, 14

Checks, 99

Choke ties, 34

Cloth (fabric) beam, 15

Cloth diagrams, 137

Color, 112, 115, 161, 169, 180

Computers, 140

Counterbalance loom, 213

Countermarche loom, 213

Counting thread, 31

Craft schools, 195

Cross (lease), holding, 38; making, 31; purpose of, 30; removing threads from, 39; tying, 31

Dents (see also Reeds), 14, 18, 21; sleying, 39

Direct tie-up, 61, 62, 104

Double weave, 149-157; double width, 153-155; one shuttle, 153; sett, 150; tubes, 155; two shuttle, 151-153

Drafts, 101-108; altering, 131-140; basket weave, 111; four parts of, 101-106; from cloth diagrams, 137-140; honeycomb, 160; log cabin, 116; overshot, 186, 187, 191, 192; periwinkle, 131, 132; plain weave, 110; profile, 174-175; reading, 101-108; rib weave, 112; summer & winter, 176, 178, 181,

Drafts (continued)
183; tabby, 110; twills, 122, 123, 124, 129, 133, 134, 135, 143, 147, 148; waffle weave, 144

Draw-down, 106-107; cloth diagram, 137-140; twill, 131-133

Draw-in, 21; calculation, 95; minimizing, 67-68

Ends per inch, E.P.I. (see also Sett), 21; determining, 25; in lace, 168-169; in overshot, 190; in summer & winter, 181

Errors, repairing, 80-81, 227-229; sleying, 41-42; threading, 48-49, 73

Evaluation, self, 89-90

Fiber content, cotton, 200; linen, 200; silk, 199; wool, 199

Finishes, 221-222; fringe, 93, 221; hemstitching, 77, 93; machine zigzag, 77; overhand knots, 77; twining, 222

Finishing, fabric, 80; washing, 81

Floor loom, 16, 43-44, 61

Fringe, 93, 221

Front (breast) beam, 15

Guide strings, 29

Glossary, 20-22

Harnesses, 14

Headers, weaving, 65-66

Heddles, 14, 209-211; directional twist, 45, 209; distribution, 211; hooks, 44, 45; marking, 210; moving, 210; positioning, 44-45; repairing, 210; threading, 42-49; types of, 209

Hemstitching, 77, 93, 222

Honeycomb, 159-162; draft, 160

Jack loom, 104, 106, 127, 209, 213

Knots, lark's head, 52; overhand, 46, 51, 77; square, 58; surgeon's, 58

Lace weaves (see also Atwater-Bronson), 163-170; sett, 168-169; tabby treadling for, 166; threading, 165-166

Lamms, 104

Lark's head knot, 52

Lash cord, 52, 60

Lease (see Cross)

Lease sticks, 21, 42

Levers, table loom, 14, 104

Log cabin, 115-166, 120; draft, 166

Loom bench, 17

Loom(s), buying, 211-216; counterbalance, 213; countermarche, 213; designs, 43; floor, 16, 43-44, 161; jack, 104, 106, 127, 209, 213; parts of, 13-16; price, 215; rising shed, 105; sinking shed, 105; table, 16, 44, 61, 104; types of, 211, 212; X style, 44

Loom waste, 21, 77-78, 94-95

McMorran yarn balance, 18

Overhand knot, 46, 51, 77

Overshot, 185-194; diagram, 186-188; drafts, 186, 187, 191, 192; sett, 190; threading, 186-187; tie-up, 188-189

Pick-up stick, 19

Picks per inch, P.P.I. (see also Weft), 21, 96, 97

Plaids, 113, 199

Plain weave (see also Tabby), 109-120; basket weave, 110-111; log cabin, 115-116; plaids, 114; rib weave, 111, 120; stripes, 113; tabby, 110

Projects, 216-220; bags, 156; blankets, bedspreads, afghans, baby blankets, 219-220; clothing, 217-218; curtains, 219; granny shrug, 156; planning, 91-100; rugs, 217; sample, 23-25; shawl, 97-98; towels, placemats, napkins, etc., 93, 218; wall hangings, 218-219

Quill, 19

Ratchet and dog or pawl, 55, 70, 71, 213

Record keeping, 84-85; sheet, 88

Reeds, 14, 18, 22; positioning in beater, 37-38; sizes, 206; sleying, 36-41, 151; substitution chart, 208

Rib weave, 111, 120; draft, 112

Rising shed loom, 105; tie-up, 106

Samples, 23-25

Sectional warp beam, 20

Selvedges, 22, 67; draw-in, 67-68, 95; floating, 68-69, 127-128, 154, 190; special considerations, 68-69

Separators, 55, 57

Sett (see also Ends per inch), balanced, 97, 201; chart, 208; choosing, 207; double weave, 150; lace weaves, 168, 169; overshot, 190; summer & winter, 181; twill, 126

Shaft (see Harnesses)

Shed, 14, 22, 49, 65, 70; problems, 227, 228; rising, 105; sinking, 105

Shuttles, 14; boat, 19, 70; placement during weaving, 190; rag, 19; rug, 19; ski, 19; stick, 19; two, 112, 151; winding weft onto, 66

Sinking shed, 105; tie-up, 106

Skeins, 26, 203; using, 27

Sley hook, 19, 22, 36; alternatives, 36

Sleying, 36-39; double weave, 151; errors, 41-42; where to start, 37

Spool rack, 20

Square knot, 58

Straight draw, 45, 102, 151

Stripes, 113

Summer & winter, 177-184; drafts, 176, 178, 181, 183; sett, 181; threading, 178

Swifts, 26; squirrel cage, 27; umbrella, 17, 26-27; yarn reels, 27

Tabby (see also Plain weave), 64, 66, 110; in lace weave, 166; in summer & winter, 180; treadles in overshot, 188

Table loom, 16, 44, 61, 104

Take-up, warp, 22, 94; weft, 96

Temple, 19, 68

Tension, beaming, 56; evening of, 60; problems, 227; warp, 53, 56

Tension box, 20

Texture, 116-117, 120

Threading, Atwater-Bronson, 165-166; cloth diagram, 138-139; double weave, 150, 156-157; draft, 102-103; errors, 48-49, 73, 228; heddles, 42-49; honeycomb, 160; method, 47-49; overshot, 186-187; position for, 43-44; straight draw, 45, 102, 151; summer & winter, 178

Threading hook, 19, 22, 36

Threads (*see* Warp; Weft; Yarns)

Tie-up, direct, 62; draft, 103; multiple, 61-62; overshot, 188; systems, 213

Time, 84-85

Treadle minder, 20

Treadles, 14; six, 62; ten, 62; tying up, 61-62, 188

Treadling, 104-105; cloth diagram, 138-139; draft, 102; overshot, 188; summer & winter, 181-182; twill, 134

Twill, balanced, 126; basic, 121-130; broken, 143; characteristics, 125-126; combinations, 145, 147; diamonds, 130-136; double faced, 148; drafts, 122, 123, 124, 129, 133, 134, 135; extended, 147, 148; herringbone, 124; Jeans, 125; mock satin, 147; offset, 143; point, 124, 148; point twill-herringboned, 147; ratios, 122-123; reverse, 124; satin, 147; selvedges, 68; 2/2, 64; undulating, 147; waffle weave, 143-144, 148; warp predominant, 126; weft predominant, 123, 126

Twining, 222

Tying on, back apron rod, 49-53; front apron rod, 58-61

Warp, 13, 204-205; advancing, 70-71; beaming, 53-57; broken thread, 73-74, 76; calculations, 93-95, 97, 99, 232; chaining, 34-35; crossed thread, 48-49, 72; formula, 95, 232; loose threads, 72; materials, 25, 93; measuring, 28-30; problems, 80-81, 227-228; removing from loom, 76-81; removing from warping board, 33; separators, 55, 57; tension, 53, 56, 60; tying on apron rods, 50-53, 58-61

Warp beam, 15; direction of turn, 55; removing, 43-44

Warp emphasis fabric, 109

Warp-faced fabric, 109, 112

Warp floats, 68-69; twill, 134

Warping, 27-63; method, 212; process, 28

Warping boards, 17, 28, 29; mill, 19, 29; paddle, 20; pegs, 17, 29

Washing fabric, 81

Weaving, headers, 65-66; on opposites, 146; sequences of, 69-70

Weaving guilds, 195

Weft (*see also* Picks per inch), 13; calculations, 96-97, 98, 99, 232; ending and starting, 71-72; repairing errors, 80-81; using two, 180

Weft-faced fabric, 109, 112

Weft floats, 134, 181, 187

Woof (*see* Weft)

Yarns, 25, 26, 93, 116, 117, 157, 161, 168, 180, 188, 197, 203; construction, 201; content, 198; conversion, 203; novelty, 202-203; packaging, 203; sizes, 202; warp, 25, 204

Formula For Figuring Your Warp Needs

<table>
<tr><td>+ project length
+ fringe
+ take-up (10% av.)
+ shrinkage (10% av.)
+ loom waste</td><td></td><td>+ finished width
+ draw-in (1-2″ av.)
+ shrinkage (10% av.)

on loom width
× warp sett</td></tr>
<tr><td>total length</td><td>×</td><td>warp ends needed = total in inches ÷ 36 = total in yds.</td></tr>
</table>

Formula For Figuring Weft

length of one weft shot in inches
× shots per inch
= inches needed to weave one inch of fabric
× inches to be woven
= inches of weft needed to weave all of project
÷ 36
= yards of weft needed

Answers to warp and weft calculations, page 98:

Warp needs—about 1,834 yards

Weft needs—about 1,466 yards

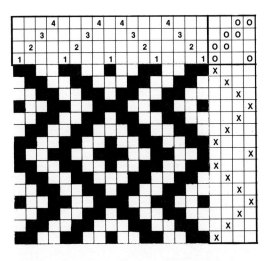

Completed draw-down from page 107.